EVERYDAY LIFE AND FESTIVITY IN A LOCAL ETHNIC COMMUNITY: POLISH-AMERICANS IN SOUTH BEND, INDIANA

Janusz Mucha

EAST EUROPEAN MONOGRAPHS, BOULDER
DISTRIBUTED BY COLUMBIA UNIVERSITY PRESS, NEW YORK

1996

EAST EUROPEAN MONOGRAPHS, NO. CDXLI

CONTENTS

INTRODUCTION

The subjects of this work are the ethnic aspects of everyday life and ethnic aspects of festivity is a single, relatively small Polish-American community in South Bend, Indiana. I would like to present the processes of marginalization of ethnicity in this community that have occurred first and foremost under the influence of the structural and cultural phenomena of the all-American character. These phenomena on the macro scale have had an enormous significance upon everything that has taken place in South Bend. I will not offer here, however, my own interpretation of the processes of the emergence and transformations of American society. The literature on this subject is ample and very well known. This text is not intended as a study in the field of the theory of American ethnicity nor as a comparative analysis. It is a case study.

I did not find myself in South Bend in 1990 by accident, but I had not been aware of the existence of the Polish-American community (or the Polonia) in this city. My teaching obligations did not give me an opportunity to study the Polonia in a deep and systematic way, but this ethnic community, at a certain moment, is a certain sense and for a few months absorbed me and persuaded me to participate, at least partly, in its everyday life and festivities. The idea of participant observation came a little later. These facts have their important, negative consequences. They prevented me from making the proper theoretical preparations for the observation. They limited the scope of sources that could be used. The result is, effectively, a kind of "coincidence". Obviously, this is nothing exceptional in research practice. Two Polish scholars, Michal Buchowski and Wojciech Burszta note, based on the examples of leading anthropologists, that "researchers...seem to assemble larger wholes of the parts and sources that happen to be at their disposal" (1992:8). I am fully aware that other scholars, being in a different cognitive and social situation, and having access to other sources, could put forward other books on the same topic and at least some of them (assuming one does not question their subjectively defined reliability) would be equally good interpretations of the studied phenomena.

South Bend is a city inhabited by a little over one hundred thousand people now. It finds itself nearly one hundred miles east of Chicago. It used to be an important center of machine industry.

After World War II, it was affected by the decline of the Midwest industry. Today, there are no big factories in town. The main employers are the Notre Dame University, school corporation, health service and many small and medium-sized construction, manufacturing and service companies. The nature of work available in town changed dramatically after the Second World War.

The Polonia has lived in South Bend since the 1870s. Its members used to be employed by big industry. They used to live on the west side of town. In that quarter, they established several Roman Catholic parishes and created their own shopping and service areas. For decades, Polonia's everyday life (except, to a certain extent, in the sphere of work) was carried out in its own ethnic world. For several decades, the Polonia dominated (although not totally), the political life of the whole city, creating successful coalitions with other ethnic groups.

At the beginning of the 1990s, the South Bend's Polish-American community underwent all the changes of the whole US Polonia, transformations profoundly analyzed in many works that will be discussed later. Nowadays, the Polish-Americans make up only around ten percent of the city's population. Only a few Americans of Polish heritage still live in the western part of town. The others, particularly better-off and younger, live in suburbs. However, many of them have not lost a psychological and even organizational contact with the ethnic center of their community, and they often visit the Polish-American "areas of concentration".

Other European ethnic groups of South Bend are first of all the Germans and Hungarians, and in the neighboring town of Mishawaka — the Belgians. Besides these groups, there are some non-European communities here also, namely Blacks and Mexican-Americans. These communities are growing in numbers and in political significance. They have become more visible than the European minorities. Now, except for the names of certain Roman Catholic parishes and some companies, the exterior signs of the former European ethnic mosaic are hardly visible. However, the memory of this mosaic seems to be alive, resulting in the maintenance of the ethnic symbolic space. The mosaic itself, and the Polonia within it, are still there, but they are undergoing deep transformations.

Any research in the field of ethnicity, including the ethnic identity of a single community, should consider the intergroup relationships. Identity shapes in the network of relations between "us" and "them", "us" and the "strangers". In my research, it was not possible to collect sufficient systematic empirical material to address this important topic. Relations between the Polonia and other ethnic groups of South Bend will obviously be mentioned several times, but will not be analyzed in a systematic way.

South Bend is a city quite well known to many Americans. The reason for this relative fame lies in the Notre Dame University, and particularly its great football team. Despite the existence of the Polonia, thought, the city is almost completely unknown in Poland. The South Bend Polish-American community is not very popular among the Polish and Polish-American students of the ethnic field. In Poland, it was mentioned for instance by historian Andrzej Brozek (1985:108), in the US by Donald Pienkos (1987:48-49, 269) and Joseph Wytrwal (1969:55, 223) and the authors of unpublished (quoted here) dissertations, but this book in my opinion is the first larger work based on the materials of the South Bend Polonia.

The main theme of this book is the everyday life and festivity of the Polish-American local community in South Bend until the beginning of the 1990s. The presentation of this topic demands that I first outline the research area, put forward basic concepts, major research directions and interpretation possibilities, even if they will not be fully exploited due to a lack of empirical material.

At the beginning of this Introduction, I mentioned that this work is not of an "analytic-theoretical" character. The conceptual framework is not the end in itself but is purpose is to serve the analysis of the empirical data. The basic categories to be exploited in my analysis of the empirical situation are that of local community and particularly ethnic local community, ethnicity and ethnic group, ethnic identity and everyday life. These categories are very closely interconnected and interdependent, regardless of the order in which they are presented.

The problems I am concerned with could be particularly extensively researched if I were able to begin my analysis with a discussion of social consciousness in situations of everyday life: people's convictions which are comprised of the conceptual categories of natural language, language being used by people in their natural everyday situations. Natural language contains the group's stock of knowledge. This stock is founded upon the group's image of the works: everything that is treated by it as natural, self-explanatory. In the study of everyday life, a very ambitious task would be to grasp the essence, the core of this imagined and assumed world. This core is being transmitted from generation to generation in the process of "primary socialization". It is being consolidated through direct, everyday interactions. It is very difficult to reach it because of its prereflexive character. One cannot simply ask people to explain it rationally. The most fruitful method seems to be to analyze biographies. This old method is being extensively used again, also in Poland. One example is a book on the life world of the native inhabitants of the Upper Silesia region. The book's authors, Krzysztof Lecki, Kazimiera Wodz, Jacek Wodz and Piotr Wroblewski analyze biographies and natural language: the Uppersilesian dialect (1992:11-12, 22, 27). The authors note, however, that even the exploitation of this fruitful method did not prevent them from meeting serious research problems.

The work I am presenting to the readers had to follow a different methodological approach. It was impossible for me to study life histories, to analyze language in a systematic way. Instead, I had to base my study of the documents available during my stay in South Bend and on participant observation. A short survey was a supplementary source for collecting data. The survey was possible thanks to the grant I received in 1991 from the Research and University Graduate School of Indiana University in Bloomington. I would like to express my thanks to Dr. John M. Kennedy of the Center for Survey Research of this school. The elaboration of data was possible thanks to the grant I received in 1992 from Nicolaus Copernicus University in Torun, Poland. Ms. Maria Nawojczyk of the Department of Sociology was very helpful in calculations and in the preparation of maps.

The theoretical background of this book is introduced in the first chapter. The second chapter presents the city of South Bend and particularly, the history of the settlement and ethnic composition. The third, and very long chapter, analyses the process of transformation of Polish everyday life of the collectivity of immigrants into Polish-American everyday life for the descendants of immigrants. The fourth chapter deals with the everyday life of

Polish-Americans institutions in the South Bend of today. The fifth chapter is the discussion of survey findings. The last chapter deals with festivity. The presentation consists of a single "Polish-American Year" in South Bend with its ceremonies and festivals that help retain the Polish ethnicity.

A large part of the first chapter appeared earlier in *Studia Socjologiczne* (2, 1993:75-91), a Polish sociological periodical. I would like to express my thanks to Grzegorz Babinski, Andrzej Piotrowski, Jaroslaw Rokicki, Andrzej Szahaj and the anonymous referee for their comments. Large parts of chapter V appeared in *Przeglad Polonijny*, another Polish periodical (XX, 4, 1994:25-41). The earlier drafts of the whole text were read by Grzegorz Babinski, Rev. Leonard Chrobot, Hireonim Kubiak, Bronislaw Misztal, Krzysztof Piatkowski, Aleksander Posern-Zielinski, Jaroslaw Rokicki, Brother Donald Stabrowski (CSC), and David Stefancic. Their comments were very helpful. (Obviously, I am the single person responsible for the final result.) I am particularly grateful for their comments to Professors Chrobot, Stabrowski and Stefancic. They are both the attentive and competent observers of the cultural processes of transformations of the Polish-American community in South Bend and active participants of these processes.

At the end of this Introduction, I would like to thank all those members in the Polish-American community in South Bend with whom I spoke and to some extent cooperated. I appreciate the interest of those Poles in Poland and in America, as well as of Americans (whatever their ethnic heritage), many of them professors of Indiana University, who encouraged me to start and to finish this project.

CHAPTER ONE

THE EVERYDAY LIFE OF A LOCAL ETHNIC COMMUNITY: TOWARDS A THEORETICAL MODEL

1. Local Ethnic Community

Nearly twenty years ago, the Polish scholar Jan Turowski wrote that there was practically no sociological concept to which more books and articles had been devoted than to the concept of local community (1977:105). Turowski's thesis refers also to the Polish literature: sociological and ethnographical publications on rural and urban communities in Poland and communities of people of Polish heritage living abroad (see, eg, Babinski 1977, 1979: Frysztacki 1986; Morawska 1971, 1978, 1988).

The concept of local community is equally: popular and unclear. Already in 1955, George A. Hillery tried to find "areas of agreement" within various approaches. He found three points. Firstly, local community is an aggregate of people who reside in a geographically distinct area. Second, these people share most of the same values, norms and attitudes. Third, this aggregate is characterized by relatively stable and intimate interactions (1955:111-123; see also Schwab 1982:348). Ewa Morawska defines local community as a "system of interactions limited in space, supported by social institutions and social control and comprised of a consensus in the field of cultural values" (1878:43, 1988:371). I will generally follow Morawska's ideas. She stresses the fact that both the meaning and the scope of the concept, as well as the directions of transformations of local communities in modern societies are still discussed by many theoreticians. I will not engage in these conceptual and theoretical controversies. Instead, I will concentrate on those ideas that in to my knowledge are fruitful for the presentation of the problems considered in this book.

I will assume local community to be a social space in which the locally oriented social interactions take place. I will follow the "interpretive" approach stressing, after Max Weber, Florian Znaniecki but also "the Chicago School" in urban sociology, the sense of belonging, the subjective meaning of social situations, the "we" sense. These senses and meanings are of a dynamic character. When analyzing the Polish-American community in South Bend, I will, for instance, have to consider the impact that some technological innovations have had on its internal organization and its transformations. The car, for example, has changed the traditional concept of local community. When it became popular, it separated spatial contacts from social contacts, it made personal interactions independent of spatial interactions. It made it possible to visit the group's centers of concentration even if one lived quite far away. The "we" sense lost its dependence on spatial closeness. Local community lost several of its former functions. It ceased to be a "primary group" in the traditional sense. It became a collectivity less and less socially engaging, it has become "the community of limited liability," retaining, though, its character as an important subject of collective actions (see, eg, Janowitz 1961; Schwab 1982:361).

The post World War II continuation of the Chicago School observed another factor, too. Traditional ethnic ghettoes, inhabited by descendants of immigrants from Europe, are undoubtedly in the process of decline, but the spatially defined local communities have neither disappeared in "reality" nor in collective memory. They still have, for many people, symbolic significance. Typically this results from the fact that, even if a majority of the members of a given ethnic community move out, institutions constituting the backbone of the group remain in the old location. This is the situation of many ethnic communities in South Bend. Therefore, traditional territory can continue to be the actual and permanent or actual and periodical area of concentration of the group. The weekly arrivals of those who live in suburbs, to the parishes and ethnic clubs located in down-towns, or more rare arrivals of larger numbers of them to particularly important ethnic celebrations can serve as an example.

Because of the above mentioned symbolic significance of space, George Suttles' (1972) ideas concerning the recognizable boundaries of local communities should be considered here. Individuals develop a mental or cognitive map of their city. This map consists of three symbolic structures. Firstly, the "face-block," a network of acquaintances in a small neighborhood, who are recognized from face-to-face relations. Second, the "defended neigh-borhood," a small quarter that has an identity (and sometimes a name) known to both its residents and outsiders. It is the area where the residents feel secure. In South Bend, such Polish-American defended neighborhoods have been given their own individual names, after "Polish" churches. The same neighborhoods have also been given other names, referring to the regions of Poland from which the majority of the population of the area had originated. These names had no significance for anybody except the Polish-Americans; practically no one was even able to pronounce them. The third of Suttles' structures is the "community of limited liability." It is a larger quarter, having its own name known not only to the residents but also to inhabitants of distant areas. The boundaries are shaped by interactions based on tradition. They are often institutionalized (see also Schwab 1982:371-74). In South Bend, the Westside having been called "Polonia" or "Polska" is such a community of limited liability.

Transformations of traditional ethnic local communities have studied for decades. These transformations do not mean their complete decline but rather alterations as to their structure and social functions. Formal contexts and organizations have been relatively concretized. Community members have had more contacts with the outside world than within the group. Spatial segregation has been decreasing because of the influx of "strangers" and the outflow of young "natives" to other quarters (this process can be interpreted as the expansion of the interaction space of the traditional communities). Communities have been based to a larger extent on voluntary and selective participation. Many traditional functions of the local communities have been transferred to specialized institutions. Ethnic ties and contacts have increasingly adopted an individual as opposed to a collective character (see, eg, Turowski 1977:129; Morawska 1988:371, 390-97). In this text, I will show how all these transformations affect the Polish-American community in South Bend.

2. The Ethnic Group, Ethnicity

Local community is a social collective characterized by specific interactions. Ethnic local community is an ethnic collectivity. Therefore, the second basic conceptual category of this book is ethnic group. As I have mentioned before, I will follow here the interpretive approach to the local community of Weber and Znaniecki, stressing the sense of belonging, the sense of "we." I think that these classical approaches are very rewarding in the contemporary analysis of ethnic groups.

Weber presented an influential analysis of the ethnic group. Florian Znaniecki did not define ethnic groups (we can read in his book about the "racial" and "cultural" groups, though) but he paid special attention to the concept of the social group. Therefore, we will start with his insights. Some of his ideas are of particular significance here. Firstly, the group is an aggregate of people who, in their own consciousness, constitute a separate social entity, which means that they establish symbolic boundaries between themselves and others. This consciousness of separateness can have an "internal" origin: it can result from various kinds of interactions between members. It can also have an "external" origin when the group is an object of social actions of other individuals or groups. Separateness does not mean the lack of spatial interactions with these groups. It means a lack of conscious communication resulting from the fact that each member of a given group, shares with other members of this group, certain experiences and consequently excludes other people from this communion. The principle of cultural communion (or separateness that is in practice an inversion of the former concept) is, in a sense, "empty": anything can be its foundation. The idea of communion/separateness does not have to be equally strong in the consciousness of all members of the group. What is important is that it exists in the "core" of the group (see 1973:38-69; 1986:302).

What do these ideas mean for my analysis of a Polish-American community in South Bend? Znaniecki suggests that whatever the "objective," "real" foundations, a social group exists (retain its identity) if its members are aware of the group boundaries, that is boundaries between the members and non members. These boundaries can emerge because of cooperation but can also be forced upon the group. The group as such is, however, a result of interactions between its members. If these interactions decline, the collective identity of the group will undergo a process of transformations, On the following pages, I will present various aspects of the "objective," "real," ascribed "foundations" of the ethnic groups as well as of the "subjective," often intentional, determinants of the ethnic groups' boundaries.

I do not see any direct impact of Znaniecki's thought on the contemporary concepts of the ethnic group. I see many similar ideas in the work of scholars influenced by symbolic interactionism, though. They will be discussed later.

"Subjectivistic," "interpretive" understanding of the ethnic group directly follows the thought of Max Weber. His concept (that was published earlier than Znaniecki's) is similar to the more general ideas developed by Znaniecki. Any cultural trait, says Weber, no matter how superficial, can start a tendency toward "monopolistic closure." When we observe sharp boundaries between different lifestyles, we can conclude that they result either from conscious monopolistic closure or from migration and the following co-existence of groups who previously lived far from each other. The belief in the affinity (or, to the contrary, disaffinity) between groups that attract (or contrast) of physical types or habits (1978:388). Based on these observations, Weber puts forward his own definition of ethnic groups. "We shall call 'ethnic groups' those human groups that entertain a subjective belief in their common descent because of similarities of physical type or of customs or both, or because of memories of colonization and migration; this belief must be important for the propagation of group formation; conversely, it does not matter whether or not an objective blood relationship exists" (1978:389).

Some authors believe that Weber's idea is not very useful because it does not distinguish between on the one hand ethnic groups in "immigrant societies," groups that are the outcome of complex processes of migration and settlement and on the other hand groups of autochthons or minorities (see, eg, Kubiak 1980a:55; Babinski 1982). However, the concept has proved to be fruitful for the analysis of the American situation, particularly from the second half of the 1960s, when the parallel processes of "politicizations" (see, eg, Bell 1975:141) and "subjectivization," individualization and privati-zation of ethnicity of a European origin became visible.

There are many reasons why ethnicity was "looked for" in social consciousness. The most important of these were the decline of traditional white ethnic ghettoes (and transformations of ethnic local communities) and difficulties in distinguishing "ethnics" from "non-ethnics" based on obvious visible features, such as appearance, language and habits. Older theories, describing ethnicity in terms of "objective" cultural traits and/or primordial attachments seemed no longer adequate. Moreover, ethnic ideologies came under more extensive discussion (see, eg, Paleczny 1988; Rokicki 1992:19). According to Ewa Morawska, "recent sociological and sociohistorical scholarship treats [ethnicity - JM] as a dynamic category: a 'strategic tool' or 'resource' situationally activated and mobilized in the process of interaction between the immigrants and the host system" (1985:8). The author refers to Anthony Giddens' concept of structuring as a sustained, dynamic interpretation of the everyday, personal world and social environment. This environment is a normative system both constraining and mobilizing individuals (1985:5,6).

Dynamic, interactive, subjective ideas of ethnicity and the ethnic group, having been developed since the early 1970s, are strongly influenced by the scholarship of Frederik Barth. His ideas are similar, in my opinion, to the more general thoughts of Florian Znaniecki, mentioned above. Barth does not agree that there are strong and univocal ties between cultural groups and concrete, "objective" cultural traits. He questions the thesis that geographical and social isolation is the crucial facto in sustaining cultural diversity. Two observations support the scholar's skepticism. Firstly, he thinks that apparent boundaries between ethnic groups persist in spite of a flow of personnel across them. Distinction into ethnic groups is, therefore, not based on the lack of mobility, contact and information. Instead, it is based on the social processes of exclusion and incorporation. Secondly, some stable and often important social relations are maintained across group boundaries and they do not blur them. Barth concludes that ethnic groups are the outcome of ascription and identification by the actors themselves. They are social categories that organize interactions between people within the group and across group boundaries (1969:9-10).

Origin and cultural background are also important, but their significance has a subjective character. According to Barth, "A categorical ascription is an ethnic ascription when it classifies a person in terms of his basic, most general identity, preemptively determined by his origin and background. To the extent that actors use ethnic identities to categorize themselves and others for purposes of interaction, they form ethnic groups in this organizational sense" (1969:13-14). For Barth, individuals are actors capable of reason, who depending on the situation, select cultural traits or differences that will be important for them to identify group boundaries. Where we are concerned with interactions between different cultural groups, cultural rules must emerge, enabling communication across boundaries as well as rules enabling maintenance of identity. The proof, that it is not prescribed cultural traits but rather values and features consciously selected by active social subjects which create group boundaries, lies in the fact that even a drastic reduction of cultural differences between ethnic groups does not correspond in a reduction of ethnic identities or with a breakdown in boundary-maintaining processes (1969:33).

The concept of the group presented by Florian Znaniecki and the ideas of the ethnic group put forward by Max Weber and Frederik Barth have, in my opinion, important common features. "Something" can "objectively" lie at the foundation of the group. However, the most important thing is what the group members define as common for all of them, whet in their opinion distinguishes them from the "others," how they define boundaries between themselves and the strangers, and what kinds of social actions maintain boundaries. This "something" that lies at the foundation of ethnic groups does, however, exist to a certain extent" in that some phenomena are more important than others and more real for people. In Znaniecki, the sense of belonging can have an external, constraining origin: a social environment can locate us in a group and in this way determine our life's potential, opportunities of interactions, access to social resources. The "extra-conscious" and "extra-subjective" foundations of ethnic groups are not neglected in modern theoretical approaches but, as we will see, they are rarely stressed. Some modern ids referring to them seem to be very helpful in the empirical analysis of contemporary ethnic local communities.

In 1887, Ferdinand Toennies introduced the concept of Gemeinschaft (community). Since then, it has become one of the basic notions in sociology. The kind of collectivity it denotes embraces "natural" and "ascribed" relationships (1963). Wsevolod W. Isajiw refers to this idea in his discussion on the definitions of ethnicity. He notes that the Gemeinschaft implies involuntary participation, and a sense of peoplehood and a sharing of the same culture.

One's participation in culture means that one has been formerly socialized into it. Socialization is a social process, in many respects intentional. Sometimes, though, after three or four generations, the ethnics do not undergo any ethnic socialization (referring to the group of distant origin) but the "subjective identity' remains.

Subjective approaches to ethnicity have, therefore, some advantages according to Isajiw, who seems to prefer definitions stressing involuntary participation. Subjective identity is for him somehow based on the real link between a certain person and a group of his/her ancestors that shared certain cultural values and norms. The link with ancestors, and therefore with history, is, according to Isajiw, quite often forced upon people form outside, giving them no opportunity to forget their ethnic identity (1974). Traditional culture, group history, both before migration and after resettlement, is obviously constructed, and the link with ancestors has a symbolic character. Concerning the whole Polish-American group, this problem was not so long ago discussed by Jaroslaw Rokicki (1992:151-82).

Gary B. Cohen has presented a model similar to that of Isajiw. In Cohen's opinion, the ascriptive, primordial traits are at the foundation of ethnic groups. On the other hand, an individual has to learn his/her group's culture and its persistence is a result of social activity. A group's culture must somehow be clear and distinguishable for the others. Therefore, ethnicity must be treated as a dynamic phenomenon of an interactive character. The more frequent the intergroup contacts, the more mutable the group's definition of cultural traits considered particularly significant (1984:1031-37).

Some "objective" (and at least not fully controlled by immigrant minorities) ascriptive features that unify people into ethnic groups, are discussed by Jonathan D. Sarna. There are various kinds of unifying features. The most noticeable are language and religion. Systems of ethnic classification are sometimes based on both of them but more often on one selected trait. There are collectivities classified as one ethnic group because of a common religion whatever the language (or rather languages) spoken by their members. There are collectivities classified as one ethnic group because of one language regardless of the religions practiced by the people. "Objectivity," "outside character," "ascriptive" character of these features are beyond question. However, these "objective" criteria were applied "subjectively." Classification had, according to Sarna, an outside character. All groups making up a host society (and not only the dominant group) employed, when looking for common similarities, the selectivity by the "lowest common status." Consequently, Jews, regardless of their country of origin and language, became classified by a religious criterion. Some Germans and Irish were considered to be primarily Catholics. Most of the immigrants, however, were classified by language whatever their religion and regardless of their own identity. In addition to this informal outside ascription, there also emerged the institutionalized outside ascription of the *Immigration Commission's Dictionary Of Races*, published in 1910. Immigrants were classified by politicians, churches, schools. Often, the levels were accepted by immigrants because they gave them symbolic opportunity for collective defense (1978).

The symbolic and not "technical" significance of the previously vivid cultural features and ethnic organizations is stressed by Herbert J. Gans. He believes that historically speaking ethnicity is an immigrant working class phenomenon. Increasing visibility of ethnicity results, in his view, from the socioeconomic upward mobility of the white immigrant groups. The old cultures of the countries of origin have no significance for the ethnic middle classes. On the other hand, its members wish to avoid the total uniformization and atomization of modern mass society. They want to be distinguishable but in a way that causes as little trouble as possible and is acceptable to the host society. They refer to symbols that somehow represent ethnic culture and that can be easily expressed. Therefore, ethnic culture and ethnic organizations must somehow exist. It is enough if this essence is residual (from the point of view of the situation in the traditional ethnic ghettoes) and the ethnic group, in this symbolic sense, can continue to the next generations (1979). According to Gans, participation in the ethnic group is no longer prescribed. Now, it results from choice but this choice must refer to features that exist independently of the will of a concrete individual. I believe that this model describes ethnicity very well for many of the groups making up the Polish-American community in South Bend (the examples will be presented in the following chapters) and perhaps in other towns and cities.

Donald Horowitz accepts the idea that ascription distinguishes ethnic groups from voluntary associations. However, he pays special attention to the fact that individual persons are often able to manipulate (enhance or hide) traits socially defined as ascribed and ethnic groups can shift their own boundaries (1975:113-14). I will return to this interesting problem later. Some authors, like Nathan Glazer and

Daniel P. Moynihan seem to question the very existence of primordial aspects of ethnicity. They say that "One problem with the primordial is that we know how many of the groups that have engaged in "primordial" conflicts are themselves recent historical creations. We know to what degree attachment to one group or another, or the intensity of attachment to any group, depends on accidental circumstances" (1975:19).

There are arguments that no primordial elements or "givens" are relevant for white ethnicity in modern, complex American society. Stanley Lieberson and Mary Waters cite the findings according to which ethnic categories gradually shift and new categories emerge. Because of many reasons, among the white Americans, the knowledge of ethnic origin weakens. Distortions occur in the transmission of family traditions. People of multiple ethnic origins tend to simplify ancestral history and they transmit this simplified, distorted picture to their children. Spouses tend to stress the marital homogeneity and sometimes invent it. In families questioned about origins year after year, inconsistency is quite common. The authors draw the following conclusions. If, among the whites in America, ethnic origin were to decline as a sociopolitical issue, these distortions would increase. Other social characteristics may become more important than ethnicity and people may declare their ethnic origins depending on their own class situation. Hence, the segment of the population who are unable to provide. any picture of their ethnic origins will expand (1986).

A different kind of connection between the "primordial character" of ethnic traits and the social situation that contributes to the fact that ethnic identities fluctuate, is presented by George M. Scott, Jr. (1990). His analyses are also important for the issue of group solidarity and the identity of ethnic groups, to be discussed in the next section of this chapter.

According to Scott, the phenomenon of continuing, emergent and reemergent ethnicity can be explained by two approaches: "primordial" and "circumstantial." The first, psychological theory refers to the ineffable affective significance of ethnic and the second, behavioral, refers to social circumstances. The first explains effectively ethnic attachments continuing over time in different environments but does not explain the fluctuations of ethnicity. The second has the opposite advantages and disadvantages. Scott's synthesis draws upon Edward Spicer's (1971) model of fluctuating oppositions.

Scott believes that we should forget the dichotomy of persistence and fluctuation of ethnicity. The dependent variable in our explanations is the degree of ethnic solidarity. The independent variable is the degree of opposition experienced by a given group in its social environment. "Primordiality" of ethnic sentiments is also important. In this theory, it is considered an intervening variable. The higher the degree of opposition, the stronger the "primordial" ethnic sentiments and, therefore, the higher the degree of ethnic solidarity. Primordial sentiments are also significant for the specific content of ethnic identity, since they are attached to those symbols against which the opposition is particularly strongly expressed: language, territory, group heroes, music, clothing, etc. The opposition itself can occur in various fields. The group's perception of the opposition is important as well. "The greater the opposition — economic, political, social, religious, or some combination thereof — perceived by an ethnic group, the greater the degree to which its historical sense of distinctiveness will be aroused, and hence the greater its solidarity or the more intense its movement towards redress (1990:164).

Scott believes that his model considers the "circular causation" which can explain the escalating nature of ethnic conflict: the belligerent expression of ethnic solidarity of a given group leads to a greater opposition against it which, in turn, increases group solidarity. The model also explains the fact that the opposition to an ethnic group can have a selective character and be stronger against some, rather than other socioeconomic strata. Those members of the upper strata of a minority who are not opposed by the dominant group, can define their position only in class terms. However, if their economic interests become endangered, the almost forgotten ethnic consciousness, solidarity and even membership of an ethnic movement can return (1990:165-6). I find Scott's model very useful for the interpretation of ethnic phenomena and will use it later, particularly in Chapter III.

What is the significance of membership in an ethnic group or in more loose ethnic categories? What are their social functions? Some are psychological: to fulfill the need to distinguish oneself from the rest of the mass society or to base personal contacts on the primordial attachments. On the other hand, ethnic groups may also be treated as interest groups. Both factors will be important to the Polish-American community of South Bend. It seems that in the area of realization of interests, ethnic groups are particularly efficient. Their power lies in the fact that they connect interests with emotions (see, eg, Bell 1975:160: Cohen 1984:1038: Glazer and Moynihan 1975:19: McKay and Lewins 1978:419) which stimulate activities that can contribute to the realization of those interests.

The discussion presented in this section proves that there are many different aspects of ethnicity and of determinants of ethnic groups' boundaries. "Objective," "real" elements as well as individual and collective ethnic consciousness can be conceptualized in several ways.

3. Ethnic Identity

Subjectivism, stressing the significance of the idea of consciousness of the ethnic group, analysis of group boundaries, their persistence and their shifting due to individual and collective activity, all lead us directly to the next problem area: individual and collective identity. The problem has important philosophical (see, eg, in Polish literature: Lipiec 1972:124; Witkowski 1988:111-117, 122-23, 219-23), psychological and sociological aspects. Drawing to some extent on the philosophical and psychological, I will concentrate on the sociological ones.

The concept of identity can be considered for every entity. Usually it is applied to anything which decides that a changeable entity persists in the integral way. As we can see, dynamics lie at the foundation of the analysis of the problem of identity. In the social context, we are using this term primarily to consider such systems as the human individual and social group. In both cases, an essential (but not the only important) issue is the consciousness. The problem has a complex character. The first point can be the individual's self-distinguishing him/her from other individuals. This self-feeling can have a prereflexive character but it can also be shaped by the perception and understanding of normative aspects of social situations in which the individual operates. The second point can be the identification of the individual with this or that group. The third point can be collective consciousness (and collective actions that follow it), the collective sense of distinction from other groups, the understanding of the criteria of belonging to the group and exclusion from the group.

Besides self-consciousness, we can deal with an equally important issue: with the potential judgment of a competent outside observer who, based on the analysis of structure and actions undertaken by the given social system, can pronounce if, and to what extent, with the passing of time, the given social system retains or loses its crucial characteristics.

Sociologists are studying the problems of identity of individual human beings and their attachments to social groups, rather than problems of identity of larger social units. When Andrzej Piotrowski, analyses the concept of identity in theories of symbolic interactionism (1985), he is interested in the identity of individual persons. Malgorzata Melchior, in her work on ethnic identity stresses the fact that the notion of social identity can be applied both to individuals and to groups, but she concentrates on the first possibility. Individuals identify with social groups or with culture. Individual's identity determines his/her place in the social world (1990:21-23). Another Polish, Zbigniew Bokszanski, presents a sociological analysis of the self-experience of social actors (1989:3). An individual person is the only actor taken into account here. On the other hand, Bokszanski also analyses the action sociology of Alain Touraine (see, eg, 1977, 1981). In this theory, the collective and not the individual actor is important. The new found self-consciousness of this actor manifests itself in the increasing conviction of the self-determination of social systems, of the possible designation by them of their own life world. Group identity is determined by the group itself by means of its own actions. The social order does not seem to be impersonal to the collective actor. It becomes a creation of the group. The collective actor's identity emerges as a result of its dynamic relations (first of all conflict) with other collective actors. Self-identification is possible by self-definition, by definition of the adversary, by the collective project of the new social order (see also Bokszanski 1990:217-28).

Krzysztof Kwasniewski attempted to conceptualize collective identity in a cultural context. It refers, in his opinion, to the social agency, subjectivity. He says that "This subjectivity (or the agency - JM), even if unconscious, establishes, in historical-territorial communities, an objective cultural and ethnic identity. On the other hand, social subjectivity (agency) of collectivities which are more dispersed and culturally heterogeneous is also possible, particularly where it is an object of social actions of another, outside, social collectivity. Then, this subjectivity is connected with the growth of consciousness of identity and becomes a subjective-objective cultural and ethnic identity or social identity" (1986:14).

Modern literature on ethnicity uses the concept of identity very often. Two terms are being applies: "identity" and "identification." In the majority of cases they are not very precise. According to Irvin T. Sanders and Ewa Morawska, in the works on ethnic issues, at least four different implicit theoretical concepts are being applied. The first is subjective, psychological ethnic identification or better, the conscious self-identification of individuals. The second refers to a more complex phenomenon in which self-identification, as reported by respondents, is combined with other characteristics of ethnic attitudes and behavior. The third concept of ethnic identity is expressed only in terms of patterns of attitudes and behavior. Finally, the fourth concept includes in the analysis the ethnic community dimension and introduces the idea of "ethnic identification with community" (1975:236). Identity has four basic dimensions: a vague, subjective self-concept (self-identification); "ethnic attitudes;" "ethnic behavior" (both attitudes and behavior have their own indices), and finally relations between the individual and the group.

Not all these dimensions must be (and are) considered in concrete ethnic studies. Neither is their list closed. Tadeusz Paleczny stresses the emotional dimension too: not only perception, but also the "positive evaluation" of one's own, individual participation in the ethnic group (1989:66). It corresponds to the McKay and Lewins' (in the work quoted above) concept of two types of ethnic identification. Obviously, "negative evaluation" is also possible.

As we can see, the notion of identity is applied first of all to the relationship between an individual and his/her reference group (or cultural environment). Conceptually and emotionally, it divides the world into the "us" and "them," into the "we-group" and "they-group." Ethnic identity is a particular kind of identity. Boundaries between an ethnic group and its environment, as earlier mentioned, are built or constructed from the inside or from the outside. Ethnic identity will therefore be, at least to some extent, determined by the "others" (see, eg, Bell 1975:159; Rokicki 1992:19-20).

When, in the literature on ethnicity, the concept of identity refers to groups, two ideas seem to be particularly important. First is the above mentioned idea of collective action and the second the also previously mentioned idea of shifting group boundaries. Persistence of the group's ethnic identity depends, amongst other things, on the maintenance of its boundaries. Change in group identity depends, amongst other things, on the boundary shift.

How can a group shift its boundaries? The answer is through individual or collective, faster or slower, more or less violent, more or less deliberate actions. A group can create possibilities for the change of the individual identity of its members, for example, through religious conversion. It can take steps towards modification of its own habits and customs, becoming more or less ethnocentric in its relations to other groups, more or less rigorous in stressing the ascriptive aspects of membership. In South Bend, some large Polish-American organizations firstly decided to accept the non-Polish husbands or wives of their members, secondly to accept people of non-Polish but Slavic origin and finally to accept even Hungarians, defined (falsely) as Slavs. The president of one of the big Polish-American associations is a German-American, the husband of a lady of Polish extraction (formerly, he was an activist of a German-American club). A group can assimilate and become absorbed by another group. Various groups can unify into one, one group can divide into several.

Changes in the identity of ethnic groups can also occur without the boundary shifts. A group can completely transform its own economic structure, increase or decrease its status in the social hierarchy (see, eg, Horowitz 1975:113-18). The typical activity being undertaken so far by the group as a collective agent can change. One reason for this situation can be the alteration of the problems which the group faced. The dominant factor in the group attitudes and personality types can change. The scope for the continuation of cultural tradition can also change: some aspects of this tradition can be given up others can be picked up.

The change in the group identity can, but does not have to, be perceived by and reflected in the consciousness of the members of the group. Therefore, we must not treat identity as the phenomenon limited to the sphere of social consciousness. Group identity, when it becomes considered as a "theoretical" problem, for the whole or for some of its parts (for instance — some particularly sensitive or interested members), can become an object of manipulation and even of ideological conflict. Various subgroups can expose various aspects of the group's symbolic structure as those forming its core and deciding on its persistence or, to the contrary, transforming its core into an advantageous or disadvantageous direction.

The problems of identity and change will be considered again in the next chapters of this book.

4. Everyday Life

After having discussed the concepts of local community, ethnic local community, ethnic group, ethnicity and ethnic identity, I should discuss the meaning of "everyday life." It seems to me that there are various ways of conceiving "everyday life." They can be located on the continuum. On its one extreme, there are historical descriptions of daily activities of different social collectivities. A prominent example of this kind of "description" is the well known work of Fernand Braudel (1992) devoted to the analysis if "structures of daily life." However, this scholar deals not with any local community but with the whole world during a period of four centuries. What belongs to the "daily life" according to Braudel? He describes in this volume the agriculture, food, housing, clothing and fashion, technology, transportation, the functioning of the economy and the financial system, city life. The second extreme of the continuum are, in my opinion, analyses completed by social phenomenologists, ethnomethodologists, symbolic interactionists. We have in mind first of all their contributions during the last few decades, when we think of sociological studies of everyday life.

Historical description, even if referring to the present time, seems to be the simplest approach to everyday life. However, even this kind of description demands some analytical categories. Braudel does not pay particular attention to them but he provides some interesting directions. "Daily life — he says — means petty facts hardly visible in time and space" (1992:25). "Talking about economy, we depart from the routine of daily life, from the un-conscious existence (1992:469). I will return to these ideas later.

I should stress the fact that in this book the conceptual analysis is treated instrumentally, and not as an end in itself. We should also bear in mind the fact that within the socio-philosophical approaches to the world of everyday live we can find proposals that are difficult to coordinate. The examples are on the one hand Juergen Habermas's ideas and on the other theories developed by Alfred Schuetz and his followers. Despite the difficulties, the category of everyday life has been, for about one decade, applied in Poland for the empirical studies of religion (see, eg, Borowik 1990; Pawluczuk 1990) and for studies of regional consciousness (see the works quoted in the Introduction).

Jacek Sojka, in his book on Schuetz's phenomenological sociology, discourages his readers from applying this approach to the empirical analysis of social phenomena. According to the empirical analysis of social phenomena. According to Sojka, Schuetz's ideas can be empirically useful, but only regarding research on the social situation in the fluid, unstable state, where the intersubjectivity is only emerging or where, due to certain reasons, the reality of the world is being questioned by its participants (1991:11, 144-50). Neither does Zdzislaw Krasnodebski encourage us to apply in field research the achievements of phenomenology. He believes that this philosophy can be used only as inspiration for sociological research and interpretations. However, he presents examples of how phenomenology and ethnomethodology are being actually applied in research. Under the label of "sociology of everyday life," peripheries of social life, unusual phenomena, extreme situations are being successfully studied (1989:49). He does not mention local communities. Maurice Roche, who is interested in the phenomeno-logical approach in sociology, thinks that ethnomethodology, dealing with everyday life, concentrates on conventional methods of operation of bureaucratic organizations, but also on the ways the people act beyond the official rules and directions (1989:468). Neither of the examples presented above is attractive for me as an approach to the analysis of the everyday life of a local community. In a sense, however, I will follow some of these ideas, paying attention to ethnic local institutions, and to formal and informal aspects of their life.

Institutions as examples of "interpretive field research" are interesting for Marek Czyzewski: "The effect of these analyses is a new type of sociological literature that might be described as ethnography of everyday life. What is meant here are first of all monographic studies of everyday life in various social institutions" (1990:102). Czyzewski mentions research on the health service, education, courts of justice, jurisdiction for adolescents, scientific labs, etc. As we can see, the ethnic community is not listed here as it is not presented as a subject of studies by other social phenomenologists. However, a methodological postulate of Czyzewski is interesting. He says that there is no necessity that sociologists, using their regular field technics, construct a new social phenomenon: "sociological research." They can observe in a "natural," careful way, everything that goes on in the world that surrounds them. "There is a reality moving along before our eyes. We guess the way it is arranged but — I do not know why — we do not consider this arrangement worthy of our systematic study" (1990:1020). This suggestion to conduct research by means of various kinds of observation of what "goes on" was taken on board in this book. This anthropological method is obviously more than one hundred years old but its value seems to be eternal.

The authors I quoted above, despite their skepticism for empirical research, are enthusiasts, theoreticians and practitioners of interpretive sociology. What is interesting, in Polish sociological literature an encouraging conduct of field research of local communities from the point of view of phenomenological sociology of everyday life can be found in an author who, practicing it, overtly presents his general skepticism towards it. Jacek Wodz is interested in the actual and potential object of empirical research of local communities within the phenomenological perspective. He says that the scope of this object is wide: phenomena of everyday life in concrete social situations, social time and space, rhythm of social activity within time and space, normative order, social construction of boundaries in space. Like authors quoted above, Wodz is also interested in the breaking of norms, in unusual social phenomena that glue a community together, which make up the cadence of social time, which give meaning to social activity because of its relation to the exceptional (1989:33-40).

As I have mentioned above, empirical analyses of everyday life have been conducted for decades by social anthropologists.

5. Everyday Life and Festivity in an Ethnic Local Community: Summary

What is the significance of the former conceptual analysis for the chapters to follow? The everyday life of an ethnic local community is a world of a common, paramount, normal, pre-arranged, intersubjective but unconscious (in the sense that it is not the subject of constant reflection), unquestioned "ethnic reality," a world that is not considered by its participants as their practical problem but which can always break down. This world is a correlate of subjective experiences of individuals. For each of them, it seems to have an intersubjective character: it had existed when they entered it, it is shared with other individuals (Berger and Luckmann 1967:19-28, Szahaj 1990:157). The reality of everyday life is always, in a hidden way, a "given," it is a world preconstituted in social constructions, in already existing knowledge. It refers to implicit knowledge, structured but unconscious, based on cultural "pre-understandings." Using the Ryle-Habermas language we could say that it refers to intuitive "knowledge how" and not explicit "knowledge that" (see, eg, Szahaj 1990:65). Using terminology of Jerzy Kmita, a Polish philosopher of culture, we could say that it refers to "respected knowledge," being used in the routinized activity and not consciously recognized, reflexive, "accepted knowledge" (1982:47-48). Everyday life will form a conceptual scheme that determines specific styles of experiencing the world (Grathof 1989:449).

In the analysis to follow, the everyday world will be, like in Richard Grathof, a world of work. It will also be a world of close friends, relatives, social clubs, associations, parties, and to some extent of local politics. In my observations, I did not have access to all these worlds. From the point of view of the ethnic aspects of social life, some of them seem to me more and some less important, though. For the active maintenance of individual ethnicity, the world of social clubs and associations during the last couple of decades became even more important than the world of work, politics and family. All the worlds, to which I had access, will be presented here, though.

The "life world" reproduces itself in the cultural tradition. Therefore, this tradition must somehow be constantly reinforced, or there must exist (be sometimes invented) symbols and rituals that always refer to it. As we know, the identity of ethnic groups can shift and the way it shifts should be analyzed. The problems (mentioned earlier) of language are very important in this context: what happens to the everyday life of an ethnic group when it ceases to use its traditional ethnic language, the social code that determines the way of perceiving and understanding the world?

In the analysis to follow, it is not possible to agree fully with the thesis of Berger and Luckmann (1967:44) that the everyday world is "a zone of lucidity behind which there is a background of darkness." The ethnic world of life of a local community is its most important aspect, a singled out sphere, but the other spheres are not a background of darkness nowadays. Relations between the ethnic world and the world which is there behind it should also be a subject of research.

The ethnic world of life has its local space and its local calendar. It has its everyday activities and its uncommon activities, its festivity. Festivity, clearly visible against the background of everyday life, manifests itself in the contact with that reality which is particularly important for the culture of the group, with the sphere of sacrum. Festivity means a temporary breaking with the routine, with the unconscious, unreflexive being.

The ethnic world is maintained and reconstructed by the individual and collective actions, by relationships between individuals and subgroups. The world of life of an entire ethnic local community is maintained to different degrees by different individuals and organizations. Some of them act in a very routinized way and participate in this world only, or nearly only, by conforming to the norms of the world that they maintain. Others reproduce this world in a more active way, sometimes even make it shift. Such constructs of the social ethnic daily world, like language, implicitly accepted group ideology, normatively understood social structure, undergo slow transformations. Old constructs do not cease to exist but they rather take the symbolic, festal meaning and may return in a new form when the group intends to give witness to its ethnicity. "Knowledge how" can transform itself into "knowledge that" ("respected knowledge" into "accepted knowledge') when, under the influence of changes of the outside situation, the previous routinized ways of activity cease to be efficient. Then, some actions can leave the sphere of everyday life and enter the sphere of reflexive group consciousness. However, new "knowledge that" can become routinized and be transformed into a new "knowledge how." Everyday life and festivity overlap. Calendrical ceremonies and rites of passage are always long awaited and prepared. They mean the contact of the group with the sacrum, but obviously must be performed in a routinized way.

••••

The theoretical categories presented above were not discussed in a equally detailed way. The reason for this was that they have been and still are used for the empirical analyses in varying degrees. Ethnicity, having many particular aspects, was discussed at length. The most important problems appeared to be with the central concept, the concept of everyday life. The following pages will show to what extent it was possible to combine the interpretive approach with more routine ways of sociological and anthropological analysis.

CHAPTER TWO

THE URBAN COMMUNITY OF SOUTH BEND AND ITS GROWTH

South Bend is a city located in the northern part of Indiana, very close to the border with the state of Michigan, and about 45 minutes drive from the beautiful dunes of Lake Michigan. It lies more or less half way between, on the west, Chicago and the border of Indiana with Illinois, and on the east, the border of Indiana with Ohio. South Bend makes up one urban agglomeration with neighboring (on the east) town of Mishawaka. The two towns together have approximately 150 thousand inhabitants. The nearest town, more than ten miles east, in another county, is Elkhart, once having the highest per capita income in the States. Some inhabitants of Elkhart work in South Bend and vice versa. A very small subcampus of Indiana University at South Bend (IUSB) is located in Elkhart. Another close little town is Niles, being the border with Michigan. Some people commute from Niles to work and/or school in South Bend.

South Bend and Mishawaka belong to St. Joseph County. In 1980, the county had 241 thousand inhabitants when the Standard Metropolitan Statistical Area (SMSA) of South Bend had 280 thousand inhabitants. The metropolitan area of South Bend is, therefore, larger than the county to which it belongs. The name of the county comes from a picturesque river that "bends" within the town and that flows through northern Indiana and part of Michigan.

The name for the whole region that I am discussing is Michiana. The word contains parts of the names of both of these bordering states. Three local television stations, based in South Bend, as well as an uncountable number of radio stations, broadcast for the whole Michiana. The only remaining local newspaper, *The South Bend Tribune*, is distributed also in southern Michigan. I have already mentioned that many people from southern Michigan commute every day to South Bend. Between the city of South Bend on the south and the state border on the north, there are many suburbs. The big Notre Dame University is also located in this area. The university has its own postal address and code that cover the neighboring St. Mary's College, too. Nearly all students and employees of both schools live in South Bend and its suburbs. The second university, one of eight campuses of Indiana University, finds itself in the southern part of town. Some students from Niles and other places in southern Michigan commute also to this school. In the city of South Bend, there is a busy Michiana Regional Airport, the third biggest airport in Indiana. Nine airlines connect the area with six large Midwestern cities.

According to the 1980 Census reports (when I was writing this text, reports of the 1990 Census were not yet available), there were nearly five million inhabitants in the whole state of Indiana. In the South Bend SMSA, a little more than 280 thousand lived and in the town as such - nearly 110 thousand (much more people had lived here earlier: in 1960 - 132,445 and in 1970 - 139,400; see Stabrowski 1984: 54). Among the South Bendians, according to the Census report, 11,056 people were of single Polish ancestry and 6,399 people of Polish and other ancestry (*Census of Population*, 1983: table 60). Demographically speaking, the Polish-American community is a significant part of the city's population.

In 1980, the South Bend SMSA lived 8,198 people born outside the US, including 5,230 people born in Europe. The largest communities were made up of people born in Germany (995), Hungary (817), Poland (693) and Austria (344). Slightly more than 57 thousand children between the ages of five and 17 lived in the area. Among them, 55 thousand spoke English at home. Of the rest, the highest number of children speaking Spanish (904), German (516), French (167) and Polish (147). Nearly 203 thousand people were 18 years old or more. Nearly 190 thousand spoke English spoke English at home. Among the rest, the highest number were persons speaking Polish (4,533), Spanish (2,431) and German (1,799) (*Census of Population*, 1983: table 116). This information illustrates that, at least in the Polish group, transmission of ethnic culture through language is not very successful.

We will now return to the city and its ethnic characteristics after this consideration of the standard statistical area. Half the population (58,584 people) declared themselves to be of single ethnic ancestry. If we exclude the category of "others" (relatively large, embracing 21,206 people, probably Blacks and Hispanics), the Poles will emerge as the largest aggregate. There were 11 thousand of them. The second were Germans (9,842). The next aggregates were the people of "English" (5,541), Irish (3,485), Hungarian (3,446) and Italian (1,201) ancestry. (In the neighboring Mishawaka, the order of precedence is different and the Poles are in fourth place.) As for the people of multiple ancestry in South Bend, the largest aggregate were people of German and other (19,677), then Irish and other (14,044), English and other (10,086), Polish and other (6,399), French and other (4,689) and Italian and other (1,383) origin (*Census Of Population And Housing*, 1983: table P8). It seems therefore, in my opinion, that the Polish, French and Italian groups had more endogamic character than the German, Irish and English groups.

As often happens, statistical data is contested by representatives, and particularly leaders of the ethnic communities in question. They believe that the real numbers are higher. They rarely present their own estimates and when they do, there are no reasons to consider them more reliable than the Census data. Until now, there is no systematic analysis of the ethnic composition of the whole population of South Bend, its SMSA nor the county. Some attempts to collect materials have been undertaken, though.

Indiana University at South Bend (later IUSB) established in the early 1970s the Ethnic Heritage Studies Program, that soon published two small, interesting booklets. The topic under consideration in one of them is the Polish-American community (Breza and Pieszak 1975) and in the second one - the Hungarian-American community (Scherer 1975). In addition to these, a "resource guide" about the main ethnic groups of the city was published (Calvin, Rasmussen and Gollnick [eds.] 1975.) It contains text on the Blacks, Hungarian-Americans, Italian-Americans, Mexican-Americans and Polish-Americans. Each chapter informs us about the ethnic associations operating in town, on ethnic parishes, festivals and cuisine.

There is also an interesting amateur "publication" prepared by The Forever Learning Institute, run by the Fort Wayne-South Bend Roman-Catholic Diocese. The booklet presents ethnic groups of the city and county that were of interest to the participants of the research project (they were not specialists, though, in the fields of history, sociology, ethnicity, etch.). The chapters discuss the following groups: Polish, Hungarian, Belgian, French, Irish, Greek, Italian, Croat, Jewish and German (Scheuer [ed.] 1982). It is not clear what the reason was for this particular choice and for this order of precedence. No numbers, not even estimates of the membership of particular groups were given. The stylistics of individual chapters are different. Some of them (unfortunately not of the Polish-Americans) present and quote at length memoirs and life histories. They make a very good resource for the research on everyday life of these groups. In the following pages, I will draw upon the booklets mentioned above.

The city of South Bend is divided into 35 Census tracts. We can compare them with the town map (that is a part of the Census report). People of single Polish ancestry live in each tract. In 33 tracts, there are people of Polish and other ancestry. People of single Polish ancestry live mostly in the western part of town, constituting, in the tracts close to each other, 15 to 40 percent of the population. The numbers of people of mixed (Polish and other) ancestry in the same tracts is lower, sometimes significantly so (see, *Census Of Population And Housing*, 1983: table P8). Based on this data, it is possible to conclude that the Westside of South Bend is still concentrated by most of the people of single Polish origin and that people of mixed ancestry tend to move out to other parts of town.

Today's ethnic mixture, and the Polonia within it, was shaped by early processes of settlement. The areas on St. Joseph River, where South Bend lies now, belonged until the late 18th century to the colonies that later became Canada. They had been visited for the first time by white people in 1679, who left some memoirs of this fact. A prominent discoverer, whose name is noticeable on the street plates in most Midwestern towns and cities, Rene Robert De La Salle, came to the region at this time. In his expedition, the purpose of which was to search for tracts to transport furs, there were three French Roman-Catholic monks. One of them Father Louis Hennepin, came to the particular site where South Bend is located today. Then, Indian tribes of Miami and Potawatomi lived here. In 1686, Indians transferred their land to the Jesuit Order. A chapel and a temporary Niles St. Joseph Mission were founded. After the American revolution, the whole region was taken over by the US and included the Northwest Territory. The Roman-Catholic jurisdiction of the diocese of Montreal was maintained until 1830, when it was transferred to the diocese in Baltimore (see, McAvoy 1953).

The region, earlier inhabited only by Indians, attracted some French and later French-Canadians at the end of the 17th century. Until the early 1800s, there were no permanent settlements here.

Only in 1820, Pierre Navarre, the next of both the historic and legendary figures, decided to build a home and storage facilities in the area. Like many before him, he was trading with the Indians. According to the source literature, Navarre was under the influence of the beautiful St. Joseph River valley and located his household on the northern bank of the river. It was not Navarre, however, but Alexis Coquillard who was considered to have been the first citizen of the future town.

In 1829, the first post office was opened. The settlement was called Southhold then, nobody knows why. It belonged to the then very large Allen county. (This county still exists but is much smaller than at the beginning of the 19th century and contains the area of the city of Fort Wayne, about 100 miles southeast of South Bend.) In 1830, the town was called South Bend and soon became the capital of the new St. Joseph county, much larger than the same county now. Only in 1835, were all the legal problems with the localization of the county capital and incorporation of the town solved (Brown 1920: 20-27).

In November 1842, a group of priests of the Congregation of the Holy Cross (CSC) with Father Edward Frederic Sorin came to town. This fact had an enormous impact on the future history of South Bend, the region and even on American higher education. The monks built, on the northern outskirts of town, a chapel dedicated to Notre Dame and established a school. This school developed into Notre Dame University. Two years later they opened a school for girls nearby. This later became St. Mary's College.

The area lies in the river valley and on the important cross roads of trade tracts. In addition to this communication advantage, iron ore was discovered here. All of this meant opportunities for fast growth. The chance was used well. In 1833, the first metallurgic works were established. In the late 1830s, the first factory of tolls and carriages was opened. In the 1840s and 1850s, the railroad was being built and soon it connected South Bend with the northern parts of the country. The factories needed workers to fill the increasing number of available jobs. They were not on the spot and had to be brought from outside the region. The first immigrants to the town, besides French-Canadians, were Americans from the states of Ohio, Pennsylvania and New York. Europeans came as well. Germans from Bavaria are said to have been the first of them. Soon, at the railway construction, others got employment too: the Irish, Belgians, Swedes, Englishmen, Poles, Hungarians. All of them made up their own local communities, building their own churches and schools (McAvoy 1953). It should be mentioned here that since the mid-19th century South Bend has not been a Roman-Catholic town. Despite the presence and even sometime domination of Notre Dame University, most inhabitants have belonged to various Protestant denominations.

Throughout the 19th century, several industrial enterprises were opened in South Bend. Very soon they brought fame to the town and, because of the jobs they offered, attracted many people. In 1852, two blacksmiths, brothers Henry and Clement Studebaker came to town. They started to manufacture carts and carriages. Soon, the very famous Studebaker Brothers' Wagon Co. began its operations. In 1855, South Bend Iron Works, later renamed (after the founder) Oliver Chilled Plow Works was opened. In 1868, two new factories were established. The first was Singer Sewing Machine Company, manufacturing sewing machine cases and the second was Birdsell Manufacturing Company (less important for our analysis). In 1873, Studebaker was said to be the largest carriage factory in the world. In 1899, the company started production of combustion engine cars. In 1900 it experimented with cars with the electrical engines. Up until the Korean War, the factory was also building military vehicles.

Industrial growth contributed to the growth of the town. Between 1850 and 1880, the number of inhabitants was doubling every decade. In 1850, there were 1,652 inhabitants, in 1896 - 3,803, in 1870 - 7,206, in 1880 - 13,280. In 1865, South Bend received its city rights. Encouraged by their employers, particularly by James Oliver, the workers were moving in their families and building or buying houses. They resided in the city. Individual ethnic groups were constructing their own neighborhoods with stores, workshops, banks. In the late 1870s, members of the immigrant groups began to enter local politics. In order to vote and to be elected, they had to become US citizens. Just after the Civil War, because of the large influx of immigrants, their naturalization and their political preferences, the previous domination of the Republican Party came to an end in South Bend. A new era, with lasting continuity and with only short breaks up until today, the domination of the Democratic Party began (see, e.g., Renkiewicz 1967: 29-69; Swastek 1941: 8-

16). What is interesting, is that Mishawaka remained Republican. Perhaps this is connected to its ethnic composition.

The companies mentioned above were initially very much interested in their actual and potential employees. James Oliver is said to have been bringing immigrants form New York City personally at his own expense. Job offers were sent to the East Coast and even to Europe. Because of these actions, in the 1870s not only individuals and families, but also groups of families were coming to South Bend. Initially, the companies were paying very good wages for unskilled labor. As I have mentioned above, they were helping in the buying and building of houses. It should also be noted that up until World War I, the labor market in South Bend was strongly concentrated. According to Frank Anthony Renkiewicz, at the beginning of the century, Oliver, Singer and Studebaker together employed seven out of nine thousand laborers of the city (1967: 104).

Living, in principle, in a state of social peace but witnessing significant social tensions sometimes, the city was growing. Between 1900 and 1930 the number of inhabitants tripled. The dynamics were stopped in their tracks though only a few years after the end of the First World War, because of two simultaneous social processes. One of them was the new law that seriously limited immigration, particularly from Eastern and Southern Europe. The second was the Depression. A few years before the Depression, in 1923, Vincent Bendix opened a workshop in South Bend producing car breaks. Since 1929, Bendix Aviation Corporation has manufactured various instruments for automobiles and airplanes. In a sense it has continued to do the same up until now, under the new name of Allied-Signal, Inc. Depression and limits on immigration caused, however, both a decline in the industrial sector of the South Bend economy and, between 1930 and 1940, in the city's population.

After World War II the city recovered. The population was growing from decade to decade. Postwar prosperity made renovation and development of the city possible. The downtown area took particular advantage of this. Quarters inhabited mostly by Eastern European ethnic groups until now, found themselves on the outside of the improvement.

Meanwhile, new immigrant groups emerged on the urban scene. On the one hand, the Blacks started their mass migration from

the South to the industrial, urbanized North. On the other hand
Hispanics, mostly Mexican-Americans, were also moving to the
North. This general pattern was true in South Bend, too. In 1940,
3,679 Blacks lived here, and in 1980 - 20,066. Until 1950, city
statistics did not register Hispanics at all, and in 1980, 2,594 people
of Hispanic origin lived here. Both groups moved into Westside,
inhabited until then by Eastern Europeans (see Stabrowski 1984: 57).
Eastern European groups were no longer growing through the
process of immigration. A small number of individuals came in
1939, just after the outbreak of the Second World War. A few
hundred Poles came in 1950 and 1951 under the status of Displaced
Persons. In 1956, a few hundred Hungarians came during the civil
war in their country. After the declaration of martial law in Poland
in December 1981, less than one hundred activists of the Solidarity
movement came but very soon left for bigger cities. Changes in the
character of immigration were to have a strong impact on the city,
particularly on the white, European local communities.

The increase in population continued until the late 1960s.
South Bend, like many other cities of the American Rust Belt, the
existence of which was based on metallurgy, became witness of the
decline of heavy industry. At the end of 1963, Studebaker company,
then employing around 12 thousand people, was closed. Now, only
recollections, unemployment, huge empty shops and a beautiful
Studebaker National Museum are all that remains of the firm that
once manufactured many kinds of vehicles, including very elegant
ones. The Bendix Corporation, employing in the 1950s about 10
thousand people, laid off one third of the labor force. As the Allied-
Signal Inc., it is still one of the largest employers in the region and
one of the most modern tool-manufacturing companies. The Oliver
corporation, employing in the mid-1960s around four thousand
people, was reduced in the late 1970s to a small factory. As we can
see, South Bend experienced a serious outflow of well-paid jobs,
particularly interesting for people without high formal
qualifications. The consequence was economic problems for many of
the inhabitants and a decrease of population (Stabrowski 1984: 53-
56: Renkiewicz 1967: 311-312).

Parallel to the decline of big industry and growing
unemployment among skilled blue collar workers who came mostly
from Eastern European immigrant groups and lived on the Westside,

we had, during the last two decades, the slow but continuous growth of small manufacturing, constructing and service companies, employing first of all people with much higher formal qualifications, people of different ethnic backgrounds, who lived in newer city quarters or in suburbs. They employ also unskilled laborers, typically new immigrants to the city. The city's economy has changed profoundly, and with it its class structure and ethnic composition. In 1993, in St. Joseph County (which means mostly in South Bend), about 10% of the active population were employed in government, nearly 6% in finance, insurance and real estate, nearly 20% in retail trade, 6% in wholesale trade, 5% in construction, 5% in transportation, communication and utilities, nearly 19% in manufacturing and 28% in services (*St. Joseph County*, 1993: 30). The four largest employers in the county were: Notre Dame University with 3,500, Allied-Signal Division with 2,300, South Bend Community School Corporation with 2,300 and South Bend Memorial Hospital with 2,250 employees (ibidem: 29).

St. Joseph County, which means mostly South Bend, Mishawaka and their suburbs, is a major educational center nowadays. It is divided into three school districts. They cover seven high-schools, nine middle-schools, thirty-eight grade schools. Besides these, there are also many private schools, including parish schools. There are several two-year colleges, such as Indiana Vocational Technical College, Michiana College of Commerce, Bethel College, Davenport College, Holy Cross Junior College. There are colleges and universities like St. Mary's College (offering BA programs), IUSB, being the third largest campus of the state university (offering BA and some MA programs) and internationally recognized Notre Dame University.

There are two big, modern hospitals in South Bend. Two others function in Mishawaka. There are numerous parks and recreation areas here. Symphonic and chamber orchestras and the city choir present regularly the classic repertoire. Four departments of drama at the colleges perform quite often in the city.

Despite the huge transformations which South Bend has experienced in both the ethnic and employment spheres, it is a city in which one can still live quietly and quite easily.

CHAPTER THREE

FROM POLISH TO POLISH-AMERICAN EVERYDAY LIFE

This chapter has a historical character. I intend to present here processes that shaped the Polish-American local community in South Bend. The chapter will embrace around 120 years of establishment and expansion of this ethnic group, since the immigration of first the Polish settlers, until the late 1980s.

The processes shaping the whole American Polonia have been analyzed by many Polish (and American) social scientists, mostly historians and sociologists. I will draw upon some works published after the Second World War. We should also remember, however, the pre-World War II classics of the research on Polish immigration to America, like Krystyna Duda-Dziewierz (see, e.g., 1938). Jozef Chalasinski (see, e.g., 1934, 1935, 1936), Mieczyslaw Szawleski (1924), not to mention Florian Znaniecki (see, e.g., Thomas and Znaniecki, 1918-20).

This volume concerns a regular, typical, everyday life of a Polish-American community. I will be trying to follow the process of marginalization of ethnic daily life. Initially ethnicity, as a system of specific cultural traits, based on common language and tradition, transmitted from generation to generation, filled the whole life of immigrating individuals and groups. It made up the zone of lucidity (mentioned at the end of Chapter I) behind which an outside background of darkness spread. Only (or, more precisely, mainly) the everyday world of work, also mentioned in the first chapter, was the window to another world. This other world meant an unknown language; strange folkways; a previously unknown industrial work discipline; the necessity of getting new skills; new material objects to deal with, etc. Unfortunately, I do not know of any written recollections presenting the way the South Bend Poles had been entering the new world, the world that, with the passing of time, was to become their everyday world, not Polish and not ethnic. I doubt if these recollections are available at all. I should add that Adam Walaszek, who studied the history of Polish-Americans in Cleveland, Ohio, succeeded in collecting this kind of material (see 1994; his work was published after I had finished this book).

The world of a regular job was only partly a strange, dark background. Frequently, the job was done together with compatriots who belonged to the same team. Therefore, the job belonged to a certain extent to the same, ethnic world. It seems to me that only in the last decades, with the increasing necessity to have formal education and qualifications and in conjunction with the decline of the old types of industry, the full removal of the world of work finally occurred, separating it from the zone of the world of ethnic, local community is, then, determined by cultural, structural and economic processes of the all-American character.

In other spheres of existence of immigrants and their descendants, particularly visible and known to the students of the problem, the daily life lost its ethnic everyday life character earlier than the work life. Ethnicity shifted to the important and highly valued world of festivity. Initially, however, just after arrival in the new country, the everyday life of religious and cultural activities of the immigrants had a solely ethnic character. This everyday life maintained the ethnic identity of the group, made up its world. It filled the social time and space of immigrants. It gave rhythm to their social activities. This type of solely ethnic everyday life is still visible today but it concerns only a few members of the ethnic group, its core. The situation in the spheres of politics, urban life, voluntary associations, is similar.

The above observation refers to the settled ethnic groups that are not being continuously revitalized by immigration. This is the case of the Polish-American local community in South Bend since the First World War.

This chapter is to present processes of the marginalization of the ethnic everyday life. I will be trying to do that partially in a direct way, showing how some aspects of Polish-American everyday life were being removed by the all-American everyday life. I will be attempting to do that indirectly also, showing how the number of people of Polish heritage, in whose everyday life ethnicity continued to be significant, was decreasing.

South Bend has always been a provincial American city. Its Polish-American community used to play a significant role in the social life of the all-American Polonia, but only exceptionally and for very short periods of time. Both everyday life and festivity of this provincial ethnic community were, however, not autonomous but determined by very general processes. The big growth of industry in the last decades of the 19th century, then a decline of this industry in the rust belt, the development of mass culture, the development of an educational system, the shifts in the religious culture, the slow evolution of the political system, all affected the situation of the immigrant groups. I mentioned those points before and will be returning to them quite often. There are many details in this work but I hope that they will not obscure the whole picture. They should help the perception of how the general processes manifested themselves in a particular ethnic local community.

In this chapter, I will not occupy myself with everything. Because of a lack of data, I will not discuss the everyday family life. Instead, I will concern myself with several spheres, which in my opinion are particularly important: work (and economically motivated immigration to South Bend), religion, voluntary associations, politics and urban life. These scopes of social proactive obviously overlap. This will be clearly visible, even if each of them will be discussed separately. One history of the community will, therefore, be told several times from the beginning. I will start with work, the sphere that is the most important for a man's livelihood.

I will use as my sources first of all the findings of some historians of South Bend and its Polonia. These reports have various levels of professionalism and they were not, until now, published and broadly distributed. My discussion will also, to some extent, draw upon the yearbooks and bulletins of some Polish-American institutions. Caution is necessary here, because of their "partisan" character is out of the question.

3.1. Immigration "For Bread and Butter" and the Polish-American World of Work

The first Polish immigrant came to South Bend looking for work, but it was not the lack of work which induced him to immigrate from Poland. Unlike the Poles who came here later, he did not stay in town for long. We do not know very much about him. Literature does not even give his first name. According to Thomas McAvoy (1953), this first Polish newcomer was Dr. G. Bolinsky, who appeared in 1840. We can find more information about him in Joseph Swastek's dissertation (1941: 1-2). Bolinsky was to come to town in June 1840. He took a hotel room and until mid-August was placing ads in the *South Bend Free Press*, announcing his services as a physician and surgeon in the Polish army of 1829-31 and as a midwife. According to the ads, he brought with him all the instruments necessary to practice his profession and the best German medicines. In spite of this, he did not find enough patients and left South Bend without a trace. The next Polish influx offered completely different services to the city. Consequently, the picture of Poles in the collective consciousness of the whole urban population was not based on the mythical person with the university education and the respectable profession. The one-man Polonia of Bolinsky was in no single aspect similar to the very large Polonia collectivity, which would soon be coming to South Bend.

The first Poles who came after Bolinsky and who are mentioned in historical sources, arrived in the area in 1865. According to Chas Chapman, the author of a history of St. Joseph County (1880: 781; quoted after Deka, 1990: 1-2), an entrepreneur named Fred G. Miller brought a group of Poles (Polanders) and settled them in "marsh and timer land in the area called Terre Coupee in the prairie region west of South Bend." The laborers were to pay for their transportation by working in Miller's saw mill. Two years later, the Terre Coupee area was described as very well cared for, having been turned into cultivated fields and pastures. The Poles we are talking about worked well and efficiently. There were at least two factors that might have contributed to that. First, they were, most probably, occupied with what they had known very well and done at home before leaving for America, and secondly, they came in families. We can safely say that despite emigration from Poland, their world of work did not change very much. Before 1880, Miller settled thirty-five Polish families on his land close to South Bend.

Historical research conducted by Swastek shows that several Polish families settled within the borders of South Bend in 1866. In 1868, there were already fifteen Polish families here. The naturalization documents show that in this year a few Poles of South Bend gave up their Prussian (German) citizenship and applied for the US citizenship. The same names that are quoted by Swastek, we can still find today, after more than 130 years, on the membership lists of Polish-American clubs and parishes in South Bend. In 1870, there were around sixty Polish families in town. Some of them came from other places in Indiana, and some directly from the Poznan Duchy, a German-occupied part of Poland (the best history of Poland is: Davies, 1982).

Polish laborers who lived in South Bend, worked initially mainly on the construction of the railroad. They were unskilled workers, but earned much more than they could dream of in Europe. According to Frank Renkiewicz (1967: 30), in the very good year of 1870, it was possible to make in South Bend $1.50 a day, working as an unskilled railroad laborer. Concrete data, presented by various historians concerning the earnings of the workers, and their relative buying power, are not fully consistent though.

The railroad company took pains to bring many Poles to South Bend to do the construction work. According to popular myths, being repeated by historians, they were recruited even in Poland. They were definitely recruited in New York City harbor. On site, in South Bend, the railroad company was faced with a strong competition, offering even higher wages for equally unskilled labor. This came from the rapidly expanding industries that, since the early 1870s, had badly needed employees. Some workers were "bought" from the railroads. Others had to be brought from out of town.

Cathy Deka states that between 1870 and 1880 the number of Prussian citizens with Polish names grew in South Bend from 160 to 1,577 (1990: 5). Swastek says that in 1876, around 150 adult Polish men worked in local industry (1941: 10). Deka quotes a story, according to which James Oliver met twelve Polish families in New York in 1875. He moved them at his own expense to South Bend, gave them jobs in his company and built them homes on the city's Westside (1990: 5). Although we cannot preclude the possible truth behind this story, it has all the characteristics of a myth on the beginnings of South Bend Polonia, and particularly the Polish-American Westside. Similar stories were being told about the way in which the Studebaker brothers recruited their own workers.

Another, very well know "way" to the northern Indiana industry were the letters to the "old country," sent by those who succeeded in finding a good job there. Since 1877, an additional factor pulling the Poles to South Bend from other places in the US was the Polish church. I will return to this issue in the next section of this chapter.

The research findings of Kathleen Breza and Martha Pieszak reveal that the highest number of Poles came to South Bend between 1880 and World War I. Until the end of the 19th century, the immigrants were mostly coming from the Prussian Partition (the German-occupied part of Poland). Later, proportions between newcomers from all three partitions (Prussian, Austrian and Russian) became more equal (Breza and Pieszak, 1975: 5). The latter fact will significantly affect the symbolic structure of the social space of the Polish-American local community and the way the Polish parishes were named.

During the period mentioned by Breza and Pieszak, a very interesting and well-known process began. It was the process of the establishment of a unified Polish national group out of the masses of immigrants coming from three different economic, political, cultural and educational systems that had been developed after the third partition of Poland in 1795. Unfortunately, I did not succeed in finding information on relations between Poles coming to South Bend from different partitions. Some contemporary opinions on this topic will be presented though.

Polish immigration "for bread and butter" to Indiana was relatively small in comparison with immigration to other states of the American Midwest. "Even during the period of intensive immigration from 1899 to 1910, when over half a million Poles came to the United States, only 7,064 entered Indiana. At the end of the decade, Pennsylvania numbered 188,276 foreign born Polish settlers, Illinois - 148,809, Michigan - 62,606, and Ohio - 41,328, while Indiana only accounted for 14,530. Of this total, approximately one third lived in South Bend" (Swastek, 1941: 6; see also *Indiana Poles*...1976). Polish economic immigrants were coming to the South Bend region mainly with their whole families. The largest group of immigrants, the people coming from the Prussian Partition, did not intend to return to Europe, which is proved by their naturalization applications and the buying or building of houses.

In 1873, an economic crisis occurred in the US. It had nearly no consequences for the South Bend industry. Companies that employed Poles did not suffer. Polish workers earned well (Swastek gives lower wages than those quoted earlier after Renkiewicz), and having small needs, they could maintain their big families, buy houses and give money for the construction of Polish churches. They had a higher standard of living than in Europe before emigration. They did however, receive lower wages than the native South Benders (Swastek, 1941: 14). Comparing the standards of living of different ethnic groups, Renkiewicz even says: "If there were people lower socially and economically in South Bend than the Poles in 1875, no one saw them in any great number" (1967: 39).

Why were the Poles at the bottom of the social and economic structure? The hypothesis that they were discriminated against because of their ethnicity, that there was a particular opposition against them, does not hold water: I did not find any arguments supporting it. Two other explanations seem to be more reasonable. First, it seems that initially their efficiency of labor was low. Industry, particularly heavy industry, demanded from workers a different work discipline and different skills than those in agriculture and forestry, with which the Poles were much more familiar. Therefore, it was necessary to learn new skills, and until they were apparent, to work as unskilled labor. Secondly, the Poles arrived unable to speak English. Immigrants from the Prussian Partition could read and write in Polish and often also in German (Swastek, 1941: 16), but it took a lot of time to learn to speak, read and write English. Until that time, they had to rely on the good will, patience and honesty of their supervisors and their German colleagues with whom some of them could communicate. For some employers, perfect command of English was a precondition for giving somebody a position of responsibility.

Polish workers in South Bend took pains to earn as much as possible. It meant that they were ready to adapt to the new conditions of the work environment. *The South Bend Daily Tribune* praised them in 1876, writing that they were even better mechanics than Americans, Germans, Irishmen and others, and that, because of this fact, they earned more. As I have mentioned before, these higher wages must have been exceptional. Moreover, Swastek says that the high productivity of some Polish skilled workers led to the lowering of wage scales and, in effect, of income. Strikes were the consequence of this situation. In the 19th century, the Poles of South Bend actively participated in three serious industrial conflicts. The employers won all of them.

In the first strike, in 1876, about twenty Poles who worked in one team, participated actively. Press discussions concerning this conflict suggested that it did not involve workers of other nationalities. Polish grinders at Oliver's protested against the lowering of their wage scale. Because the job was attractive and many candidates waited for openings, the striking grinders were fired. Despite the intervention of some newspapers, they were not hired again.

At the turn of 1885 and 1886, a more serious conflict occurred in the same firm. Because of the wage reduction, about two hundred out of the total of nine hundred workers went on strike. The conflict was presented by the media as having an ethnic character, as initiated by the Poles who were, this time, presented as the "bad guys." Actually, workers of various nationalities participated in it. The "communist agitators" came from Chicago. According to Breza and Pieszak, Polish and Hungarian workers attempted together to establish a trade union. They succeeded, but only temporarily. The union did not achieve anything and very soon disappeared. The company's owners closed the factory for two months. The Roman Catholic bishop intervened condemning the striking workers. Oliver threatened that his company would leave the city. In this case, the city's economy would have been endangered. Other local businessmen organized a citizens' committee that supported the manufacturer. The committee assured him that the city would not tolerate the breaking of the work discipline. A large number of Swedish laborers were imported. The factory was opened again and former workers were rehired very selectively. Those Poles who lost their jobs were taken care of by the pastor of the Polish parish, having been in existence for about ten years.

The third strike took place in 1898 at Singer's. It was for the same reason as the above mentioned cases. The wage decrease was particularly painful this time because the living expenses were increasing quickly in this period. The Poles having big families suffered severely from the growing costs of living. *The Goniec Polski*("The Polish Messenger"), a Polish newspaper already operating in South Bend for two years, printed a warning to its readers. The editor expressed his hopes that this time the Poles would be cleverer than during the strike at Oliver's and would not be provoked by representatives of other nationalities. Excessive striking activity of the Poles would, in the opinion of the editor, endanger their formerly good reputation (Swastek, 1941: 17-22). Singer, like Oliver, threatened that his company would leave the city if the strike continued. On the other hand, Singer and the Studebaker brothers differed from Oliver in the fact that they did not allow the organization of ethnic work teams. Formally speaking, people of various nationalities worked together. It was to lower the probability of the (mentioned in the first chapter) combination of class interest with emotional factors, the primordial ethnic attachments. It was to lower the probability of the founding of ethnically consistent trade unions and the organization of successful strikes (see, e.g., Breza and Pieszak, 1975: 16).

Until the end of the 19th century or, in other works, during the first three decades of the existence of the Polonia in South Bend, the Poles worked there in the same way as in many other industrial centers, in Poland and abroad. They worked in big teams, mostly together with other Poles. Their supervisors and the owners of the factories were strangers. Despite the fear of unemployment, the Polish workers attempted to defend actively their class interests. Most of the time, they were not winning industrial conflicts but their economic situation was still much better than the situation of Polish peasants or the unemployed, wherever they lived. During industrial conflicts, representatives of higher levels of the church hierarchy were against them and supported employers but the parish priests attempted to do their best to help their families avoid poverty when the strike was lost. Industrial conflicts had very important ethnic aspects (even when the employers were trying to prevent that) increasing national solidarity and hindering assimilation.

At the end of the 19th century, the Polish community was a very important element in the economic and social life of South Bend. Renkiewicz says that then "the Poles had also become the city's largest and most aggressive bloc of unskilled workers, a position which had put them at the center of the major local debate in those years on the condition of the laboring class" (1967: 102).

The work of the adult men in factories, particularly in heavy industry, was not, during all these years, the only source of income of Polish working-class families in South Bend. We should bear in mind three other sources, very important for the entirety of family life of that period. The first of them was the work of children, most of whom were quickly (after I Communion) leaving school. The second was the renting out of rooms to the single Polish laborers who had not yet bought or built their own homes. The third was the work of women. Most of them were cultivating vegetables and fruits in gardens and around their homes which decreased the family's costs of living. Some of those who did not have little children, were breaking with the traditional division of labor and took jobs outside the household. Breza and Pieszak say that these women found work in various cigar factories. Their main employer, however, was a garment company, Wilson Brothers Shirt Factory (1975: 6). It seems that the outside jobs of Polish women, being of a more individual character than the jobs of men, could have led them out of the purely Polish world of everyday life. However, family, church and the local community did not accept this. According to historians of the South Bend Polonia, even among those Polish women who had outside jobs the command of English was much lower than among men. The work of women was an economically necessary, but socially marginal aspect of their lives.

At the beginning of the 20th century, the second generation of the South Bend Poles were entering active life. The new generation was born and raised in this city and did not compare the situation in America to the conditions in which peasants lived in Poland. New ambitions were being expressed. New ways of earning one's living became possible along with the growth of the Polish local community. These new ambitions and new opportunities slightly changed the collective identity of the Polish group but also strengthened its boundaries and isolation.

In the previous chapter I wrote that at the beginning of the 20th century, the three main companies of South Bend employed 80% of the labor force. The city economy was based on the production of agricultural equipment, sewing machine parts, carriages and soon automobiles. New immigrants were arriving, first of all were Hungarians. According to the estimates of the Immigration Commission, the Polonia of the first and second generation counted sixteen thousand people. It was now the second largest (after the "native" Anglo-Saxon Americans) ethnic group in the city. The third largest group were the Germans. It numbered eight thousand members (Renkiewicz, 1967: 104-07). The fact, that in South Bend there were several large ethnic groups, helps ups compare the ways in which they coped with the basic vital problems.

Most of the Poles, as well as the representatives of other ethnic groups, looked for jobs in big industry. Employment was not equally permanent or secure for all of these groups. The best situation was that of Germans. Whatever the place of birth (German or America), they usually had a permanent job during the whole year. "Native" Americans as well as Jews, Poles and Hungarians of two generations were, in this order of precedence, employed in a less systematic way. Children of school age worked regardless of their ethnic origin but in the Polish families this phenomenon was particularly apparent. Around 40% of these families depended partly on the income brought home by youngsters. The parents were even forging their birth certificates so that the work in factories and stores appeared legal. This fact was noted by the afore mentioned immigration commission.

As we know, at the beginning of the new century, two generations of Poles worked in South Bend. The younger generation differed from the older one in its higher concern with the fast increase of income. Trade unions, for a long time ephemeral, enjoyed more appreciation among the young Polish workers than among the old ones. The older workers were reluctant to engage themselves in activities directed against the employers, particularly against violent actions jeopardizing the company's property. They paid more attention to the reputation of the Polish community than to their own income. They approached life form a more collectivistic vantage point than did their children whose attitudes were more individualistic. On the other hand, they supported such activities that could result in the increase of the workers' income without endangering property and the Polonia's reputation (Swastek, 1941: 32-34).

In the 1930s, strong union leaders emerged among the Poles of the South Bend Westside. They organized two shops of the United Auto Workers: one at the Studebaker corporation and the other at the Bendix company. The shops were large and consisted mostly of Poles. Their leaders had an increasing influence on the city's political life (Stabrowski, 1984: 202).

According to the popular stories, big employers appreciated the political involvement of Polish workers. One of my informants, a lifelong activist of the (in fact Polish-American) West Side Democratic and Civic Club, told me a story about participation of Poles in Dyngus Day. This originally Polish, now in South Bend all-city feast, shapes the political time of the urban community. It ends the winter stagnation and begins (not equally significant every year) political season. It has been organized by the Club on Easter Monday which is a regular workday in America but a day off in Poland. The Polish workers had, according to this story, permission from their employers to participate in festivals and discussions with local, state and sometimes federal politicians from lunch time onwards. In this way, the American everyday world of work, done by Polish employees, met with a Polish religious feast, applied to strengthen American democracy.

At the beginning of the 20th century, other forms of economic activity of the Polonia emerged, or rather developed on a large scale. From the early 1870s, the city's Westside, inhabited mostly by Poles, grew very quickly. Soon, it got its own name, know not only to Poles but also to other citizens: Polonia. The Poles began to establish stores, mostly groceries, serving their own tastes. Small ethnic businesses made up this new field of activity that developed between 1890 and 1910.

The growth of Polish ethnic businesses in South Bend had strong support from the first generation of immigrants, from the Polish parishes, voluntary associations and from the *Goniec Polski*. All of them were in favor of those activities that would strengthen the Polish identity and closeness of the local community. The *Goniec* propagated the slogan: "support your own." It reminded its readers that they should patronize Polish stores. It doubted the Catholicism of those Poles who did not shop at Polish bakers, butchers', etc. It clearly divided the social world according to the ethnic criteria, identifying Polishness and Catholicism. It stressed the contrast between the "we-group" and the "they-group." Polish merchants advertised in the *Goniec* with slogans and rhymes directly promoting their own businesses, better than the "other" businesses because Polish and Catholic.

This propaganda campaign was very successful. In 1901, on the Westside, there were eleven Polish groceries, fifteen meat markets, two bakeries, two confectioneries, eight barber's shops, one clothing store, two drug stores and five tailor's shops. During the next decade, new businesses emerged, for example, a contractor's firm, four bottling workshops, one billiard and pool room and two real estate offices. The Poles owned four cigar factories and one of them was the largest in the city. Now, there were thirty-one

groceries, eighteen meat markets, eight bakeries, eight confectioneries, four clothing stores (Swastek, 1941: 30-32); other authors give
slightly different, but essentially similar figures). In effect, the
Polonia ceased to be a totally working class ethnic group. All these
firms were very small, however. They employed very few people
each. They often gave work to children. They strengthened the
isolation of the Polonia and were not visible form the point of view
of the city's economy and the all-city business community. In 1908,
among 322 members of the South Bend Chamber of Commerce,
there were only seven Poles (Renkiewicz 1867: 131).

In 1926, Polish entrepreneurs established an organization
called the West Side Businessmen's Association (now - the Polish-
American Business and Professional Men's Association). Five years
later, a similar organization of women, actually an association of
wives, was founded - the Polish-American Business and Professional
Women's Organization. The purpose of the larger and more
influential men's organization was initially to take care of the
economic aspect of the Polonia's Westside. The organization was
blooming, especially just after the Second World War, when many
Poles started to invest their wartime savings and higher postwar
earnings in business. The association helped in the economic
development of the South Bend's Division Street (now - Western
Avenue) area. The business center of this area became (for a short
time), after downtown, the second largest shopping and service
center of the whole city. After a spectacular but short success, this
Polish business center lost its significance because the center of
economic life moved to still further westerly located districts of the
city and to the suburbs (Renkiewicz, 1967: 308-312).

The Great Depression that started in 1929, obviously did not
help the Polish business community. All firms except the Sobieski
Federal Savings and Loans Association, a small bank that still
functions today, had problems. The post-Depression recovery
brought with it a completely different economic and political
situation. Now, employment opportunities were more strongly than
ever before connected with federal contracts controlled by
government agencies.

In the period presented above, that is at the beginning of the
20th century, there was not yet a group of Polish professionals with
university degrees in South Bend. I have already mentioned that the

concern with the long-term education of children was not very popular among Poles. Moreover, their income was relatively low and tuition was expensive. In 1912, there were in South Bend two Polish lawyers, one physician born and educated outside the US, one public accountant, one choir director and one pharmacist. This situation was to change, but slowly. Due to the close proximity of Notre Dame University, the number of professionals in the fields that could be studied there, was growing.

The last sphere of employment to be discussed here is closely connected with first urban politics and later, to some extent, with federal politics. In this part of the chapter, I will draw upon the findings of penetrating research conducted in the first half of the 1980s by Donald J. Stabrowski (1984). He was studying the political machine of the Democratic Party in South Bend and its relationships with the Westside Polonia. These relations were profitable for both sides. The party organization and the political machine of the Democrats could provide the Polonia with relatively stable jobs in the public sector and the Polonia could in exchange give the Party its votes. In order to do that, the Polish immigrants would have to successfully go through the process of naturalization and become US citizens. Relations between the Party and the Polonia are a very good example of the "patron-client" relationships, discussed by political anthropologists (see, e.g., Rosman and Rubel, 1984: 140; Silverman, 1965; Weingrod, 1968).

In the following sections of this chapter, I will discuss the rhythm and strength of the political support of the Polonia for its patron - the Democratic Party. Now, I will concern myself with one particular kind of profit the clients - the Westside Polonia - received. I will concentrate on the work opportunities, other issues being left aside. It is therefore necessary to say that the Polonia seems to have been concerned first and foremost with non material gains. It was interested in these expressions of gratitude of the patron that were not connected with fulfilling the material needs of the clients. The Polonia succeeded in establishing an elaborate system of ethnic institutions and the Poles in need could rely on them and did not have to approach city hall. Public jobs, on the other hand, were very prestigious and because of that were desirable. To be employed by the city meant for the Polonia that its members were as good

Americans and citizen of the city, as the members of other, more
established ethnic groups.

The Democratic Party machine began its growth in South
Bend at the beginning of the 20th century, when the second
generation of the Polish group entered adult, active life. Already in
the 1920s, the effects of cooperation between the Polonia and the
Party were visible. More and more Poles were getting prestigious
public jobs, controlled by the Democrats. We can assume after
Stabrowski that at least until 1950 the Polonia made up the
overwhelming majority of inhabitants of the Westside. Stabrowski
was studying the South Bend register of public jobs. He was
concerned with those people from the register who lived on the
Westside and who had, in his own (undoubtedly competent)
judgment, "Polish names."

In 1920, inhabitants of the Westside constituted around 30% of
the total population of the city and the Poles occupied 21% of the
city jobs (in 1928 - 25%). In 1930, the Westsiders made up 24% of
the total population and the Poles occupied in 1932 18% and in 1936
- 28% of the city jobs. In 1940, the Westsiders constituted 38% of
the total population and the Poles had in 1940 - 25%, in 1944 - 30%
and in 1948 - 48% of the city jobs. In 1950, the Westsiders made up
37% of the total population (Blacks and Hispanics also live here now)
and the Poles had in 1952 37%, in 1956 - 45% of the city jobs.
Later, the proportion of public jobs in Polish hand dropped. Between
1960 and 1964 it equaled 38%, in 1968 - 33% and between 1972 and
1980 - 31% (Stabrowski, 1984: 60 and 103).

As the statistics show, when the political machine was strong,
the Poles' access to the city jobs corresponded to their participation
in the whole population. In the last decades, when the political
machine ceased to function, but the city hall controlled jobs paid by
the federal funds, the participation of Poles increased for a short
time. Therefore, we can conclude that in fact the Poles were not
preferred by the Democratic political machine. However, the opinion
that they were preferred was shared by the whole city population,
including the Polonia. In my opinion there are three explanations of
this situation. First, the correlation between the growth of the
machine and the increase in the number of public jobs in Polish
hands (from pre-machine level) is spurious and public opinion was
wrong. Secondly, the correlation is not spurious and the machine

helped the Polonia in equalizing proportions, rectifying former discrimination. Public opinion properly reflected the real patronage relationships but was incorrect as to the over representation of Poles. Thirdly, the patronage of the Democratic Party machine was real but was not expressed in the quantity but in the quality of jobs. More than one of these explanations may be true. I have no source to test the first two hypotheses but Stabrowski's findings help us show that the third one might be true.

In December 1958, the mayor of South Bend published in the *Goniec Polski* his Christmas Greetings to the Polish community. In the greetings, in a full page advertisement, he listed all 354 Westsiders of Polish ancestry on the city payroll. The list consisted of, for example, 107 firefighters and 62 police officers. These positions were very prestigious and coveted. Perhaps in securing these kinds of jobs, the Democratic Party realized its obligations as the patron (Stabrowski, 1984: 101).

The South Bend Fire Department was, under Democratic administrations, a Polish stronghold. According to some stories, the firemen were recruited by the earlier mentioned (in fact Polish) West Side Democratic and Civic Club. The job application forms were said to have been handed out in the club's rooms, only to its members. Obviously, the firemen showed their appreciation by voting for the Party. Moreover, they were taking care of the election turnout, driving in the sick people who would probably vote for the Democrats. They were also serving as "checkers." Stabrowski says that "Almost half of the city firemen since the 1950s have come from the westside" (he means the Poles; 1984: 257). When the Democrats lost power, these prestigious jobs stayed in Polish hands.

Let us sum up this section of the chapter. The Poles came to South Bend in the 1860s, looking for their "bread and butter." The city had industrial character and it was relatively easy to find an unskilled job there. Industry was growing in South Bend along with the growth of the Polonia. Until the decline of heavy industry in the second half of the 20th century, the Poles worked primarily in big factories. They lived in a separate quarter of the city and quite soon on arrival, began to organize their own infrastructure. This infrastructure was simultaneously a job market. With the second generation of the Polish community that began its active life in the early 1900s, many businesses of different character appeared on the

Westside. They employed Polish staff, including children. The effect
was the closing of the community. In the second half of the 20th
century, the Polish businesses disappeared almost completely. Some,
but not many Poles had university education and worked as
professionals. Some Poles were city functionaries. Their prestigious
positions could be considered a reward for loyalty to the Democratic
Party.

Until the decline of the South Bend big industry, the Polish
everyday life of work and economic activity was first and foremost
the everyday life of factory workers. During several decades it was
also, to some extent, the everyday life of small family business.
Then, this whole sphere of work became dispersed. There is now no
Polish or even Polish-American everyday life of work. Obviously,
Poles and/or Polish-Americans still produce goods and perform
services. However, they exceptionally do that together with other
Poles or Polish-Americans. They do not speak Polish during work
hours, they rarely live in the same or close neighborhoods. It is
difficult (not impossible, though) to find Polish store owners now.
Those who are there, employ as assistants and clerks the staff of
various ethnic origins. They sell their goods to representatives of
many groups, not only to Poles. The Polish lawyers, physicians,
engineers, realtors, sell their services to the customers whatever
their heritage. Most of the time, they do that outside of the Westside.
The world of work for a long time maintained ethnicity but relations
between the two are now severed.

3. 2. Polish-American Parishes and their Everyday Life

The immense influence of the Roman Catholic Church on the
functioning of the Polish communities in the big cities and small
towns of America has been stressed by many scholars (see, e.g.,
Buczek, 1980; Les, 1981; Mocha [ed.], 1978, particularly Part II).
There is no need to quote these well known observations here. What
I would like to present in this chapter, is the way in which
membership of the Roman Catholic Church has structured the
everyday life of the Polish-Americans in South Bend. I would like to
show which problems it has helped to solve and which problems it
has created in South Bend. As in other places in the US, Roman
Catholicism has been a minority denomination in South Bend (the

largest single denomination among the Christian ones, though). Because of the simultaneous presence of the University of Notre Dame and various institutions closely connected with it, the influence of Roman Catholicism on the city life has been significant. I will deal not only with Roman Catholicism in this chapter; as there is also a parish of the Polish National Catholic Church in South Bend.

According to historical sources, the first Roman Catholic church in South Bend, St. Alexius Church, was built in 1853. It was destroyed by fire but was rebuilt in 1869 as St. Joseph Church. Forty-seven families or 210 persons belonged to the parish. The first Polish families were already living in town. Before the above mentioned church was rebuilt, another Roman Catholic Church, St. Patrick's Church, had been established in 1859 by the Irish who worked on the railroad's construction. In the 1860s, the German masses were said here which gave a chance to active participation in services to the Poles, who came from the Prussian Partition. The Germans established their own ethnic parish (St. Mary's) only in 1883, many years after a Polish church had already existed.

The first Poles in town participated in services at St. Patrick's. In 1868, the first Polish child was baptized there. In 1871, seventy Polish families belonged to this parish. In the same year, Father Adolph Bakanowski started a mission in the Polish language for these people (McAvoy, 1953). They wanted their own parish. The reasons for the desire to separate were the tensions between the Poles and the Irish, both at work and in church. There were significant differences in the religious customs of the two groups (Breza and Pieszak, 1975: 6). The cultural contact with the "others," favored the shaping of the homogeneous Polish ethnic consciousness.

According to the information collected by Kathy Deka, some Poles participated in services at the Sacred Heart Church in Notre Dame. In addition to this, once a month a mass was also given, especially for Poles in private homes (1990: 3).

The increasing immigration of Poles to South Bend, led to the organization of their own, "national" Roman Catholic parish. In this kind of parish, they could fulfill their various needs in Polish (the "national" as opposed to the "territorial" parishes have been in accordance with Canon Law). The Polish group in South Bend was concentrated in one, expanding quarter of town and consequently its parish, (and later parishes) acquired a secondary "territorial" character later. When this process of the "territorialization" of the "Polish" parishes was very advances, it converged with another process, which started later. This was the process of the "marginalization" of the ethnic character of these parishes. Both processes, very much advanced nowadays, have not yet been completed.

In around 1871, 75 Polish families are said to have lived in South Bend. According to the historians, one of the main topics of their conversations was the organization of a Polish parish. In 1874, nearly twenty men established the St. Stanislaw Kostka Society, the first Polish association in town and in the State of Indiana. In the same year, another group of Polish men organized the St. Kazimierz Society. The aim of both associations was the unification of the Polish community in South Bend, the mutual confirmation of its Catholic faith and its Polish national solidarity, as well as mutual assistance in the case of misfortune. These associations also took pains to organize the parish. It was to be located close to the main factories and to the shopping center of the town. In 1875, much of the land was bought and in 1876 the work started. The first Polish-American Roman Catholic church was emerging in the town and it was only the second in Indiana (after Otis, 1871).

To build the church, an enormous financial effort by the Poles was necessary. Swastek quotes calculations, according to which an average Polish family contributed in 1877 $22 (the equivalent of nearly one month's wage) for the parish. After five years, when the devastated chapel was being rebuilt, the contribution equaled more than $33 for each adult man, or in practice, for each family (1941: 23-24). Later, it became necessary to contribute for the maintenance of the existing parish and also for the construction of new churches. The contributions were made in various ways: regular Sunday pew rental, annual donations, special collections for special needs, fees for church services (for instance, in 1877, 50 cents for a funeral without a sermon and one dollar for a funeral with a sermon), school fees and parish societies' contributions. Moreover, the profits from the parish's social events and picnics went to the church (Swastek, 1941: 24-25).

On 1st January 1877, Father Valentine Czyzewski became the pastor of St. Jozef's (St. Joseph's) parish, which was being organized. Czyzewski was born and educated in Poland, then went to schools in

America, was a member of the Congregation of Holy Cross and had just been ordained at Notre Dame. He was to become one of the most influential public figures of South Bend, the organizer of all four Polish Roman Catholic parishes in town and several in the vicinity.

The construction of the new, wooden St. Joseph's Church was finished in June. It was consecrated on the 1st July 1877 in the presence of 125 Polish families and some German and Irish friends. The erection of the church stimulated the organizational growth of the Polish community. The next associations were emerging. Unfortunately, in November 1879 the structure was destroyed by a windstorm. It was rebuilt in brick, in the Romanesque Revival style, now as St. Jadwiga's (St. Hedwig's) Church, in 1883. Many Polish groups contributed to the project. Polish farmers from Terre Coupee helped cover the footings with dirt. The main altar was a present from the Hedwig Society. Two side altars were given to the church by the St. Stanislaw Society and the organ by St. Kazimierz Society (Swastek, 1941: 40-42); Breza and Pieszak, 1975: 6-7; Deka, 1990: 7).

The 1880s were the period of mass immigration of Poles to South Bend. During the two decades after the erection of the first Polish parish, the number of families that belonged to it grew from 125 to 1,300. A Polish parish school as well as 23 associations (during the next sixty years their number was to increase by 23) were associated with the church. The parish was becoming too large and must be divided. In fact, quite soon after, the new parishes were established. In 1899, Father Czyzewski organized St. Kazimierz Krolewicz's (St. Casimir's) parish and in the next year, St. Stanislaw's (St. Stanislau's) parish. About seven hundred families moved to the new parishes. In 1910, the Poles established their last Roman Catholic parish in South Bend. It was St. Wojciech Biskup and Meczennik's (St. Adalbert's) parish. About 150 Polish families, out of 1,600 Polish families inhabiting South Bend at the time, joined the new organization (Swastek, 1941: 44; *St. Hedwig...*1977).

The fact that St. Hedwig's parish was becoming too large was not the only factor responsible for the emergence of new parishes. Other reasons were of a social-ecological character. The Polish group was shifting westwards. A larger and larger proportion lived behind the railroad tracks that separated it from its only church and church school. The situation was increasingly dangerous for the children crossing the tracks every day when going to school. It seems that this was the main reason for the organization of St. Casimir's parish. St. Stanislau's was established for the Poles who lived on the north-western and St. Adalbert's for those living on the south-western side of town (see: Swastek, 1941: 43; Breza and Pieszak, 1975: 6-7). Consequently, the Polish local community was divided into four parts, easily identifiable thanks to the church buildings. I will return to this issue soon. Now, I will present some details connected with the life of the new parishes.

The organization of St. Casimir's parish began in the spring of 1893. It was then that Father Czyzewski announced that the Poles who lived on the southern side of the Grand Trunk railroad were to meet and select a lot for a new church. Only those people who owned land were expected to participate in the meeting. Three years later, the selected lot was bought and the new parish associations were organized. The construction work started in 1898. One year later, the new church building and the parish school building were consecrated. In 1907, the debt which had been contracted for the construction was fully paid. In 1924, a lot nearby was consecrated. Soon, the new church building (serving the parish to this day) was built there. The school moved to the old church building. There have been about twenty clubs and associations functioning at St. Casimir's Church. In 1912, when the last Roman Catholic church was being built by South Bend Poles, St. Casimir's parish numbered 527 families or 2,857 members (*Pamietnik Srebrnego Jubileuszu*,1929; *Jubiliee Book*, 1949).

Organization of St. Adalbert's parish also began several years before its official opening. In 1905, St. Adalbert's Fraternal Aid Society was established. Its members made house-to-house collections to purchase land for the church building and for the school building. When they had slightly over $400, they bought two lots. In the fall of 1909, the construction work started. The first building completed was the church, but later a school and still later, the Polish Heritage Center were moved there. In the summer of 1910, the first pastor arrived and in the fall of that year the first mass was celebrated in the open air. In the winter, the masses were given in a parish hall of St. Hedwig's Church. During these years, all four Polish parishes were closely tied together, actually forming one, large national and religious community. The present church building (considered the largest and most beautiful church in the diocese) was ready only in the spring of 1926 (*St. Adalbert Parish*, 1985).

During the first years, the pastors and assistants at the Polish parishes were always the priests from the Congregation of Holy Cross (more on the relations between the Congregation and the Polonia in South Bend, as well as on the religious life of the poles in this city can be found in Stabrowski, 1991). This fact had various consequences. Undoubtedly, it stimulated close cooperation between the pastors. It gave the parishes strong support from a powerful Roman Catholic organization. On the other hand, the Congregation had a policy of moving pastors and assistants every few years (fortunately for South Bend and its Polonia, this rule was never applied to Father Czyzewski). This policy made it difficult for the priests to become and later continue to be, the local leaders. In the case of a priest acting in such a role successfully and being moved to a parish out of town, serious conflicts between the parishioners and the Congregation would emerge. The only Polish pastor from outside of the Congregation, nominated by the bishop from among the diocesan priests (until now always a Pole or Polish-American), was the pastor of St. Adalbert's Church. At St. Hedwig's Church, the priests were nominated by the Congregation until 1964. From 1975, for more than ten years, the pastor was not even a Polish-American (see, e.g., Swastek, 1941; Stabrowski, 1984: 153, Stabrowski, 1991).

Polish parishes in South Bend, as everywhere under conditions of emigration, have served several important social functions. Obviously, they have fulfilled the religious needs of the faithful, but they have also been the centers, fortresses of the Polish identity and have helped the immigrants in their gradual assimilation into the American everyday life. Actually, they have been trying to outbuild, step by step, the American aspects of everyday life compared to its Polish aspects, the maintenance of which was considered by them for a very long time the crucial aim of their activities.

Before the Vaticanum II, the liturgy was celebrated in Latin, sermons were given in Polish. Christmas carols, Lenten songs and some other hymns were sung in Polish. Actually, until World War I, all religious matters had been dealt with in this language. Later, and particularly from the end of the 1930s, the situation started to change quickly. In each of the Polish parishes, the number of members who did not understand Polish, began to increase. Some of them were of

Polish, some of "other" descent. The above mentioned process of "territorialization" of formally "national" parishes continued.

In 1938, the English language was introduced to the sermons at St. Hedwig's and in the next year at St. Stanislau's. At St. Casimir's, the English sermon is said to have been introduced only in 1970 (see Swastek, 1941: 79; Renkiewicz, 1967: 214; Breza and Pieszak, 1975: 17). It is difficult to believe this. The jubilee book of the parish, published in 1949, discusses all events that took place after 1924, solely in English. The jubilee book of 1929 was still published totally in Polish. Now, in none of these churches is there a Polish sermon nor are Polish hymns sung regularly during mass. One "Polish mass" every Sunday is given at St. Adalbert's (also at St. Mary's Polish National Catholic Church), though. All of these changes mean undoubtedly, a serious transformation of the ethnic identity of the Polish-American group in South Bend. One of its significant, "objective" cultural features has disappeared. On the other hand, Polishness was maintained for a long time by the parish associations and clubs, by parish schools and through social events organized by the Parish.

The fact that the South Bend Polonia, led by Father Czyzewski, was able to organize four Roman Catholic parishes in a period of thirty-five years, seems to be proof of its strength. It does not mean, however, that the relations between the Polish community and the Church's hierarchy were very smooth. On the contrary, they were in conflict.

The South Bend Polonia owes a lot to its strong Roman Catholic parishes. However, the Polonia's second generation, more self-confident, feeling at home in America, having no peasant-like habits, wanted more organizational independence from control, on the part of the priests. The Protestant milieu favored new attitudes. This milieu did not jeopardize Roman Catholicism in the doctrinal sense, because the Poles had neither theological interests nor competences. The Protestant parishes were organized in a different way though, from the Roman Catholic ones. The lay persons had much more input and the control on the part of the clergy over the secular aspects of the life of the parish communities was small.

Except work and later, local politics, almost the total everyday life of the Poles in South Bend was organized by parishes and parish associations. Therefore, the control over the parishes was very important for the lay persons. Their first conflicts with the clergy began already in around 1900, but until 1912, they did not jeopardize the loyalty of the faithful to the Church (see Swastek, 1941: 56-57); Renkiewicz, 1967: 194; Breza and Pieszak, 1975: 7). The conflicts that occurred later were much more dramatic and found a partial solution in a schism.

The first strife took place already in the first year of the functioning of St. Casimir' parish (what is interesting, is that the jubilee books do not mention it). The first pastor, who enjoyed great sympathy and popularity among the faithful, was routinely moved by the Congregation of Holy Cross to other work and replaced by another priest, also a Pole. The parishioners did not like this move. A new idea, original within the Roman Catholic framework developed amongst them. They came to the conclusion that they had the right to make decisions also who their pastor should be. The conflict between the parishioners submitted and were even praised for that by the Polish-language journal, the *Goniec Polski* (Polish Messenger) (see Swastek, 1941: 58). Soon, the lay persons were not so meek and their newspaper was not so enthusiastic about total submission to the clergy.

In the following year, another incident occurred. For a certain period, some lay Polonia organizations had attempted to deprive the Roman Catholic parishes of their monopoly over the organization of Polish patriotic celebrations. Local branches of such associations like the Polish National Alliance (PNA) or the Falcons were organizing some celebrations without the priests. Lay leaders, politicians and businessmen and not the pastors were invited speakers. This process of demonopolization and partial secularization did not mean, however, that it was possible to do without a mass. The conflict occurred when Father Czyzewski, pastor at St. Hedwig's and a respected Polonia leader, did not allow the Falcons to enter his church in uniforms. They must stay behind the door (historical sources differ also whether this incident really took place). It was in disagreement with the former South Bend practice. A similar incident occurred (here the sources have not doubt) at St. Casimir's in 1911, when the assistant, in accordance with the diocesan regulations mentioned above, forbade the Falcons to enter the church in uniforms during the service for one of their deceased members. The Falcons treated this as a personal insult and were to remember it (see

Breza and Pieszak, 1975: 9; Swastek, 1941: 58,64; Renkiewicz, 1967: 20).

The above mentioned actions of the priests were inconsistent with the routine, with the everyday, "natural" definition of the Polonia's world that was thought to form a unity, without any autonomy or separation of the sacred and secular spheres. These actions disturbed the smoothness of the everyday life of the ethnic group in which everything was perceived as obvious and foreseeable. This meant, in a sense, the questioning of the factual character of the Polonia's social world, the necessity to suspend the binding until then implicit knowledge. This world was actually changing very much. Contradictory definitions of the situation were emerging and each of them was inconsistent. The lay leaders wanted to be independent from the Church but did not accept the independence of the Church from them. Religious leaders still considered their total domination as natural but the canon rules demanded that they withdraw from a part of the secular sphere.

Another crisis took place in 1903. A group of Poles wanted the bishop to agree to the establishment of a Polish cemetery (the first Polish parlor, St. Joseph's Funeral Home, had functioned since 1901, though). The bishop was unwilling to give the required permission and the disciplined Polish priests stood by him. Despite this, they lay delegates of all the Polish parishes met and wrote a declaration on this issue. Father Czyzewski protested against the declaration and against the fact that the incident was reported in the *Goniec Polski*. He threatened that the editor and publisher would be excommunicated if they continued to engage themselves on the part of the lay activists. The editor was not afraid of the prominent cleric and replied that "to remain under someone's thumb in order to be a good Catholic is no longer in style among us" (Swastek, 1941: 60). The communication between the two parties was not broken, though. The cemetery was created and has continued to serve to this day as St. Joseph's Cemetery. According to the agreement with the bishop, finally signed in 1908, the cemetery was recognized by him but not consecrated. Each grave was to be consecrated individually. Very soon, this compromise was to become very useful (see Stabrowski, 1991: 25-28).

According to Swastek, some pastors understood and shared the ambitions of those lay people who wanted to influence the decisions made in their parish communities. In 1904, St. Casimir's pastor introduced a rule for electing the parish council, which was to be a secret ballot in which all adults were to take part. The matters affecting the whole parish were to be decided by general ballot. The parish council supported the Polish cemetery project and the pastor did not oppose for much longer (1941: 60-61). The spirit of independence and the ambition to participate in the decision-making process strengthened in the parish. The next time, when the Congregation and the bishop wanted to impose their will upon the parishioners, it was very close to an overt conflict.

Strong tensions which occurred at the beginning of the next decade and led to a schism had their origins in strictly secular, organizational, administrative matters. Within the institution of the Roman Catholic Church and its individual parishes, these were the tensions between, on the one hand, those who had no power and wanted to gain it and, on the other hand, those who had power and, generally speaking (some exceptions were presented above), did not want to share it. The authority of the priests was simultaneously recognized (and, by the same token, it contributed to the integration of the institution) and contested (contributing to the emergence of the overt conflict). It reflects well the situation of imperatively coordinated associations, analyzed by Ralf Dahrendorf in his conflict model of society (see, e.g., 1972: 168).

As I have mentioned above, the tensions in the Polish parishes in South Bend had no doctrinal background (this also corresponds to Dahrendorf's model). The lay people did not question Roman Catholic dogma. The Protestant theology was not interesting for them because they considered it completely strange. Ideas, propagated by the independent from the Vatican "national churches," were known in South Bend at the turn of the century but they were met only with derision. Emissaries of the schismatic organizations were coming to town, but for a long time were unsuccessful. The breakthrough came when the tensions in the authority relations became very strong. These tensions occurred first at St. Adalbert's and St. Casimir's. Through normal social contacts and particularly through publications of the *Goniec Polski*, they became a problem of the whole Polonia community in town. Because the police and the judicial system also became involved, these tensions became a problem for the whole town. Reports of historians on the course of events are not very consistent. I will try to put them in order, though.

The contestation movement and the schism that followed it were a consequence of the "political" tensions within the Polish parishes of the Roman Catholic Church. The fact that the movement and the schism happened in this place and at this time, was due to the existence of some social resources in South Bend or, in Dahrendorf's wording, social conditions of conflict group organization. These resources (or conditions) were in the form of a "national" Catholic parish, already functioning in town, independent from the Vatican.

In 1912, because of strife between the Hungarian lay Roman Catholics and the priests of their St. Stephen's Roman Catholic Church in South Bend, the Sacred Heart Independent Hungarian Catholic Church was established. This church was accepted by Bishop Francis Hodur into his all-American organization, the Polish National Catholic Church (relations between this church and European immigrant groups like Slovaks, Czechs, Lithuanians and Italians are discussed in Kubiak, 1970). The bishop dispatched a young Polish priest who spoke seven languages, including Hungarian, to his new parish. The priest proved to be a very good organizer of the new Hungarian parish and was capable of attracting dissatisfied members of the Polish Roman Catholic parishes.

The tensions had lasted in the Polish parishes for the whole previous decade and were to continue for the next several years. In 1910, St. Adalbert's parish was organized. Its pastor was not a member of the Congregation of Holy Cross. This fact in itself generated tensions because the Congregation took its monopolization over the religious life of the Poles for granted. Moreover, the pastor of the new parish, obviously a Pole, represented ideas that were strange to his own compatriots. He was educated in the Polish-American seminary in Orchard Lake, Michigan (and not at Notre Dame), but was an enthusiast for the fast process of Americanization of the Polish group. He was considered (and he considered himself) a "progressive" and "reform-minded" person. Simultaneously, he considered himself the sole authority in the running of his parish and did not allow any control on the part of the lay parishioners. He was also fighting against the bishop's attempts to control the finances of the parish.

The pastor believed that, for a good cause, he had the right to interfere in the private and personal lives of his parishioners. He was a prominent activist, and was even the national president, of the Polish Catholic Abstinence Society of America and therefore propagated the ideas of abstinence vigorously. His parishioners, admonished by him severely, were writing letters to the *Goniec Polski*. Some of them were published in the summer and fall of 1911. The authors of these letters, and other people later also, accused the priest of behaving brutally and tactlessly, and of administering the parish "with the czarist disposition." His reaction was to call them "numskulls" (see Swastek, 1941: 65-6). The parishioners organized a delegation of the representatives of the whole Polish community to the bishop with a request to replace St. Adalbert's pastor. The bishop did not consent. Consequently, several families moved to St. Casimir's parish. In 1913, 75 families organized, without publicity, St. Valentine's Independent Catholic Church. This initiative was never fully institutionalized and the Association of Polish Societies attempted unsuccessfully to heal the schism. The dissidents dropped their idea of organizing their own church and began to meet at the above mentioned independent Hungarian church that already belonged to the Polish National Catholic Church.

At the same time, new tensions arose at St. Casimir's parish. The earlier conflict between the assistant and the Falcons had not yet been forgotten when the next problem (resulting from that one) occurred. In 1913, after the death of Father Czyzewski, the Congregation of Holy Cross moved the pastor of St. Casimir's to St. Hedwig's. The new pastor of St. Casimir's died soon afterwards and the Congregation nominated the next one. It was the same priest who, two years earlier, had not allowed the Falcons to enter the church. Moreover, the faithful had their own candidate for the pastorship: a young assistant who had worked there for one year. The Congregation did not want to concede and to establish the precedent that the Roman Catholic parishioners elected their pastor. The official nominee was forced by the faithful to withdraw but the Church authorities sent in another priest, again not the one the parishioners preferred. They had nothing against him personally, the only problem was that he was not the candidate of the parish community.

A new phase of the conflict began. The parish community split into two parts. The majority wanted full control over the parish. The minority was ready for a compromise with the bishop and the Congregation. The majority began demonstrations and appealed to the court of justice to prevent the pastor from entering the church. The Church authorities called for the police. Early Sunday morning, on 15 February 1914, the sheriff and his deputy escorted the pastor secretly to the church. The parishioners, warned by their lookouts and the ringing of the bells, again prevented the entry of the pastor. Soon, he returned with much stronger police support but about one thousand parishioners waited for them. Fighting started and some people were seriously injured. From Monday, the "war" again moved from the street to the courts. Eventually, in the next month, a compromise between the Congregation, the bishop and the parishioners was reached. The pastor was introduced to the church (he kept his position for one year and a half) and the bishop dropped his charges against the leaders of the parishioners. Peace was slowly returning.

The social situation had completely changed from the summer of 1913, though. Already in October 1913, a part of St. Casimir's parish community joined the new, now Polish (national) Catholic parish, led by the pastor of the Hungarian schismatics. This new parish of St. Mary's, had been initially and informally organized in the summer of 1913, and in November of 1913 a large and important meeting of the community was held. An "official" organization committee was elected. In February 1914, after the "bloody Sunday," new dissidents joined the St. Mary's group. About 500 people came there from St. Casimir's parish. Another 500 left St. Casimir's for other Polish Roman Catholic parishes (see, Renkiewicz, 1967: 196-209; Swastek, 1941: 64-71; Breza and Pieszak, 1975: 8-9; Bentkowski, 1990: 1-2).

It should be mentioned here that the conflicts between the parishioners and the Roman Catholic hierarchy, in which the Polish National Catholic Church had been involved, were not only specific to South Bend. A conflict of this kind, between the Polish parishioners and the Irish hierarchy, over Christmas Midnight Mass, was analyzed by Jaroslaw Rokicki (1986b). Returning to the South Bend case, I should add that the jubilee book of St. Casimir's parish from 1929, only mentions some misunderstanding between the

Church hierarchy and the parishioners in 1913 and 1914, and the book from 1949 does not even touch upon these events.

After 1914, conflicts occurred between the pastor of St. Adalbert's and the bishop, resulting in 1920 in the retirement of the former. Besides this, the life of the Polish Roman Catholic parishes carried on smoothly. The problem was that the ethnic composition of the Westside was changing. The Polish language was becoming obsolete, even in church. The St. Casimir's jubilee book from 1929 was published in Polish but the book from 1949 describes all the events that happened after 1924, in English. The St. Adalbert's jubilee book from 1960 (*Fifty Year*, 1960) was published in both languages but the Polish test is of slightly shorter and of poorer quality. The above quoted book from 1985, was published entirely in English. St. Hedwig's jubilee book (also quoted) of 1977, was published only in English. There have been fewer and fewer Poles and, fewer inhabitants generally, on the Westside. The number of priests with understanding of the Polish language was decreasing. Looking from today's perspective, I would agree with the sentence written by Donald Stabrowski in 1984: "At least three of the four parishes: St. Hedwig's, St. Casimir's, and St. Stanislau's could be closed with little inconvenience to the west side community" (1984: 267).

The South Bend case, of the marginalization of ethnicity in formerly Polish, Roman Catholic parishes in America is not exceptional. Stanislau Blejwas analyses a similar situation in a small town in Connecticut. He shows, how, since World War II, the Polish language has been disappearing from church activities (see Les, 1980).

I will close this section with a presentation of the functioning of the Polish Catholic parish and its relationship with the Roman Catholic majority of the South Bend Polonia. I will not discuss the Polish National Catholic Church as such, its history, structure and functions, because they have been described very well earlier (see, e.g., Kubiak, 1970; Kubiak, 1980b).

Joseph Swastek, a Roman Catholic priest, presented the collectivity that had established St. Mary's parish in such a way: "The five hundred Hodurites represented a relatively unimportant numerical group in the total Parish (Roman – J.M.) Catholic population of approximately thirteen thousand persons. Social, they were nondescript: several saloon-keepers and would-be socialists who assumed positions of leadership in the revolt, and the rest, honest but misguided hardworking people, deluded into a belief that ecclesiastical authorities were depriving them of the rights they had acquired by organizing the parish and participating in its administration" (1941: 71).

Deluded or not, these hardworking people succeeded for a second time in organizational matters. Not so many years before, they had actively participated in establishing the Roman Catholic parishes of St. Casimir's and St. Adalbert's. In 1913 and 1914, they established another, Polish Catholic parish, which has functioned, like the former ones, to this day.

At the end of July 1914, The Secretary of State of Indiana recorded the articles of association of the "Polish National Catholic Church of St. Mary's of the Holy Rosary." Its members found a suitable location for the church close to their own homes, i.e., close to the Roman Catholic parishes from which they had originated. The leaders sent an official letter to Bishop Hodur, notifying the registration of the parish and requesting him to accept it into his Church. In January 1915, the organizers of St. Mary's received two handwritten letters in Polish from the bishop. In the first one, he informed them that at the present time, he did not have a suitable priest on hand. He showed interest in the new parish, its membership and its potential dynamics. He asked if it could support a priest independently. In the next letter, mailed a few days later, he informed them that he would immediately send a temporary administrator to the parish. Instead of the administrator, a regular and permanent pastor arrived in February (see Bentkowski, 1990: 1-7).

In the fall of 1915, the bishop blessed the first, wooden chapel and confirmed children. Before the blessing, a procession led the bishop to the rectory. The procession included parish associations already organized, but also societies from the Hungarian National Catholic Church (which disappeared in 1922) and one of the local Falcons nests. About three thousand people are said to have witnessed the procession. I have not found any information to their reaction.

It was soon realized that the wooden chapel was too small. On the next lot, the parishioners began to construct a permanent building. Construction worked stopped, though, due to the difficult economic situation of the community, which related to the recession and then to World War I. The parish functioned, though. The first marriage was blessed in February 1916 and soon after that, the first funeral.

Just after the war, the construction of the church building was resumed. Work was not easy because the members of the Polish Roman Catholic parishes did not tolerate dissidents. In an eye-catching way, both "objectively" and "subjectively," the identity of the Polish ethnic group was disturbed: membership in the Roman Catholic Church was one of the most important elements of this identity. The old conflict between the Polish Roman Catholic community and the schismatics took on new forms. Now, the dissenters were not only ridiculed. The religious majority attempted to prevent the new organization from functioning. What the parishioners of St. Mary's built during the day, is said to have been destroyed by other Poles at night. It became necessary to post watches and guards. What is interesting, is that the recollection of this situation is alive in the consciousness of the Roman Catholic rather than the Polish Catholic group. An amateur-historian of the second party quotes, in his description of the events, a report written by the members of the former (see Breza and Pieszak, 1975: 9; Bentkowski, 1990: 7-8) and not documents or the oral tradition of his own group.

In spite of the problems, the church construction was eventually completed. In the summer of 1921, the building was con-secrated by Bishop Hodur. Bearing in mind the tensions between the two Polish religious communities that continues for the next fifty years, two things should be stressed. Firstly, the Polish Catholic parish has never had its own cemetery and without any problems, has been allowed to bury its deceased at the Polish Roman Catholic St. Joseph's Cemetery. The fact, that (according to the earlier mentioned agreement from the beginning of the century) not the whole cemetery but each individual grave was being blessed by a priest, allowed the cooperation of the two communities to be relatively smooth. Secondly, the Polish Catholic parish has never had a school. Little children went to a public grade school (opened for them), but its graduates interested in education attended the St. Hedwig Roman Catholic High School. In 1933, the first St. Mary's member graduated from the latter institution. It was interpreted by the Polish Catholics not only as proof of the talents and motivation to study on the part of the graduate, but also on the improvement in the relations between the two Polish communities. Actually, the end of the conflict was still very far away. It took a whole generation to end it.

During the period between the two world wars, St. Mary's was a "regular" Polish-American parish in the sense that it organized Polish language classes mandatory for children (who did not attend a Polish school), organized Polish theater performances, as well as Polish picnics in a grove, bought by an affluent family nearby. In 1941, when the US entered World War II, the parish organized Polish and American patriotic celebrations. A very important event, for the parish, and particularly for its Polish identity, then took place. The American Legion Pulaski Post, located on the South Bend's Westside, and consisting almost entirely of Polish membership, organized special celebrations connected with the presenting of American and Polish flags to all the Polish parishes in town. At a very touching church service, St. Mary's received its flags as well.

After the Second World War, transformations similar to those at Roman Catholic parishes, began at St. Mary's. They are very interesting from the point of view of the ethnic identity of this community. More and more parishioners of Polish origin, but educated in American public schools, preferred to speak English rather than Polish. Moreover, due to the more general transformations on the Westside, the ethnic composition of the parish community was changing. The pastor of that time reacted to this situation in two ways. On the one hand, in 1946, he reintroduced (suspended because of the war) theatrical performances in Polish. On the other hand, he introduced sermons in English during the early Sunday mass.

The Polish Catholic church and parish were still (with only a very few exceptions) isolated within the Polonia community of South Bend. For instance, they were not invited to the federation of Polish-American associations of the town, called the Centrala. Roman Catholic parishes did not maintain any relations with St. Mary's Moreover, since 1923, there had not been any other independent Catholic church in South Bend. This situation of isolation, opposition and tension, undoubtedly favored the internal integration of the group, but this was considered to be very uncomfortable. Therefore, consecutive pastors and parish councils tried to take action in two directions. Firstly, they took pains to break the isolation on the part of the rest of the Polonia, and secondly, they attempted to contract multilateral relations with other Christian parishes of the town and its vicinity. The second direction, the strengthening of the "anti-Roman Catholic" identity but meaning also the weakening the Polish-American identity, proved to be successful earlier. The parish choir was particularly instrumental in contracting these contacts as it was very often invited for concerts, to other churches.

In 1951, in connection with the celebrations of the 35th anniversary of the Rosary Society, the bishop of the Episcopal Church's Northern Indiana Diocese, was invited and came to St. Mary's to be the guest speaker (in 1957, the seat of the diocese was moved to South Bend, which contributed to the intensification of these relations). Since 1946, the Polish National Catholic Church and the Episcopal Church have been united by formal intercommunion, due to the decisions of their supreme bodies. In South Bend, intercommunion has been practiced since 1951. Since 1963, St. Mary's has had close contact with the Serbian Orthodox Church and slightly weaker contacts with the Greek Orthodox Church. The parish choirs sing quite often in the churches with which their own parishes collaborate; priests and parishioners participate in religious ceremonies, which are always accompanied by social contacts. English is obviously the language of these contacts. Rejected by the Polonia, composed of an increasing proportion of people of non-Polish origin, the Polish Catholic parish has become one of the many small, American religious organizations. However, it has retained up until now (even more than the formerly Polish Roman Catholic parishes) many elements of Polish symbolism.

In 1961, an event, important from the point of view of the marginalization of the parish's ethnicity, occurred. The pastor performed the first all English mass. Chester Bentkowski recalls this with enthusiasm. He says that this was "truly, a great step forward." The reason was that the church wanted to serve all the parish members, and the number of mixed marriages was increasing. Bentkowski adds that the pastor's initiative was in accordance with the wishes PNCC highest authorities. The Church's Synod had earlier decided that "where two masses were held on Sunday, one could be in English if a parish majority voted in favor of it" (1990: 21). The author does not mention anything about a ballot at St. Mary's though.

The shift from the church-related Polish everyday life to the American everyday life coincided with the slow but systematic inclusion of the Polish Catholic parish into the everyday life and festivity of the whole Polish-American community in South Bend. The everyday life of this community was undergoing serious transformations, though. It was becoming less and less Polish and more and more Polish-American.

In 1964, the local branch of the Polish National Union of America presented to the parish, American and Polish flags during the observation of Flag Day. The pastor received a Haller Medal with Crossed Swords from the Haller Post, a Polish association of veterans. It seems to me, however, that the breakthrough was connected with the South Bend celebrations of the Millennium of the Polish State in 1966. During these events, the isolation of St. Mary's became a fact exceedingly visible to the audience.

The St. Mary's parish organized its own Millennium ceremony in June 1966, with the participation of priests and lay members of the above mentioned Christian churches with which it collaborated. Meanwhile, the Roman Catholic Polonia was preparing itself for great festivity. The already mentioned federation of the Polonia associations, the Centrala, was in charge of the organization. Even if various individual Polish groups had de facto recognized St. Mary's, for the Centrala leaders those Poles who were not Roman Catholics, were still placing themselves outside of the national group. They were not only the "others" (regular "other,." the Americans of non-Polish descent, if they qualified because of some reasons, were invited), they were "renegades." The main affair (I will return to it later) took place at Notre Dame University, and about one thousand people attended the dinner. The exclusion of St. Mary's, an established Polish-American institution, having functioned in the town for fifty years, puzzled not only the city authorities but also the invited speaker, then the vice-president of the Kosciuszko Foundation from New York. Not only Bentkowski (1990: 27-28) but also Breza and Pieszak (1975: 9) refer to this. It seems that the resonance was so strong, that the situation would be changed immediately. And it really changed and changed fast in a radical way.

In January 1967, the Centrala issued an invitation to St. Mary's, to participate in the activities of the federation. The pastor accepted the invitation and sent three delegates. After only three years, Chester Bentkowski, the St. Mary's parish amateur-historian, became the president of the Centrala. He kept his position for the next twelve years. In 1969, the parish was invited to the special Polish Day Dinner given by the federation. St. Mary's choir was singing and the benediction was given by the Polish Catholic pastor. For many years to come, until 1978 when he became the Polish Catholic Bishop and moved to Chicago, he was even the chaplain of the Centrala. Other Polish-American institutions followed suit and in an ever increasing way, were taking advantage of the resources of St. Mary's parish.

A little later, relations between the Polish Catholic parish and the Roman Catholic parishes of the Polonia improved as well. In the spring of 1976, during the 25th anniversary of the ordination of the pastor on St. Adalbert's parish, the pastor of St. Mary's was invited to take part in the procession, mass and banquet. In 1978, due to the fire in the parish hall, the dinner following the celebration connected with the promotion of St. Mary's pastor to the rank of the bishop took place at St. Hedwig Memorial Center. In the 1980s, the parish associations and choir regularly participated in the processions organized by Polish Roman Catholic churches.

3. 3. Polish-American Parish Schools: Growth and Decline

Ethnic School, at least in America, is closely connected with religious organizations. It is, at least in the case of Christian denominations, the parish school. It serves first, the purely educational functions. Moreover, it is, on the one hand, a very important channel of ethnic socialization, involving the transmission to the students of the culture of their ancestors and, on the other hand, a channel of gradual acculturation of students to the normative system of the host society. All these problems are, in Polish literature, discussed in an interesting way by Dorota Praszalowicz (1986). She analyses in detail the Polish-American Roman Catholic schools, German-American Roman Catholic schools, German-American Lutheran schools and their manifold social and cultural functions.

Ethnic school is an important element of the ethnic everyday life. It is connected with the regular family life through the children, Parents-Teachers Associations, the church itself. This was true in South Bend from 1877 to the end of World War II.

The first Polish parish school was established at the first Polish parish. As a Roman Catholic school, it was subordinated to the diocesan School Board. The records submitted by the superintendent of Catholic schools of the diocese inform us about the origins of Polish formal education in South Bend. In 1879, the school at St. Joseph's Church had one lay teacher who taught 143 children: 76 boys and 67 girls. It was the largest of the five Roman Catholic schools in town. Both Polish and English textbooks were used by pupils. The catechism and sacred history were taught in Polish, while geography and arithmetic were taught in English. In addition to these, there were lessons in Polish reading and writing as well as in English reading and writing. Except for Polish, the subjects were similar to those in the South Bend public grade schools.

When the previously destroyed, wooden church was being rebuilt (later also renamed as St. Hedwig's), a new brick school building was also constructed. During the next ten years, the original enrollment number increased four fold. The St. Hedwig school was educating a half of the Roman Catholic children of South Bend, attending parish schools, by 1888. There were seven teachers now, including one brother and two sisters from the Congregation of Holy Cross. One of these nuns was a Pole. The school had a library consisting of four hundred volumes and was subscribing for 140 copies of a Polish scholastic periodical, the *Dzien Swiety* (see Swastek, 1941: 92-94; Deka, 1990;8-9).

At the end of the school year 1898/99, 22 years after the first school building had been constructed, 1,025 Polish pupils attended St. Hedwig's school. It was the largest school in the city. Twelve teachers, most of them nuns of the Holy Cross, were the instructors. The curriculum was bilingual by an increasing number of subjects were taught in English. Meanwhile, another Polish school, at the new St. Casimir's parish, appeared. The Nazaren Sisters taught there. Very soon, the St. Stanislau's parish and school appeared with sisters fro the same congregation serving as teachers. When in 1910 the parish school was organized at the new St. Adalbert's Church, the teaching obligations were given to the Felician Sisters from Michigan.

The schools were under the control of the diocesan authorities. From 1904, the graduates of the eighth grade were receiving diocesan diplomas (see, *Jubilee Book*, 1949; *Pamietnik Srebrenego*

Jubileuszu, 1929; Swastek, 1941: 93-94). As it was mentioned in the chapter on the working life, many Polish children were being removed by their parents from school, immediately after First Communion. In order to give them (and to uneducated adults) a chance to continue their education, Father Czyzewski twice (in 1877 and in 1902) tried to establish a free municipal night school.

It seems that, before the Polish Catholic parish was organized, nearly all the Polish children had attended parish schools. Public schools were giving instruction only in English and were therefore considered, by Polish parents, priests and the *Goniec Polski*, to be denationalizing. Moreover, because of their secular character, they were regarded by the Poles as "schools without God" (Swastek, 1941: 95).

The retaining of the Roman Catholic faith and the Polish language and customs, was for a very long time the most important function of school for the parents. And the South Bend Polish parish schools really fulfilled this role. Donald Stabrowski believes that the majority of Polish children in the city spoke better Polish, could read and write in this language better than their parents who were born in Poland. Polish customs and traditions were fully maintained and even embellished. All of this was done at the South Bend parish schools "beyond anything imagined in an impoverished Poland. Here the immigrants had the financial ability to provide what they could not afford in the old country" (1984: 73). Here, in South Bend, the immigrants became more aware of their Polish national culture than they had ever been in Poland.

Relatively few Polish children were reaching secondary level education. According to Breza and Pieszak, the Polish parents of graduates of grade parish schools would send them to such secondary schools that would teach them a trade (1975: 16). In the mid-1920s, which means half of a century after the establishment of the Polish settlement in South Bend, the number of candidates to high school was increasing, though. Because of the reasons quoted earlier, this had to be a Polish Catholic school. These ambitions were realized in 1928. The St. Hedwig High School, known also as the Polish Catholic High School was organized in this year. Its history is not clear. The sources are not consistent. It seems that, after ten years, the school was renamed the South Bend Catholic High School. It did not operate for very long. Because of decreasing enrollment and its financial difficulties, it was eventually closed in 1950 (see, Renkiewicz, 1967: 213; Breza and Pieszak, 1975: 16; *St. Hedwig's Church*, 1977; *Golden Anniversary*, 1971).

The heyday of the Polish parish school was at the beginning of the 1930s. Thanks to these schools, both the first and the second generations of the South Bend Polonia were able to speak, read and write fluently in two languages. At the end of the period between the two world wars, the Polish language was taught as one of many subjects. The scope of education in Polish was much less than about five decades earlier, but it was still efficient. The whole everyday life of the South Bend's Westside could continue, based on a command of Polish. After World War II, though, the situation began to change in a fast and radical way. On the one hand, the Polonia could still speak, read and write in Polish. It should be added that during and just after the war a few hundred Poles came to South Bend from Europe. They were able and willing to strengthen the Polishness of the city. On the other hand, the Polish parish schools stopped all teaching in Polish (Breza and Pieszak, 1975: 17; Stabrowski, 1984: 71). All those who went to school after the war, had many contacts with the Polish language, for instance at home, in the store, sometimes at work, but they could not study it in a systematic way. It was still a language of the family group, of the neighborhood, the language of numerous institutions on the Westside, but it ceased to be the language of the children's play group. Children talked to each other in English, as they did in school. That was a very important step in the process of marginalization of Polish ethnicity.

Soon, the next step was made. In 1969, the historic St. Hedwig's parish school was closed. Then, the same happened to St. Stanislau's school. In 1975, St. Casimir's school was closed also. Young Polish couples, having children of school age, did not settle on the Westside. There was no demand for any school. The only Polish-American parish that kept its school was St. Adalbert's parish. The school is still run by the Felician Sisters but there is no systematic Polish program in the curriculum. The total number of children (including Polish) in school, is decreasing very quickly. In 1930, there were 1,045 students, in 1980 – only 216 (Stabrowski, 1984: 229).

At the end of this section, I would like to quote (from Donald Stabrowski, 1984: 72) the number of pupils in Polish parish schools in South Bend from the beginning of the 20th century. I have already pointed out the important borderline: after World War II, on the one hand, the ethnic composition of the whole city quarter, and along with it of the formerly Polish parish communities, changed and, on the other hand, Polish was no longer taught in schools. In 1900, in two schools (St. Hedwig's and St. Casimir's), there were 1,089 pupils, In 1910, in three schools (St. Stanislau's school was added), there were 1,556 pupils. In 1920, in four schools, there were 2,818 pupils, in 1940 - 1,992, in 1950 - 1,507, in 1960 - 1,641. In 1970, in three schools (St. Hedwig's school was closed one year earlier), there were 846 pupils and in 1980, in one school - 216.

3.4 Polish-American Voluntary Associations

Grzegorz Babinski, a Polish Student of theoretical and methodological aspects of ethnicity, and particularly of ethnic organizations, considers the difficulties of the very idea of "voluntary association" (1986: 91). I bear in mind all these problems. However, for my analysis, I will discuss those features of associations (some of them are analyzed by Babinski) that, in my opinion, distinguish them from other types of social institutions.

In my opinion, the basic feature of associations is the obvious fact that one joins them voluntarily or, at least, can refuse to join them without risking serious, subjectively determined negative formal sanctions and life problems. Associations are mostly the purpose-oriented organizations. This means that they serve some "external" social functions, fulfilling simultaneously the needs of affiliation and of social contact for their members. Associations have a "complementary' character which means that they do not play a crucial role in the life of their members and of the community that forms the pool for their recruitment. That means that it is possible to function without the existence of a membership.

Babinski presents an interesting typology of all ethnic organizations, including voluntary associations (1986: 78-87). Because of the fact that the aims of this work are limited and concrete, I will not utilize this typology. Most of the associations to be discussed here are sectoral (they embrace only a part of the personality and the everyday life of their members). All of them fulfill, to various degrees, instrumental and expressive, as well as internal and external functions. Polish, and later Polish-American associations in South Bend, will be divided here into organizations of strictly local character on the one hand, and local branches of all-American organizations, on the other. The first ones have mostly been genetically connected with parishes.

Associations established by the Poles in South Bend have exhibited many interesting characteristics. Initially, they were only Parish clubs. Later, the local branches of all-American Polish societies, and Polish (since territorially concentrated on the Westside) branches of some American societies were coming to the city. Some parish clubs have transformed themselves, over time, into secular societies, even if where have functioned to some extent within the parish communities, having had their own chaplains and having rendered services to their parishes. At the beginning, male and female societies functioned separately. This gender division has been maintained to a large extent to the present day, even if the participation of women of Polish descent in the public South Bend and St. Joseph County life, seems to have been immense. In the next chapter, I will discuss the recent differences between the functioning of the male and female associations. Some of the female clubs originated as auxiliary organizations to the male associations. Not all male clubs have formed their female counterparts, though. Both the local and national societies have been, to a large extent, fraternal organizations. Polish-American associations of South Bend have been to a decreasing degree interested in Polish matters, and to an increasing degree in their own local community. Ethnicity is clearly being marginalized in their everyday activities.

It is hardly possible (and necessary) to discuss all societies into which, either spontaneously or on the priests' advice, the life of various groups of Poles in South Bend was self-organized. Breza and Pieszak believe that in the 1930s there were about ninety societies (1975: 11) but this number seems to me to be underestimated. I have already mentioned around fifty societies functioning at St. Hedwig's Church. I will not discuss here the business peoples' clubs (they were mentioned earlier) nor political societies (they will be analyzed in the next section).

I will first present associations organized at the very beginning of the functioning of the Polish group in South Bend. In the section of parish life, I said that the first societies, of St. Kazimierz

(Casimir's) and St. Stanislaw (Stanislau's), organized in 1874, contributed to the emergence of the Polish churches. Both were fraternal organizations, offering in the first, difficult years abroad, something resembling life insurance and help to widows and orphans (see, Breza and Pieszak, 1975: 9). They were preparish societies, but they built the parish and they were later included in it. The next society, based on parish membership but having secular purposes, was the Star of Victory Society. This was organized in 1887 (I will return to this in the following pages). Its aim was to cultivate the Polish language, to organize patriotic celebrations and to help their own sick members and their widows and orphans. In the following year, the Polish Merchants' Society was established. What is interesting, is that its aim was to develop Polish cultural interests among its members. Soon, both societies became included into the Polish National Alliance (an all-American organization), established in Philadelphia in 1880. Another, religiously oriented all-American organization, the Polish Roman Catholic Union, established in 1874, opened its first South Bend branch in 1890, the St. Vincent dePaul Society. It has functioned, like other branches of the Union, to the present day, without special publicity. An all-American Polish female organization, the Polish Women's Alliance in America, established in 1898, opened its first South Bend branch in 1902, called the Daughters of Poland Society. Very soon afterwards, the semi-military and gymnastic societies emerged. In 1889, the Krakus Division of St. Casimir was organized. It was to add splendor to the religious and patriotic functions by its members appearing at them in uniforms, The Falcons came to the city in 1894 and have been here ever since (see, Swastek, 1941: 81-82).

All of these societies served many important social functions. I will discuss some of them. The associations organized leisure activities, secured at least minimum level of insurance, took care of the preservation of the Polish culture and physical training.

I will now present some examples of parish societies. This discussion will also present the opportunity to show, how many, social functions were fulfilled by the Polish Roman Catholic parishes in America. The quoted above jubilees book of St. Hedwig's Church, published in English in 1977 (after the dramatic and marginalizing ethnicity transformations), names all the parish societies that had ever functioned there. As long as the local Polish-American community existed, new associations, organizing time and activities around the Polishness, the Roman Catholicism and the parish, were organized. The jubilee book tells us which societies still existed in 1977.

Two societies connected with St. Hedwig's parish emerged before it had been organized. In 1877, when it was created (as St. Joseph's parish), the Confraternity of Mary and the Children of Mary emerged. In 1879, the St. Cecilia Society, the Ladies of the Rosary, and the Young Ladies of the Rosary were established. In 1880, the Confraternity of the Rosary for Men and Boys, in 1883 - the St. Hedwig Society, and in 1886 - the Apostleship of Prayer emerged. In 1888, the Men's Rosary Society, the St. Stanislau's Marching Band and the Knights of St. Casimir were established. In 1890, the (above mentioned) St. Vincent dePaul Society and in 1891 - the St. John Cantius Culture Society (an institution very important for the city) were organized. In 1892, the St. Florian's Society, the Society of the Infant Jesus, the Guardian Angel Society, the Altar Boys, and the Temperance Society of the Immaculate Conception emerged. In 1893, the third Order of St. Francis and in 1895 - the St. Valentine's Society were established. In 1906, the parish group No. 65 of the Polish Women's Alliance, under the name of the Ladies of St. Joseph as well as the Garland of Mary were organized. In 1907, the Knights of St. Michael, in 1908 - the St. Aloysius Society, in 1911 - the Name of Mary, in 1914 - the St. Bernice Society emerged. During the First World War, in 1917, the Citizens Wartime Committee was organized. After the war, in 1920, the Circle of Missionaries and the St. Hedwig Grade School Alumni were established. In 1925, the Ladies Civic Club, in 1927 - the School Safety Patrol and in 1928 - the League of St. Joseph emerged. In 1935, the St. Theresa of the Little Flower and the St. Hedwig Parents and Teachers Association were established. In 1937, the Boy Scouts group emerged, twice later reorganized, in 1847 and 1950. In 1950, the Holy Name Society was established. In 1953, the Legion of Mary, in - the Knights of the Altar (reorganized Altar Boys), in 1959 - the Confraternity of Christian Doctrine and in 1963 - the Young Catholic Students were organized.

Besides purely religious groups, there are also on this list, the cultural, musical, political, scholastic, and scout clubs. Nearly all of them also served fraternal functions. Between 1963 and 1977, when the jubilee book was published, no association was established. According to the book, in 1977, eight groups were still functioning, including a choir group and a ladies' political club.

In the earlier quoted (published partly in Polish and partly in English in 1960), jubilee book of St. Adalbert's Church, we can find not only a list of parish associations, but also interesting comments (sometimes in Polish, in other cases in English) on their activities. On St. Adalbert's Rosary Society, we can read (in quite archaic Polish) the following information: "On the 2nd of October 1910, the Late Reverend Father Jan Kubacki called upon the ladies of St. Adalbert's Parish to establish the Rosary Society. The Society was paying for the laundry of the church linen...and helping the parish with its generous donations for the purchase of church instruments as well as for the flowers for bigger celebrations" (*Fifty Years*, 1960: 124). With regard to another association, we can read (also in archaic Polish): in 1911, "a Fraternal Society was organized, named on the request of Rev. Jan Kubacki, the St. Stanislaus Society of St. Adalbert.... The Society still functions perfectly in the Christian spirit, supporting moral and material causes. Today, it numbers about one hundred members." Its members participated in parades in uniforms, carrying canopies (*op. cit.*: 133-134). The jubilee book names nineteen associates still functioning in 1960, partly purely religious but also cultural, educational, scholastic, musical, charitable, etc.

The jubilee book of St. Casimir's of 1949 names 23 existing groups, of a similar character to those presented above. An interesting point is the fact that in each of the Polish parishes, male and female political societies (Civic Clubs) were emerging. Only those parishioners who were American citizens were eligible to join them. This requirement gave a very high level of prestige to these groups. The purpose of Civic Clubs was to help other Poles to become naturalized (Stabrowski, 1984: 80-81).

After the well known events at St. Casimir's of 1913 and 1914, many societies formerly connected with that parish began to function independently (Renkiewicz, 1967: 211). Quite soon, after World War I and the resumption of the independence of the Polish State, some features became characteristic of the Polonia associations. The trend towards the organization and the strengthening of nonparish societies and towards the actual independence of the parish societies from the respective churches became noticeable. Societies were dealing less and less with Poland and more frequently with the local matters concerning the Westside, South Bend, St. Joseph County and with various insurance programs (*op. cit.*: 307); Swastek, 1941: 80-82).

An interesting example of a large club having a parish origin but actually functioning independently from its parish, is the St. Joseph Young Men's Society. It was organized in 1910 at St. Adalbert's parish, on the initiative of its first pastor. During the first two weeks after the Sunday sermon when the pastor had suggested this club, 56 youngsters joined it. It was to be open for all those men between 12 (later - 16) and 30 years of age who were Roman Catholics of Polish descent (membership in St. Adalbert's parish was not a requirement; in this sense, it was a nonparish club). According to the statute, the members were to go to communion every three months. For many years since 1912, the club had produced theatrical performances. It participated in patriotic parades and supported its church financially (to this extent it was a parish club). At the beginning of the First World War, so many members joined the military, that it was no longer possible to achieve a quorum in the meetings. After the war, the club concentrated on sports, organizing basketball, softball and bowling teams. It sponsored the Polish Boy Scouts movement. In 1939, the society bought a building on the Westside. It set up a bay, functioning to the present day, and several conference halls. The membership grew fast. In 1960 there were 750 members. One of the reasons was that the society had a very success-fully invested insurance program (*Fifteenth Anniversary*, 1960). I have already mentioned the ascriptive character of membership in the Young Men's Society. It will be present in many Polish-American associations. What is still more interesting is the way this "objective" criterion was actually applied.

Two other, still operational, local but nonparish societies that are worth further consideration, here, are the Chopin Fine Arts Club and the Achievement Forum. The first was established in 1940 and the second in 1953. This was the time when the processes of the marginalization of the Polish ethnicity in South Bend were just beginning, and were soon to become quite visible. Both societies have been the associations for people having social and occupational characteristics different from those in other Polish-American organizations. They have been the clubs of people well (but not necessarily very well) educated, fully assimilated, who hardly (or not at all) spoke Polish, earning more than the South Bend's average.

The goal of the Chopin Club, established by 84 young men and women of Polish descent, has from the very beginning been the propagation of the Polish culture not only within the Polish-American community but also among people of other ethnic extractions. The initiators wanted to "return to the roots," to manifest the values of the culture of their country of origin. It seems to me that they also wanted to redefine the Polish group identity. They wished to call the South Bend population's attention to those elements of this identity that until then had not been exposed and noticed by members of the Polish-American group and by its cultural milieu. The first meeting took place in the house of a Polish-American doctor and two Polish-American students of Notre Dame University (amongst others) were elected to the board. Being completely secular, like all other Polish-American associations, it has had a chaplain. The first one was a priest of the congregation of Holy Cross.

During the first years of its activities, the club was bringing some famous Polish artists to South Bend, like Jadwiga Smosarska, an actress, and Helena Morsztyn, a pianist. Both of them were performing very successfully in the city theater and received very good reviews in the South Bend Tribune. In the fourth year of its operations, the club began to publish its own newsletter, *The Keynote*. This monthly has been published up until the present day. In the 1940s, the society began collaboration with the Polish-American high school, helping to establish an art room. To raise money for this or other kinds of activity, since the beginning of the 1950s, the club organized successful card parties. What is interesting is that for many years from 1952 onwards, the Mexican Fiesta was organized as a fund-raiser by this Polish-American society. In 1948, the association joined the American Council of Polish Cultural Clubs, actively participating in its works. In 1954, a congress of the Council took place at Notre Dame University and Florian Znaniecki, the famous sociologist, was the key speaker. The Chopin Fine Arts Club was in charge of the organization of the whole event. In the same year, it organized the first Art Fair in South Bend, which was actually an ethnographic affair. Since then, the club has participated in it every year. In 1956, the society celebrated the one hundredth anniversary of the death of Adam Mickiewicz, the famous Polish poet. On this occasion, it even had its own program on the local radio. In the same year, a journalist of the *Goniec Polski* became the president of the society. Now, much more information on the activities of the club were reaching the Polonia. In the next year, the one hundredth anniversary of the birth of Joseph Conrad was celebrated. In 1958, the club hosted two famous Polish actors. Over 400 people came to the concert. In 1966, the Chopin Club participated in the celebrations, of the Millennium of the Polish State, presenting a show and cooperating at the organization of the Festival of Polish Art.

Since 1954, the club has been giving scholarships to those needy graduates interested in art of the South Bend high schools. Now, it gives three scholarships a year, $750 each, and three special awards, $100 each, for young winners of a competition in Polish art. These scholarships and awards became possible thanks to a special agreement with the local Sylwester and Tessie Kaminski Foundation. In 1981 and 1982, the club participated in the city celebrations of the birth of the Solidarity movement in Poland, and later in manifestations against martial law. Since the mid-1980s, the interests of the club have been divided between Polish art and the life and artistic creativity of Polish immigrants in America. The club also organizes the well known Chopin piano competitions in northern Indiana, for the youth (Hosinski and Stabrowski, 1990).

The Chopin Fine Arts Club meets every month in various cultural institutions in South Bend. There is always a speaker, giving a talk or presenting slides. The meetings are followed by potluck dinners. It is interesting, even if typical for this kind of organization, that the society is dominated by women. In 1941, amongst 72 members, there were 54 women. In 1990, amongst 70 members, there were 59 women. Among 30 former presidents, 23 were women (*op. cit.*).

The sources I am using do not inform us, as to how many people regularly participate in the club's meetings. Based on conversations with recent activists, I do not think that there are many such people. Moreover, the interests of the club members have not been shared, on an everyday basis, by the poorly educated, working class Polonia of South Bend. This is due to the increased likelihood of their having weak ties with Poland. We should not conclude, however, that the Chopin Fine Arts Club has been located outside of the everyday Polish-American life in the city. After all, it has belonged to the Centrala. The *Goniec Polski*, particularly in the last years of its operations, regularly informed the Polonia about the club's activities. On the other hand, most of its members have not lived on the Westside. It has never been a Polish parish organization. It has never had a permanent location on the Westside. Therefore, we should conclude that it has been within the limits, but at the same time on the edges of the life of the South Bend Polonia.

The Chopin Fine Arts Club has certainly also belonged to the Polish-American festivity. At some, more important occasions, it has featured in the *South Bend Tribune*, which contributes to the increase of its own and the Polonia's prestige. It participates in all important, Polish-American celebrations in a very visible way. It is not thorough the everyday life but through festivity, that the club has maintained the ethnic identity of the slightly redefined Polish-American collectivity in the city. This collectivity is nowadays only slightly interested in the regular life in Poland but it needs institutions that will stress the great values of the culture of the country of its origin, values understandable to the "others" and fully appreciated by them.

The Achievement Forum is another kind of local and nonparish association. The history of this club has not yet been written, so the following remarks will be based only on the conversations with activists and through the observation of some of its activities.

When the members of the Chopin Fine Arts Club have mostly been interested in Polish artistic culture and have mainly been representatives of the South Bend "intelligentsia" group, the members of the Achievement Forum were first of all representatives of the city's business, politics and administration. When the Chopin Club has had no formal requirements of membership based on ascribed characteristics like ethnic origin (even if it is formed nearly only of people of Polish descent), the membership of the Achievement Forum was formally based on Polish heritage. When the members of the Chopin Club have been well off, members of the Achievement Forum have had income "considerably higher than average," in the opinion of one of its activists. When the Chopin Club has been oriented towards external activities, the Achievement

Forum has always paid much attention to itself. When the Chopin Club has mostly been interested in Poland and its culture, the Achievement Forum has been active first of all, in the field of local, South Bend community (and not the Westside, even when it was a very important city quarter). Both associations, comparable in size, have been equally exclusive; the Chopin Club because of its elite kind of interests and the Achievement Forum because of formal reasons, presented below.

The Achievement Forum emerged in 1953, that is in the last decade of the splendor of the South Bend Polonia. The founder of the club was a prominent leader of the Polish-American community, an influential leader of the local branch of the Democratic Party and a respected administrator, serving as the Fire Chief of South Bend for many years. He wanted to create an organization that would bring together such representatives of the Polish-American group of the city who had distinguished themselves in their civic and professional activity. That could mean businessmen, politicians and administrators of South Bend and the county. The candidate, only a man, would have to be of "good character." This meant that the person would have to be a good Roman Catholic (after years, a problem emerged with divorced members, otherwise considered valuable). The club was to have exactly one hundred members, or at least no more than this number. A candidate could approach the membership committee himself or could be nominated by its members. He would stay on the waiting list until the club members decided that his qualities were high enough. The club's purpose was to discuss the most important issues of the local community. It was to give one award a year to one of its own members who was not a politician (politicians were obliged by definition to serve their community and to distinguish themselves) for a particular contribution to the life of South Bend Polonia or general community. The recipient of the award would have to be a model of religious and family virtues and a respected leader of civic (not necessarily Polish-American) organizations. The club, even if totally secular, was to have its own chaplain.

The association was created and it has continued to function in this shape, without major problems and changes, to the present day. Although at the beginning of the 1950s all of its members spoke Polish fluently, the meetings have always been held in English.

Polish matters have been discussed only exceptionally, unlike local issues. The club has collaborated with other Polish-American societies. It supports in various ways their activities. It has always participated in the work of the Centrala. Regular club meetings, in which between 20 and 60 members participate, used to be held in elegant South Bend restaurants. For nearly twenty years, meetings have been held in one of the Polish-American Falcon club rooms. The key speakers have always been prominent politicians and businessmen of the city and county.

The Forum gives scholarships to Michiana students of Polish descent who have been accepted by Notre Dame University. To collect the money, fund-raisers are organized. They are, first of all, "Polish dinners," prepared by the ladies from St. Adalbert's parish in its Polish Heritage Center. Hundreds of men come to these dinners. Women are not accepted. The club only invites women at the Annual Fund-Raising Dinner-Dance and the St. Valentine's meeting. On these occasions, a woman is the key speaker.

Initially, the club consisted of middle-aged men, prominent South Bend business and political leaders. It was very attractive because of its exclusive character, an opportunity to network successfully, and a chance to strengthen one's own social position in the city. To become a member, one had to be perceived as a successful person, as somebody who has achieved something significant. This very requirement meant that the average age of the membership has increased. The initial conditions for success in politics, local administration and even in business, have changed. College education became one of the very important preconditions. On the one hand, it takes time to achieve this education, and on the other hand, education was not of a supreme value to the Polonia. Moreover, old Polish-American family businesses were collapsing, and city politics ceased to be a Polish-American domain. The pool of potential candidates to the club was shrinking. In addition, a "natural" process of the monopolization of social positions by those who had already achieved success, resulted in the very careful observation of potential candidates. Consequently, there have been more and more retired members. Some of them have been moving to the remote suburbs or even to places like Florida, and have not participated in the work of the society. By formally continuing membership, they block the succession of younger members.

Despite these problems, the Achievement Forum has not lost its prestige either in the Polonia or in the city at large. It certainly is a club for those who have achieved much in terms of financial and social status. Old networks are still active, guaranteeing hundreds of men at the charitable dinners and balls, guaranteeing media coverage of the functioning of the society. Featuring the Forum means stressing the contributions of the Polonia to the urban community's well-being, which increases the Polonia's prestige. Exposing the fact that the local Polish-Americans are also political and business leaders and professionals, contributes to the transformation of the image of the identity of the group, until now determined by other characteristics.

Like the Chopin Fine Arts Club, the Achievement Forum has belonged to a larger extent to the festivity, rather than to the everyday life of the South Bend Polonia. It belongs to the world of pride, hope and aspirations. The Chopin Club has contributed to the strengthening of the pride of the achievements of the "old country," the Achievement Forum - to the strengthening of the pride of achievements of some representatives of the Polish group on site, in South Bend.

Local, South Bend branches of all-American societies have been here for decades. I will present here one example of veteran associations and two examples of Polish-American fraternal societies. One of the veteran associations is the above mentioned Haller Post, with its auxiliary association of women. The Haller Post is a branch of the Polish Army Veterans' Association of America. The second is (also mentioned) the American Legion Pulaski Post. It was established in 1931 as the Polish Post of the American Legion but in 1935 changed its name to the present one. It is still active, in its own club building on the Westside, but since World War II it has lost not only its Polish, but also its Polish-American character. The Haller Post is still a very Polish club.

It is not clear what the reasons for the foundation of the Haller Post in South Bend. Its official aim was (translation from archaic Polish): "to carry on the work already begun for the good of the Fatherland of Poland, of adopted Fatherland America, and first of all for those who left their health and strength, far away on the fields of Champagne, Wolyn, Pomerania and Lemberg." To realize this aim, "a handful" of veterans of the Polish Army got together and prepared an address to their colleagues - former Polish soldiers. The address was published in February 1932 by the *Goniec Polski*. After several initial meetings, a board was elected and a chaplain appointed. The veterans were mostly unemployed, so they had no money for any of the activities of the Post. They began to organize fund-raising dances and other affairs. Soon, they could participate in uniforms in all Polish-American celebrations in the city. They used to invite prominent Polish officers who were visiting Chicago. They hosted, for instance, the club's patron, General Jozef Haller twice, and General Wladyslaw Anders once. The Post helped finance the construction of the monument of veterans at St. Joseph Polish Cemetery. It "was giving contributions for flood victims, for the cemetery of the soldiers killed in France, for the Moundhill of (Polish - JM) Marshall Pilsudski, for the rearmament of Poland." It presented a flag to the Polish Churches in South Bend. In 1942, it bought a building on the Westside, and since then some Polish-American affairs and meetings have been organized there. In 1932, the Auxiliary Corp. was established also, consisting of the wives of the veterans. "They were bringing assistance to sick and needy colleagues and to disabled persons and they were helping...with the organization of various affairs and receptions, and also with the maintenance of the Veteran's House" (all quotations from: *Thirteenth Anniversary*, 1962, no pagination; see also *Haller Post*, 1957; *Pamietnik Z Okaszji*, 1947).

There have been three groups forming the Haller Post: veterans, members of the auxiliary corps., and "the friends." During the time of the greatest splendor of the association, just after World War II, there were around three hundred veterans (my sources are the jubilee books quoted above and my conversations with activists of the Post). In this period, only the former soldiers who had been in combat were entitled to be called "veterans." Later, younger members of the Post were migrating to other American cities or even states. Veterans of the First World War were very old. The number of members was falling, to 14 veterans and 10 "friends" in 1990. To retain the very existence of Haller Post (the same was true about other branches of the all-American umbrella association), the definition of the "veteran," and with it the group boundaries and group identity, were changed. First, various posts of the whole association began to accept not only Poles and Polish-Americans, but also their relatives, American veterans. Retaining its Polish-American character, the association enlarged the conceptual scope of the "Polish-American group." Secondly, the posts began to accept not only the "combat veterans" but also those Poles, Polish-Americans and their non-Polish relatives, who had served, already after World War II, in the British and American sentry companies in occupied Germany. Therefore, the definition of the veteran itself was changed as well.

The official language of the Post is Polish (but the financial books must be kept in English). Therefore, some members do not understand what is going on at the meetings. According to my informants, there is no formal problem, because the English-speaking veterans and "friends" had signed a declaration of membership stating that Polish was the official language. It is not clear it they had understood the declaration. All present members are retired blue-collars. Their children, even if they live in South Bend, rarely speak Polish and belong to Polish-American organizations. The Auxiliary Corps. was dissolved in South Bend in 1988. According to my informant, the reason was that the women did not want to work and instead quarreled very much. The Haller Post is, as we can see, a dying club. In a few years, regardless of possible changes in the constitution enlarging the definition of the veteran, it will cease to exist.

The Haller Post used to belong to the everyday life of the South Bend Polonia. Most of the South Bend Polish veterans of World War I who had come to America after the war or who had participated in the war as permanent residents of the US, spent all the period between the world wars on the Westside and worked in the (mentioned in former chapters) big factories. The Post collaborated with other Polish-American associations, hosted them and visited them. It used to organize dances and picnics.

After World War II, the situation changed dramatically. The active members of the Haller Post were mostly new immigrants, veterans of the last war, so called Displaced Persons. They did not have a lot in common with the fourth or fifth generation of the local Polish-American group. They had never learnt good English. Their Polish was different from the local Polish. They had different problems. The Haller Post was already rooted in the city and for them it was a very good channel to enter the Polish-American community and city life. The Haller Post members were heroes of the struggle for the common cause, they looked very well in uniforms during the parades, processions and patriotic celebrations. They located themselves very well in the Polish-American festivity, but were in a much worse position in the Polish-American everyday life.

The problem of the building owned by the Haller Post seems to me to be interesting. During the Second World War, and particularly after the war, it served important social functions. It was a center of concentration not only of the veterans' association, but also of other Polish-American clubs, particularly those representing Poles who came to South Bend after the war. The building is located in the center of the Westside. The decline of this city quarter, and particularly of the Polish-American local community, meant the decrease of the usefulness of the Veteran House. The Haller Post which had its own problems with survival was not able to keep it. It rented it out.

The last type of voluntary associations to be discussed here are the local branches of the large, national, Polish-American fraternal organizations. These organizations were studied in detail by Polish (see, e.g., Wawrykiewicz, 1988a; 1991) and American (see, e.g., Pienkos, 1984; 1987) scholars and therefore there is no reason to present there their national history, global structure and various social functions.

Frank Renkiewicz believes that the Polish insurance fraternals arose in America as an adaptation to new conditions and a synthesis of two social trends visible in 19th century Poland. One of them was formed through social activities, leading to the transformation of the rural life and of the peasantry as a social class, and the second was the ideology of the patriotic-minded intelligentsia of partitioned Poland. Under the slogan of "organic work," Polish leaders created and developed a basically "apolitical" program of a kind of conservative reformism. According to this program, economic self-help would give the opportunity for the social progress of all classes of society (1980: 71, 73). As we will see in a moment, not only in Poland but also in the US, the apolitical character of this program could easily be questioned.

Renkiewicz analyzed the basic type of Polish-American national organizations in the following way; "On the one side stood those who favored a secular, nationalist organization for the immigrant and who had founded the Polish National Alliance in 1880. Their leaders often had an exile's enthusiasm for a free Poland, and Republican sympathies in America. The opposition preferred a clerical and Catholic orientation for the immigrant, had lately established the Polish Roman Catholic Union in Chicago, frequently took the advice of priests, and often had Democratic sympathies. Both parties wanted limited integration of the Pole into American life, but for different reasons; the nationalist, to increase pressure for Poland's liberation; the clerical, to streghthen the Catholic Church" (1967: 68).

I have already mentioned some South Bend branches of the Polish Roman Catholic Union. The Union operated mostly within parishes and though these branches, they were treated usually as parish societies. They did not have their own buildings and did not belong to the Centrala. I will not discuss them. The second type of organizations analyzed by Renkiewicz were the Polish National Alliance and later also the Polish Women's Alliance of America.

The Polish National Alliance emerged in Philadelphia in February 1880 (seven years after the PRCU had been established) as a small organization (see, Pienkos, 1984; Wytrwal, 1977: 143-145). From the beginning, the leadership assumed that it would be a union or federation of various Polish groups keeping their own identity. The idea to establish this federation was quickly met with a very positive reaction by Polish societies in Illinois, California, Pennsylvania, Michigan and New York. After a few months it was possible to start actual activity. The headquarters were located in Chicago. After seven years, the PNA was functioning in South Bend.

In the beginning it was difficult. There were only seven founders. Initially, they collected $16.50 for the activities of the above mentioned Star of Victory Society, after one month officially accepted as Group 83 of the Alliance. published in English, on the occasion of its one hundredth anniversary, the jubilee book (*One Hundred*, 1987) does not say much about its activities. It discusses the fast growth of the association, its interests in sports, particularly sport teams of children and youngsters. In 1939, the society opened a big club building which was several times enlarged later. Located on the Westside, close to St. Adalbert's Church, it began to serve as a meeting place for those Polish-American societies that did not have their own seat and for social meetings of individual members. In

1949, another building was bought for $55,000, and soon renovated for $45,000. The financial growth of this fraternal society was unquestionable. It was the same with enrollment. In 1987, there were 967 members.

What the above quoted jubilee book writes about, must have been important for the (anonymous) author of the chapter on the history of the society, and probably for its board. He analyses the enlargement of the building, construction and enlargement of the parking lot and renovation of the kitchen. Much less attention is paid to the fraternal and social activities. The latter were noticed, however. At the end of the chapter on history we can read: "Lodge #83 has spent thousand of dollars for our youth by sponsoring camps, singing classes, dancing classes, and other activities. Lodge #83 has also sponsored all types of sports such as bowling, golf, softball, basketball and a fisherman's club. Lodge #83 has also been host to six PNA National Bowling Tournaments.... The total evaluation of the property and fixtures of Lodge #83 is in excess of $500,000" (no pagation). It should be added that the fixtures include the most modern bowling line in the region.

The jubilee book does not mention Poland nor the South Bend Polonia. The reader not familiar with ethnic symbolism would hardly recognize that he/she was dealing with a Polish-American society. The PNA and its Lodge #83 are definitely a Polish-American association, though. It is an ethnic organization both in an "objective" and in a "subjective" sense. This is visible (for a knowledgeable person) in that, nearly only Polish names appear on the lists of consecutive boards, in the coat of arms of the organization and in its name, in the menu of the jubilee dinner, in the Polish anthem, and in the information on the Polish folk dance group (dissolved at the beginning of the 1990s because, as I was told, the children did not want to wear Polish folk outfits).

My conversations with several activists of the lodge brought interesting information on its recent functioning and on its membership. I will return to this issue in the next chapter. Here, I will only mention that for many years the PNA has not demanded that "insured members" or "social members" are of Polish descent. The president of the lodge of the early 1990s was a German-American, formerly an activist of German-American groups, who became a leader of the PNA under the influence of his Polish wife.

The ascriptive criteria ceased to have any formal or real significance. Symbolic elements that are not troublesome have retained their significance.

The Star of Victory Society has certainly ceased to be a truly Polish but is now certainly a Polish-American association. For several decades, the criteria for belonging to the Polonia, at least to the institutional Polonia of formal organizations, have been changing. Such associations like the Polish National Alliance, engaged first of all in insurance and recreation matters, definitely belong to the new Polish-American everyday life. It is here where Polish-Americans come to see their friends, to meet other people who, most probably (but not for sure), would be somehow related to the Polishness, to drink one (but no more because of driving regulations), to bowl, to eat a "Polish dinner," to dance to the music played by a Polish-American band that comes from time to time from Chicago. For this kind of Polish-American everyday life, it is not necessary to always bear in mind the fact that somewhere Poland exists.

Besides Lodge #83, there had functioned in South Bend, until the end of the 1980s, a second lodge of the PNA. Because of organizational problems, it was dissolved.

The movement for women's emancipation of the late 19th century influenced the functioning of the American Polonia. Although fraternal societies did not exclude women, to have their full rights guaranteed, the Polish women organized in Chicago in 1898 the Polish Women's Alliance of America. Like its male counterpart, this society had been formed of "insured," uninsured ("social") and honorary members (see, e.g., Wytrwal, 1977: 156-157).

As it was mentioned before, already in 1902 a branch of this organization was established in South Bend, under the name of the Daughters of Poland Society. In 1906, at St. Hedwig's parish, another branch, under the name of the Ladies of St. Joseph, emerged. In 1920, at St. Stanislau's parish, the Poland Resurrected Society was organized, as group number 305 of the Alliance (see, *Golden Anniversary, Group 305*, 1970). As we can see, unlike in the PNA, and like in the PRCU, the women's organization established a structure based on parish membership. I did not find any written history, but a conversation with the chairwoman of the Commission, uniting four groups active at the Polish-American parishes, brought some information.

For years, and at least since the end of World War II, membership of the parish groups of the PWA has been more or less stable. They have had about 250-300 insured members. This number embraces many children. They often do not even know about their own membership because they have been signed up by their parents or even grandparents, paying insurance dues. Very few women come regularly to the meetings. Most often, only board members are present. The groups organize various affairs like Mother's Day, a Christmas Party, and Children's Day. Then, more people participate. One of the most important purposes of the organization is the welfare of children and the youth. Therefore, until 1967, the Commission organized the Debutante Balls. Later, no people were interested. The Alliance gives scholarships to its own insured members who have graduated, with good academic results, from a high school and have been preparing for college. Lately, there has been no qualified candidate in South Bend. Earlier, the Commission organized Polish folk dance classes for insured children. Unfortunately, the volunteer-teacher went out of town and there is no money to pay a teacher's salary.

The ties between the particular PWA groups and their parishes were not very strong despite the fact that the meetings were often held on the parish premises and the groups contributed part of their income to the churches. The ties with the Polish identity were stronger. In order to be insured in the PWA, it still was necessary to meet the ascriptive criteria: to be of Polish origin or to have a close Polish relative. Some members subscribed to the periodical *Glos Polek* in which part of the text is printed in Polish. During the dinners, Polish (or at least considered Polish in South Bend) food was served. Profits from these fund-raisers went partly to the school for blind children in Laski close to Warsaw.

The Polish Women's Alliance seems to belong in South Bend to the Polish-American everyday life. About a thousand individual persons in a few hundred families were covered by its insurance plans. The families received letters and brochures from the society that stresses its Polish-American character, reminded people about Polish-American affairs, and issued invitations to them. On the other hand, it did not have its own center of concentration in the form of a club house or of sports facilities. It worked in a "diaspora," even if in close contact with parishes. The society was, in my opinion, a very good example of the marginalization of ethnicity. Many people belonged to this ethnic alliance without even knowing about it. Others knew, but ethnicity did not enter, to a larger extent, those spheres of their existence that were based on self-reflection. Ethnicity entered their daily life mostly because of financial interest and because the membership in the society connected, into an additional network, the close neighbors, and the people already tied by various kinds of social bonds, who have known each other for a long time.

The largest Polish-American fraternal organization in South Bend, having the greatest social significance, is the Falcons. The American organization of Polish Falcons emerged in Chicago in 1887. Here, the first "nests" were established. In 1894, twelve nests already existed, which formed the all-American organization, which was subsequently registered. In 1905, the Falcons became affiliated to the Polish National Alliance, keeping their relatively large level of autonomy. After four years, however, they broke those close ties with the PNA. In 1918, an insurance program was introduced to this organization that, until then, had concentrated mostly on physical training, military sports and patriotic activities. Since 1956, only those candidates who would pay insurance dues were accepted. The old "social members" who had no insurance were not asked to leave but in time, their proportion within the whole organization became insignificant (see, e.g. Wytrwal, 1977: 161-162; Pienkos, 1987).

The history of the Falcons active in the city of South Bend (there are various Falcons societies; I am writing about the association of Polish Falcons of America) is very interesting. Moreover, within a several year period, it was influencing the history of the organization on the national level. The first nest was created in South Bend in 1894, that is one year after the registration of the all-American organization. It took as its patron Mr. Mieczyslaw Romanowski (very few of the members of this nest with whom I spoke remembered the first name of the patron; nobody re-membered any particular reason why he had become the patron). The purpose of the group was the nurturing of the Polish language and customs. Friendly members of a Chicago nest sent information to South Bend referring as to how to organize a nest of Polish

Falcons and soon it was possible to start activities. It was decided to have gymnastic classes every Friday evening. Non-attendance of members was fined. Next year, the nest joined the all-American organization and was number four in it. In 1897, the nest hosted the National Convention and Field Meet of the Polish Falcons of America.

Unfortunately, after the convention, because of reasons difficult to establish today, a part of the membership of the nest separated and established their own nest. I will return to the second nest soon. The Romanowski Nest (later called simply "MR"), despite the fact of the breakup, was still very successful. In 1901, on of its leaders, the editor and owner of the *Goniec Polski*, Mr. George W. I. Kalczynski, became the third national president of the Polish Falcons of America. The all-American administration was moved for four years to South Bend. These years were very good for the association. The number of nests increased from 12 to 38, the number of members from 384 to 1,254 (see, *Czolem Ojczyzine*, 1969). Donald Pienkos, in his history of the "Falconry" in America, gives still higher figures for the end of Kalczynski's term. He attributes the success partly to the president and partly to the increasing interest of the PNA in the Falcons (1987: 49). In 1905, the Falcons joined the PNA, for four years.

Soon after the headquarters had moved to Chicago, the South Bend MR Nest bought the building it had already used, called the "Kosciuszko Hall," for its gymnastic classes. In 1926, it attempted, unsuccessfully, to publish its own monthly. The same year, it was successful in its unification with another Polish nest, named after Kazimierz Pulaski. In 1910, the MR Falconette's Nest was organized. The first attempt to establish a female group in 1898 had been unsuccessful.

The above quoted jubilee book of the MR Falcons, published in 1969 in English, entitled in Polish, devotes much attention to the year of 1931. Because of the Depression, unemployment, and poverty of the Falcons, many of them had to suspend their membership. Fortunately, these kinds of problems did not last very long. During the Second World War, in 1943, the nest began to publish a periodical entitled the *Fourth Alarm*. It continued for "many years," but the jubilee book does not specify how many. In 1969, it was out of print. The book does not say anything on the period between 1943 and the date of its own publication. Additional information was collected in conversations with the nest's leader. Now, the nest counts more than 300 insured members, and with the Falconettes - more than 700. Most of them are Polish Americans.

From the early 1930s, the MR Nest has been one of the major Polish-American golf, softball and bowling centers. It used to organize all-American Falcon tournaments in golf and softball. Some young people meet regularly at the gymnastic classes. For many years, the next has carried on a charitable activity, oriented mostly towards meeting the needs of its own members. It also used to send parcels and money to Poland.

The Polish language dominated the meetings and conversations at the bar until World War II. When, after the war was over, the veterans, speaking better English than Polish now, returned to America, transformations began. In 1952, the all-American congress of the Falcons decided that business meetings could be conducted in English. One of my informants used to be the MR nest's secretary at the end of the 1950s. During the meetings, he was taking notes in English, because this was easier for him: the board members spoke both languages but he knew English better. The minutes were to be written in Polish, though. When he had language problems, he would call his parents who helped him translate his notes into the official, Polish language. In the next decade, sometimes it was still possible to hear Polish in the company of the MR Falcons. Most of the time, this was happening during the annual mass for the next at St. Stanislau's Church. Children and youngsters were listening with astonishment to the Polish conversations, prayers and hymns of the adults, mocking them. According to my informant, this was the reason this custom vanished. In the late 1980s, the male and female nests together counted about three hundred members, 90 percent of whom were of Polish descent.

As I mentioned earlier, the second nest, active to the present day in South Bend, was established because of the separation of some members from Nest #4. The jubilee books of this new Zygmunt Balicki (ZB) Nest fail to mention this event. The group has a sense of pride in something other than its origins. Unlike the MR Nest, the newer Nest #80 attempts to keep the memory of its patron alive. This is visible both in the individual memory of some members and in the collective memory in the form of the jubilee books. In the *Ksiega*

Pamiatkowa, published in Polish in 1922, we can find Balicki's life story. In the *Ksiega Pamiatkowa*, published in the same language in 1947, we can find a chapter entitled "History of the Patron of Our Nest."

The beginnings of Nest #80 are described in the *Ksiega Pamiatkowa* of 1922 (pages, like in most jubilee books, are not numbered; the translation is from a slightly Americanized Polish): "On the day of the 2nd of October 1897, on the premises number 4115 S. Chapin Street, above the 'Kosciuszko Bank,' a company of enthusiasts of the idea of Falconry met and they initiated and brought to life, one of the most powerful Falcon Nests currently in America. The official name of this new Falcon post was: 'The Zygmunt Balicki Gymnastic Society of the Polish Falcons, Number 1, in the Polish Falcons Association Nest Number 80.'" A little further, we can read: "...the training class, in the first year of its existence, carried on 89 practices with the average participation of 24 members in each.... On the order of the Committee for the construction of its own seat, on the day of the 13th of the month of June 1898, a corner lot was bought at the junction of Division and MacPherson streets. That was the first Falcon House, owned by any Polish Falcon Nest in America.... On the day of the 2nd November 1898, a second training detachment was organized, and this was the boys' detachment, formed, initially, by seven members. The practices of this new detachment were also held twice a week. On the day of the 8th of the month of January 1899, the Society bought the necessary gymnastic equipment.... On the day of the 14th of April of the same year, a stock of uniforms was bought, following the design of the uniforms then being used by the Falcons in the Posen Duchy.... In 1906, the entire nest joined the Polish Falcons of America and received number 80. In 1907, Group Number 864 of the PNA was established at the nest." We can see in these quotations that it is not clear when the nest entered the all-American Falcon organization; it is not very important here, though.

Nineteen ten was a very important year for the ZB Falcons of South Bend. In January, the Falconette Nest #185 was established. What is interesting, is that a man became its commander, and his subordinates were 24 wives of members of the male group (see, *Ksiega Pamiatkowa*, 1922; *Rocznica Zlotego Jubileuszu*, 1960). A banner was bought. The nest was incorporated in the State of

Indiana. All its members became owners of the common estate. It was impossible to dissolve the nest if at least five members were for the continuation of its existence. In the next year, the ZB Falcon House hosted the National Congress of the Polish Falcons of America (*Ksiega Pamiatkowa*, 1922). In 1912, the nest opened an English language school and a Polish grammar school for its members (*Ksiega Pamiatkowa*, 1947).

At the beginning of 1913, it seemed most probable that war would break out in Europe. The Falcons wanted to be prepared for it. In February, a special secret meeting of the ZB Nest was held "concerning the recruitment of volunteers to the Polish Army being organized...about twenty three members enrolled...a voluntary contribution was immediately collected for the national treasury" (*Ksiega Pamiatkowa*, 1922). In March 1914, the military detachment of the ZB Next counted 112 "privates." In 1917, when the US entered the war and the government gave permission for the organization of the voluntary Polish army consisting of the Polish citizens (actually, Poles who were not American citizens) living in America, the next members started to join the military: either the Polish or the American.

During the first three months since America had entered the way, thirty-eight thousand Polish Falcons joined the US military. On the first day of recruitment in South Bend, 94 out of the first 100 volunteers were Poles, most of them Falcons. Ignatius Werwinski, a businessman, a leader of the Polish community in South Bend and a Flacon, received special recognition from President Wilson for coordination of this action (Wytrwal, 1969: 55; 1977: 223).

It is worthwhile to devote more attention to Werwinski. This insurance and real estate agent was the initiator for the establishment, by the US Congress of Pulaski Day, which is celebrated to the present day. This was not very easy to achieve. The appreciation by the whole of America of the "mythical father" of the Polonia had a particular significance for the latter. After several weeks of historical studies at the Washington libraries in 1926, Werwinski prepared a memorial and presented it to some friendly politicians. An Indiana US Representative introduced a special bill to Congress. In February 1929, in the year of the 150th anniversary of Pulaski's death, the bill was passed. The day of the General's death, 11th October, was officially announced as the all-American Pulaski Day in 1929. The issue of celebrating this day every year was to be discussed in the following decades.

In February 1929, President Calvin Coolidge appointed Werwinski as a member (soon, he became chairman) of the five-person United States Pulaski Sesquicentennial Commission. Two US Senators and two US Representatives served on this commission (*Haller Post*, 1957). It seems to me entirely justified that Ignatius Werwinski has a street named after him on the Westside of South Bend.

Let us return to the Falcons. In 1921, Nest #80 took pains to unify all the Falcon nests of the region. The MR Nest and the Tadeusz Kosciuszko Nest of Laporte, Indiana, did not agree and the initiative collapsed (*Ksiega Pamiatkowa*, 1922).

In 1926, the nest was publishing a periodical, *Pobudka*. In the following year, every month, meetings with a guest speaker were held. They dealt with "Polish and American matters" the lectures were a great success (*Ksiega Pamiatkowa*, 1947). Other cultural activities were carried on as well. In total, until World War II, the ZB Nest organized more than ten theatrical performances in Polish, more than ten "gymnastic performances," many "literary and scientific soirees" and many celebrations of Polish national holidays. The bowling league was established. I am not discussing the insurance activities because, being more and more significant for the recruitment of new members, they passed almost unnoticed in the jubilee books. Just after World War II, the nest counted 437 members, including 242 insured ones (*Ksiega Pamiatkowa*, 1947).

Similarly, as at the MR Nest, the linguistic situation changed after World War II. From 1957, English was admitted as one of the official languages. Soon, it drove Polish out.

In 1972, the ZB Nest counted 435 Falcons and 350 Falconettes. now, all of them were insured members. The South Bend ZB Next was one of the largest groups of the whole association (see, e.g., *Diamond Jubilee*, 1972; *The Golden Years*, 1969). Both in the case of the ZB and the MR, the male and female sections merged in the late 1980s.

A conversation with a prominent leader of the ZB Falcons and with her husband, also a Falcon activist, carried on partly in Polish and partly in English, brought additional information. Neither of my interlocutors knew very much about Mr. Zygmunt Balicki (but they lent me a book containing many facts from his life). They believed that there was an important difference between the MR Nest and the ZB Nest, arising from the fact that "the Romanowskis" had, for many years, been much more politically active. For instance, that nest had been one of the centers of Dyngus Day. "The Balickis" were said to have been oriented towards the Polish culture and gymnastic classes. For years, the groups of training children (older people have not trained for long) have been relatively small, counting no more than thirty people each. Once, the nest had a good choir singing Polish songs, but since the last director died, it ceased to sing. Very few people have been going to the meetings, but to the "Polish" breakfasts and dinners, if only there is nothing interesting on TV, quite a lot of people, including the young, come. They are Polish Americans and their relatives of non-Polish descent. Because of the fact that the number of intermarriages increased, it has been sufficient for many years to have at least on person of Polish origin in the family to become eligible to join the Falcons and to get insurance. Still, a vast majority of the members are the Polish Americans. In total, the ZB Nest had at the beginning of 1990 about one thousand members.

In none of the jubilee books of the Falcons nests, to which I had access, could I find any mention of conflicts between them and the local parishes before the World War I. I wrote about these conflicts earlier.

The Falcons belong to the world of everyday life of the South Bend Polonia. The number of people coming to the meetings and gymnastic classes is small. The number of people coming to breakfasts and dinners, defined here as Polish, has always been large, though. More people practice sports here. Many people are insured at the association, even if they can be insured at hundreds of other institutions. Membership of the Falcons certainly means the retaining of the Polish ethnic identity that is not connected with any troubles or inconveniences and that gives some financial, athletic and social advantages. Ethnicity is at the background of this membership, but it is a relatively unconstraining ethnicity. Ethnicity has become marginalized and has adapted to American culture.

Earlier, I wrote about the background of group membership. "Basically," one should be of Polish descent or have close Polish relatives, to be accepted into the Falcons. However, the Polishness is understood here in a broad way. One informant told me that actually, to be admitted to the society, it was enough to be a Slav. For instance, he said, to be a Hungarian. My informant was very proud of the fact that several prominent local politicians of Hungarian descent belonged to his nest due to the meeting of this criterion of "Slavicness." This is, in my opinion, an interesting case of the retaining by an ethnic association, of an ascriptive criterion. This broad interpretation is based on the lack of historical knowledge, which may result from the lack of deep interest in the "old country" and its milieu.

The fact that the Falcons are a Polish-American organization is not visible with the naked eye. If one does not know the complex symbolism, which would assume deep cultural competence, one does not see any signs of Polishness on the exterior of the club buildings or inside them. One does not hear the Polish language spoken on workdays in the bar or on Sundays at the "Polish" breakfasts.

The functioning of the Polish-American fraternal organizations in South Bend supports, at least partly, some hypotheses presented by Malgorzata Wawrykiewicz (1988b: 73) based on her all-American research project. She believes that in the period of dynamic growth of the Polish-American organizations, between the 1870s and the end of World War I, the fraternal and the ethnic types of activity, were in practice complementary. Later, a tendency of increasing the strengthening of the fraternal aspect, occurred to the detriment of a corresponding weakening of the ethnic aspect. Consequently, in terms of efficiency and regularity, these organizations took are only of the insurance of their membership. In the case of South Bend, the trend as not yet gone that far, but this direction of dynamics is clear.

The last three associations to be mentioned here are the relatively small but influential groups. The first of them is the American Relief Committee for Free Poland. It was established in 1956, at the initiative of a Pole, a professor of Notre Dame University. The Committee organizes every year, after Christmas, a "Polish Welfare Dinner." The profit goes to a "Polish cause." Initially, the organization financially supported the Polish Emigration Government in London, later the Polish library in Switzerland, and finally the Institute for Blind Children in Laski near Warsaw. The Committee, consisting of a little more than ten persons, supported in 1980 and 1981 the Solidarity movement in Poland, then it organized in the South Bend's downtown, demonstrations against martial law in Poland and coordinated the shipping of food parcels to Poland. The Committee has also invited to South Bend, Polish and Polish-American entertainment groups.

Another society, of an informal character, is the Polonaise Club, functioning as the afore mentioned Forever Learning Institute. The Polonaise Club is a continuation of the former Polish-American Club. The members are older people, mostly retired, mostly of Polish descent. Every month, they listen to lectures on Polish and Polish-American topics, given in English. They participate in Polish language classes. For some of them, these classes serve to remind them of the language they used to know well, for some it is helpful to learn some words and idioms, which is useful when they go for a trip to Poland. More often than to Poland, they go to the Polish quarters of Chicago, to the Polish restaurants and museum there. The club organizes its own "Polish" Christmas Eve dinners and celebrations of Polish holidays. It is, as can be seen, a cultural association for retired people.

Although it is quite small and consists of those older people who are neither well off nor influential, the club is considered to be an important element of the "social infrastructure" of the South Bend Polonia. Although most of the people of Polish descent are not actively interested, on an everyday basis, in Poland, although most of those who still can speak, read and write in Polish, have never been to the "old country," it is important to the existence and identity of the ethnic group that the country of origin and its culture are practically important for at least part of the whole ethnic collectivity. The American Relief Committee has been linking the South Bend Polonia to the idea of the sovereignty of the Polish nation, and the societies like the Chopin Fine Arts Club or the Polonaise Club have been linking it to the idea of the high value of the Polish national culture. It is possible to be a proud member of the South Bend Polonia without any everyday interests in Polish matters, at least in part, thanks to the existence of the associations like those mentioned above.

The last of the groups I wanted to present here is the South Bend branch of the Polish-American Congress. This branch was established relatively late, in 1975. There are about 20 members, including very few active ones. All of the latter are always on the board. The main field of activity of this group is the organization of Polish Heritage Day and distribution of the profits coming form the affairs connected with this Day. The local branch of the Congress is a prestigious organization. It seems to me that it derived its prestige form the power of its all-American mother organization (established in 1944). When the branch was emerging, the Polish-American local community in South Bend was already in a state of disintegration, so it had no opportunity to play any serious, independent role. The meetings of the board are held in Polish, because most of its members belong to post World War II immigration.

Almost from the very beginning of the functioning of the Polish-American local community in South Bend, many associations have been active here. In the late 1930s, their number was estimated at, at least ninety (Breza and Pieszak, 1975: 11). From the beginning, there were some attempts to coordinate their activities. I mentioned them when discussing the conflicts in the Polish parishes in 1913. The currently functioning federation of the Polish-American organizations in South Bend, emerged in 1921. Then, it was called (in Polish) the Polish Council of Social Care (PROS). In 1929, the Council was transformed into the Central Citizens' Committee (CKO). This Committee had an executive committee consisting of the pastors of the Polish Roman Catholic parishes. It closely collaborated with the *Goniec Polski* that was publishing all of its declarations and resolutions.

When the Polish community was still very strong, when many societies existed and belonged to the CKO, it appointed several thematic sections ("active committees"), like the Publicity section, Juvenile Guardian, Civic Improvement section. The Committee collaborated with societies that were organizing citizens classes to aid Poles seeking American citizenship. In the early 1930s, the Committee exerted pressure on the city administration to improve the technical conditions in which the Polonia lived on the Westside. It was successful on many issues, like the elevation of the dangerous railway track or the opening of Pulaski Park. In 1939, the Committee concentrated on aiding the struggling in World War II Poland. The Committee took care of 277 Poles who came to the city from Europe. They Committee assisted in opening the Polish high school. The largest event organized by the CKO was the celebration of the Millennium of the Polish State in 1966. Already in 1971, the Committee was named the Central Polish-American Organization or simply Centrala (*Golden Anniversary*, 1971).

The undated constitution of the federation (*Central Polish-American Organization. Constitution And By-Laws*) declares that it "is the only Polish-American organization which represents the Polonia in South Bend and its vicinity...in particular in matters dealing with the improvement of areas and districts inhabited mostly by citizens of Polish heritage." Regular membership of the Centrala may consist of any Polish-American parishes, any Polish-American male or female societies "covering all fields of endeavor" and professional and business persons. Every organization belonging to the Centrala, is represented there by five delegates. The official languages are Polish and English.

My conversation with the chairwoman of the Centrala gave more information on the methods and areas of its activities. For many years, the meetings have been held only in English. For a long time, sixteen organizations have belonged to it. (I was not able to see the list because its only copy was in the possession of the secretary of the Centrala who lived in Laporte. Nobody in South Bend was able to recall this list.) For years, the Centrala has coordinated the activities of these societies but it has also functioned as an individual, independent Polish-American organization. It takes care of the Polish stand at the yearly South Bend ethnic festival and on the 4th of July. It gives "Polish dinners" and card parties and the profits go for a scholarship for a Polish-American graduate of one of the local high schools who is going to college.

3.5. The "Polish Mafia" in Local Politics

In the section devoted to the world of work, I mentioned relations between the Polonia and the political machine of the Democratic Party. In this section, I intend to present this issue not from the point of view of the patronage and the search for employment but from the point of view of the participation of the Poles in the local political process.

According to the documents of the immigration authorities, as quoted by historians, the first American citizen of Polish descent, voted at the local elections in South Bend in 1868. Ten years later, a

Pole was already a candidate. He ran for a relatively low position in the police force and was defeated. In 1879 or 1880 (depending on the sources), a Pole, a welder at Oliver's and an activist of the St. Stanislau's Society, was appointed deputy street commissioner. In 1880 another Pole, the first or the second teacher in the Polish school, became the boss of the local committee of the Democratic Party and a justice of the peace. Very soon afterwards, he also became chairman of a Polish political club (nothing more is known to me about this club). In the same year of 1880, about thirty Poles established a Republican Club. This was an extraordinary event (even if not a complete exception) because the Poles were mostly (it became particularly visible after World War I) adherents of the Democratic Party (see, e.g., Renkiewicz, 1967: 60-62; Swastek, 1941: 99-100; Breza and Pieszak, 1975: 11-12).

From the municipal elections of 1881, a Pole represented the Third District in the city council (later the Second), and after the change of the borders of districts in 1890, another Pole represented the Sixth District also.

At the turn of the century, new political clubs were emerging. They were strongly supported by the *Goniec Polski* that declared a nonpartisan approach but sympathized with the Democrats. In 1898, the Pulaski Democratic Club was established. Clubs that did not declare their party preferences overtly, were also organized. Examples are the Polish-American Political Club functioning from 1896 at St. Hedwig's parish (that was not a parish citizens' club), the Polish Political Club established in 1902 and the Polish Voters' Club, organized in 1909.

Political education via the clubs was very successful. It contributed to the increase of political awareness of the entire Polish group and to the election of its representatives to various positions, including positions higher than city councilman. This development occurred soon after the turn of the century. One of the few positions that has never been occupied by any Pole is the position of city mayor. The Poles were candidates three times: in 1913, 1921 and 1967. Although in the period 1930-1963 they made up one third of the city population (earlier and later - only less than that) and they gave nearly half of their support to the Democratic Party (earlier and later - only a little less than that), the Poles have never been strong enough to overcome the resistance of other ethnic groups (see, e.g., Stabrowski, 1984: 85-89; Swastek, 1941: 104). Like in many American cities, politics has been the field of ethnic conflict in South Bend. This conflict has surfaced here only in this particular sphere of public life and has not penetrated other spheres.

A few years before World War II, the Poles became interested in county politics. In 1938, Poles were elected to the positions of the County Treasurer, the County Sheriff and the County Coroner. Since then and until today, many important posts in the regional administration and in the regional committee of the Democratic Party have been held by politicians of Polish heritage, coming form the Westside of South Bend (see Stabrowski, 1984: 171, 184).

At the beginning of this section, I listed some political clubs organized by the Polonia. I also mentioned other clubs earlier. One of these clubs deserves much more attention here, even though I discussed it in the section on the ethnic world of work.

In the fall of 1929, a group of influential Polish businessmen of the Westside decided to actively support some prominent city politicians in the forthcoming elections, including the mayoral candidate, as well as the Polish candidates for city judge and for the Second and Sixth District councilmen. All of these candidates won and the above mentioned businessmen decided in the next year to establish a political association, later known as the West Side Democratic and Civic Club. The Club was soon to become the largest, the best known and the most influential political club of the whole city, and perhaps of Northern Indiana. Initially, the club conferred on the premises of St. Adalbert's parish (even if it has never been a parish club), and since 1945 it has operated from its own building, in the heart of the Westside, very close to that church.

The Club became the center of the yearly Dyngus Day, already discussed in this work. Dyngus Day, which begins the spring political campaign, has been an important event on the scale of the whole state. Politicians from Indianapolis, including the governor, regularly come to the Club (and later go to the MR Falcons and to other institutions) to meet their electorate. Senator Edward Kennedy was here in 1968, Senator Edward Muskie (a politician of Polish descent) was here in 1972. Pictures hanging on the walls commemorate these events. Donald Stabrowski believes that in 1960 the Club's membership was around 750 people (1984: 81; *Thirtieth Anniversary*, 1960; *West Side Democratic*, 1980). In 1990, the barman and longtime activist of the Club told me that in the 1960s the association was still called the "Power House" in South Bend. All the Club members were Poles at that time. This was true even in 1990. However, there were no more than 100 members then.

The fact that the Club has fallen into decay, is attributed to several factors of the all-American character. The Poles have been moving out of this city quarter. The Blacks and Hispanics have been moving in and establishing their own institutions. Moreover, the method of functioning of American local politics has changed. The old political machine of the Democratic Party has practically ceased to exist. Therefore, political clubs are no longer the places to find a good public job. The assimilation processes of the former European immigrants have been in progress. My informant recalled that, just after World War II, all the people in the neighborhood and in the Club's rooms spoke Polish. Now, only very old, retired people speak Polish, when they see persons of their own age. The informant did not remember when Polish had disappeared from the Club's meetings.

The jubilee book of the female counterpart of the Club, established in 1932, can serve as a certain guide to the reconstruction of the period when the linguistic changes took place. The book informs us in English, that in 1966 the Women's Club began to hold its meeting in this language. This was valued positively because it resulted in an influx of new members. We can also learn from the book that in 1982 the Women's Club numbered about 600 members. The Club was open for "Any young woman of Polish descent, 21 years of age,...or any young woman of other nationality who becomes the wife of a man of Polish descent and bears his name" (*Polish Women's Democratic*, 1982).

Polish descent in the patrilineal sense also used to be a precondition of membership in the male Club. According to the earlier mentioned activist, at the times of the Club's glory, the Polish speaking men (others could not make themselves understood here) whose at least the father was a Pole, were admitted. A Polish mother alone was not enough. The non-Polish husbands of the Polish women had no chance of membership, but the non-Polish wives of the Polish men had no problems in the female Club. If we are to consider both clubs as Polish-American associations, we should pay attention to the very interesting relations between the stress on the ascriptive ("objective") ethnic criteria and their "subjective" method of practical application.

Donald Stabrowski believes that the decline of the Polish-American local community was reflected in the field of politics particularly in 1983, when a Black woman was elected as the council person of the Second District. For the first time in the 20th century, a person who had not come from the Eastern European immigrant group won a political position on the Westside (1984: 188-189). In the next elections, this Black woman lost her seat to a Polish-American politician, but after one term he lost as well, this time to a young Black man.

The political role of the Polonia was fully appreciated by the leaders of the city. Support by the Polish Americans was important for all local stores, services, banks, but also for the mayor and the county politicians. This is clearly visible in the jubilee books of various parishes and associations. Many of them were quoted above. Let us look at some of then again. In the program of a concert, published in 1932 in English (which was quite strange then), organized by the Holy Name Society at St. Stanislau's parish, many politicians canvassed for the votes of the Polonia. There were among them the Democratic candidate for the county treasurer, the candidates for the district attorney, the county sheriff, the state senator, and the state representative. In the above quoted, bilingual jubilee book of St. Casimir's Church of 1949, best wishes for the whole parish were given by many local politicians, including the mayor. In the earlier quoted jubilee books of the Haller Post, we can find examples of the same kind of greetings. In 1947, we can read (in very Americanized Polish): "On the Occasion of the 15th Anniversary of the Existence of the General Haller Post #125, I am Sending the Warmest Wishes for its Further Growth. George A. Schock. Democrat for City Mayor. Remembering me in the Primaries, Please do not Forget me in the November Mayoral Elections. Just and kind. Service for everybody (*Pamietnik Z Okazji*, 1947). In 1967, next to a large picture and also in Polish, there is a text: "The Warmest, Coming from the Depth of my Heart, Wishes on the Occasion of the Silver Anniversary, from Patrick Brennan, Prosecutor and his Whole Staff." In the same books, there are also greetings from the mayor, the sheriff and the congressmen. I was only mentioning here politicians of non-Polish heritage. There were many more greetings from the Polish American politicians and candidates. All of them had to pay for the publication of these greetings.

During almost the entire 20th century, until the beginning of the 1980s, the "Polish Mafia" (as it was described by one of my informants, a Polish-American politician) was very influential. For the reasons presented above, for instance, the role of the city hall in the filling of public jobs (of a low but also of a high level), the city hall's influence on the appearance and security of streets and parks, local politics was very important for the Polonia. These politics belonged to the Polonia's everyday life. Polish Americans, both men and women, belonged to many political clubs and had large political competence and knowledge. This was not knowledge, especially sought. It was knowledge treated as "natural," obvious. Membership of political clubs, participation in political meetings and voting, all had a "prereflexive" character. They belonged to the social role of the Westsider, the role that was acquired at home, in school and church. For a very long time, this role was played in Polish.

3.6. Cultural Activity of the Polonia. Everyday Life and Festivity

During the first decades of the functioning of the Polish ethnic community in South Bend, the participation of its members in what was broadly understood as Polish culture was very much developed, undoubtedly forming an important aspect of its everyday life.

As I mentioned in the section devoted to voluntary associations, many of them carried on cultural activity, even when their formal purposes were different. I am now talking about the Polish language cultural life. On the one hand, it was a sign of the attempts to retain ethnic identity in the foreign, strange social milieu, and on the other hand it was a manifestation of the inability to speak, write and read English.

Frank Renkiewicz's historical research revealed that the lack of the capacity of self-expression in English was a significant problem for the South Bend Polonia even at the turn of the century. New Polish immigrants were seriously behind the Jews and Hungarians, in his opinion "the most nearly comparable groups." In particular, the women dragged down the percentages. Still in 1909, in the American-born second generation, "an unusually large 7 percent" of Poles did not speak English (1967: 122-123). This was the reason why the Polish societies were permanently organizing English language classes.

Therefore, the Poles spoke and read mostly in Polish. They had no problem with access to Polish books and periodicals since many societies and parishes ran their own libraries. The first lending library was established by Father Valentine Czyzewski in his parish in 1881. Seven years later, a library was organized at the Polish Merchants' Society. Then, in 1900, libraries emerged at St. Casimir's and St. Stanislau's parishes.

Until World War I, all Polish libraries of the city together, had about three thousand volumes of Polish belles-letters and historical essays. An important source of books read by the Poles was the publishing house of the *Goniec Polski*. This house used to import and sell books. The St. John Cantius Society was buying Polish books and distributing them among the libraries. During the period between the two world wars, the PNA and the MR Falcons created their own libraries. It is not clear when all of them closed down. It is know that the books were transferred to the Notre Dame University and that in turn sent the whole collection to Ohio State University.

What kinds of books were collected and read? Breza and Pieszak write about "classical, historical and popular Polish literature." Joseph Swastek quotes the titles of the books advertised in 1901 and later in 1912 in the *Goniec Polski*. They could be bought in the office or received as a prize for subscription. According to this scholar, besides the works of the Polish classics Adam Mickiewicz and Henryk Sienkiewicz, the books "were of little, or at most doubtful, literary value…and had a strong moral tendency."

The Polish libraries in South Bend were not very often visited by the potential readers. In 1900, the *Goniec Polski* complained that the youth spent time dancing, playing cards and standing on street corners instead of reading. In 1903, the *Goniec* expressed the opinion that the Polish libraries were badly managed and did not encourage the youth to read. For instance, the Polish Merchants' library lent, during an eight month period in 1901, only 398 books (Swastek, 1941: 87-89; Breza and Pieszak, 1975: 18-19; Renkiewicz, 1967: 255).

Besides the books, the South Bend Poles read periodicals. The most important was the *Goniec Polski*, which has been in print for sixty-eight years. It was established, edited and published by George Kalczynski, mentioned earlier in the paragraphs on the Polish Falcons. After his death in 1958, his son Edwin took over. The first, "free specimen issue," appeared on 27th June 1896. It had only four pages but promised to have more in the following issues. It was to be published on Wednesdays and Saturdays. The yearly subscription cost was $1.50 and an individual issue cost - two cents.

In the note "From the Publisher," placed on the title page, Kalczynski wrote (in 19th century Polish): "...we have taken as a principle: impartiality, independence in political matters, Catholicism, Polishness, and a balance in the presentation of opinions on public issues, etc. Information of all kinds of problems will be given precisely as they occur, not otherwise." Next to this note, there was a "Local Chronicle." We can read in it, among other things, the following news of the day: "Mr. W. Niedbalski, a Polish pharmacist, moved his business from Mr. Pawlicki's building to the store at the corner of Division and Arnold streets." "The local soc[iety]. of the Polish Falcons gave, on the day of the 8th of June, in the Kosciuszko hall, a gymnastic performance, connected with the ball. The gymnastic practice was well received. The public did not come in large numbers but the people present were deeply impressed by the exhibition on the stage by our young Falcons. After the performance, the ball lasted until dawn." "A rumor is circulating that a cigar maker, Mr. Harmacinski, is soon to open a factory producing Polish cigars on the Warsaw [a subquarter of the Westside - JM]."

In 1941, the periodical became a weekly, coming out on Fridays. In the year of its closure, after 68 years of operation, it obviously looked different from its appearance on the first day. However, a single issue cost five cents and the yearly subscription - $2.50: the price did not increase much. The subtitle read "Popular Periodical" and the motto (in the form of a rhyme) - "All of us, the young and the old, must defend in concert the language and the faith of our fathers." The news on the first page came mostly from Poland. On the second page, there was a note reading that the weekly was a "Social and economic periodical, devoted to the interests of the local Polonia and the Polonia of the surrounding farm settlements."

One page was printed in English. It contained, among other things, the sports news.

The last issue appeared on 30 December 1964. In the note "For Consideration of the Subscribers of the *Goniec Polski*," the editor discussed the causes of why the weekly was closing. "The most important of them is the shortage of advertisements from merchants and manufacturers during the year.... To the closing of the *Goniec Polski*, to a certain extent, another factor contributed: the withdrawal from South Bend, exactly one year ago, of the Studebaker Corporation that locally employed over 7,000 people. ...We are sorry that we must suspend the publication of a very interesting novel entitled *Czahary*. Whoever wished to have a copy of a volume of this novel, can order it in the office of the printing shop and we will try and have it sent."

It is difficult to overestimate the significance of the *Goniec Polski* for the South Bend Polonia. Donald Stabrowski believes that nearly each Polish-American family subscribed to it (1984: 80). Joseph Swastek, 23 years before the paper was closed, presented its role in the following way. The *Goniec* was an important disseminator of the Polish cultural and patriotic traditions. It was a powerful factor in the political education and the unification of the Polonia. It was the strongest supporter of the ideal of community advancement. Every Polish activity in South Bend was important for it. Activities of other Polish-American communities were covered by it and compared with local achievements. News from all three regions of the partitioned Poland were printed here. Reprints of Polish fiction were run serially. The paper stressed the significance of the maintenance of the Polish language. It appealed to parents to see to it that their children spoke only Polish at home and that they prayed only in Polish. It called all those Poles who spoke English at home traitors. It fully supported the campaign against the membership of Poles in non-Polish organizations and in all-city celebrations of American holidays. It was a political instructor, a guide in local and in foreign affairs (1941: 96-99). These are the reasons I have been using the information and opinions taken from the *Goniec* in this work.

The *Goniec* was not the only Polish language periodical being published in South Bend. I mentioned some of the others in sections dealing with the Polish-American parishes and associations. They functioned in various decades and mostly for very short periods. They never had the significance of the *Goniec*. I will list here some titles that have not been presented before. In 1922, St. Stanislau's parish began to publish the *Poznanczyk*, in 1926, St. Hedwig's parish - *Nowe Zycie*, in 1929, St. Casimir's - *Varsovienne* (Breza and Pieszak, 1975: 18). Two of these titles (*Poznanczyk* and *Varsovienne*) are interesting because they come from the informal names of settlements or subquarters forming the Polish-American Westside in South Bend. I will return to this issue soon.

The South Bend Polonia read Polish books and papers but also listened to its own radio programs. The South Bend Polish program was the third permanent radio program in Polish broadcasted in the United States. It was run by Francis K. Czyzewski (Froncek), a relative of (mentioned many times here) Father Valentine and the well known journalist. He began working in 1921, in the *Goniec Polski*(initially as a printer) and in 1929 he joined the staff of the *South Bend Tribune*. Here, he covered weather and science (although he had only high school education). He was also the Westside reporter for his daily. In the same year, he began broadcasting the *Polish Radio Hour* on the waves of the WSBT station, owned by his paper. He conducted his program on each Sunday between 13:35 and 14:30 (*St. Joseph County Observance*, 1966). Jozef Migala stresses that the Polish-American bands, representing very high artistic values, took part in Czyzewski's program. "The Polish radio programs were eagerly listened to not only by the Polonia but also by other listeners and therefore they were presented in both Polish and English" (1984: 22).

From time to time, the *Polish Hour* was being bought from the WSBT station by the Polish-American associations like the Chopin Fine Arts Club or the Falcons. They were broadcasting their own programs. In March 1930, on the waves of the *Polish Hour*, the pastor of St. Casimir's parish produced a radio theater play entitled "Innocence Persecuted." It was said to have been the first Polish radio play in the United States (*Jubilee Book*, 1949).

After the death of Froncek, in the late 1960s, the *Polish Hour* was broadcast by his wife and later, until the second half of the 1980s, by activists of the local branch of the Polish American Congress. The rapidly decreasing number of listeners who could understand Polish resulted in the liquidation, after nearly sixty years, of Polish broadcasting in South Bend. What is interesting, is that even in 1991, one radio station broadcast programs in Hungarian. There were much fewer Hungarian Americans than Polish Americans in the city and its vicinities.

I have mentioned in this work several times the Polish-American orchestras, bands and choirs. To summarize, there were many of them during the whole period of the functioning of the Polish-American local community in South Bend. Some of them played on the *Polish Radio Hour*, others recorded their music. Some had their own hits, sung by "the whole town." In the 1970s, director George Zygmunt Gaska, who collaborated with the Chopin Club, conducted the neighboring Elkhart Symphony Orchestra. From time to time, he presented to the Michiana music lovers, programs devoted to the Polish classical composers (Breza and Pieszak, 1975: 19).

An important cultural role was played by various Polish-American associations. This role was not limited to the running of libraries. Societies and clubs organized Polish balls and picnics, in which mostly the youth participated. The St. John Cantius Society and the St. Casimir Society organized literary soirees. In the first decade of the 20th century, they were held regularly. During these soirees, Polish poetry was recited, Polish songs sung and Polish novels read. Most of the participants were women. The men came rarely. However, according to Swastek, men rather than women read prose and literary essays. The soirees were devoted to the acquaintance of the members with Polish classical poetry and prose. They did not promote original expression (Swastek, 1941: 87).

At the turn of the century, many Polish theatrical performances were organized. They were produced by the parishes and by the lay associations. The actors were mostly immigrants but educated by parish schools in South Bend. "The theatrical presentations of the eighties and nineties were strongly moral in tone, designed to teach rather than to appeal to the aesthetic or literary sense. Melodramatic in structure and language, they possessed little or no literary merit." (Swastek, 1941: 86). In the early 1900s, a lighter vein appeared in the presentations. On the eve of World War I, "the interest swung back to more serious themes" (*op. cit.*: 87).

The Polish-language theater in the United States is the subject of ample and penetrating analysis by Emil Orzechowski (1989). He deals mostly with theaters in Chicago, but also in smaller settlements of the Polish ethnic group. He pays attention to the parish and nonparish, amateur and professional stages. I have not found in this book any remark on the performances in South Bend. It seems that, from the point of view of the author interested in dramatic art, rather than in the social functions of theater, their standard was too low. Orzechowski's lack of interest in the South Bend Polish theater is an indirect confirmation of Swastek's analysis.

The intensity of the cultural activity discussed above, could not meet the demands of the particularly patriotically oriented persons and institutions, and its standard - of the criteria close to that of the connoisseurs. However, it was an activity of an everyday character. It belonged to the world of everyday life that had, for decades, retained the Polish ethnic identity in this strange environment. The opposition between the "our own" and the "strange" was strongly stressed in this activity. The particular role of the *Goniec Polski* in the spreading of this method of structuring of the world has been underlined in this work several times.

The cultural activity of the Polonia has belonged not only to the world of everyday life but also to the world of festivity. This festivity has been breaking with the regular course of events, with the normal course of the social time. It has, in fact, been structuring this time.

Festivity will be divided here into two types. On the one hand, we have the calendrical ceremonies, regular holidays within every year. On the other hand, we have special events, occurring rarely. They are mostly prepared a long time in advance, and in a particular way so as to integrate the whole ethnic collectivity. Some of them do not have a lot to do with the colloquially understood cultural life. I will discuss them because of their above mentioned integratory function and because they break with the continuity of the social time.

If we ignore the feasts of individual institutions, for example parishes or voluntary associations, the yearly celebrations could be further divided here into the religious, the Polish patriotic and the American patriotic ones. They have structured the social time in different ways. The first ones are first of all Christmas Eve, the Epiphany, Easter, and Corpus Christi. These celebrations were connected with public processions, the decorating of the exterior of homes, etc. The second ones, celebrated particularly at the turn of the century, were the anniversaries of the January Uprising (1863), of the adoption of the Third of May Constitution (1791) and of the November Uprising (1830). Breza and Pieszak believe that the anniversaries of the adoption of the Constitution were celebrated by the South Bend Polonia, and sometimes by the whole city, as Polish Day. It began with a big Polish-American parade and closed with a picnic in a local park. The quoted authors think that in the 1930s the anniversary was solemnly celebrated every year. After the Second World War, this custom disappeared.

American patriotic celebrations that gathered many Poles at the turn of the century, were in particularly Memorial Day and Independence Day in particular. Memorial Day was concluded for the Polonia with religious celebrations at St. Joseph's Polish Cemetery. Obviously, Independence Day had a different character. Picnics, dances, feasting and drinking were organized. The Fourth of July was the favorite holiday of the youth (see, e.g., Breza and Pieszak, 1975: 19-21; Swastek, 1941: 82-85).

All of these celebrations were organized so that the cultural boundaries between the Polish group and its cultural milieu were not blurred. This might be obvious in the case of the Polish patriotic feasts that had no significance for the American cadence of time. However, it was also true in the case of all-American feasts. Joseph Swastek stresses that the Poles very rarely participated in the all-city celebrations of any occasion. Even the 400th anniversary of the "discovery of America" by Columbus was celebrated by the Poles separately.

The blurring of ethnic boundaries, in the form of the participation of Poles in various celebrations together with other ethnic groups, was being strongly condemned by the *Goniec Polski*. It used to warn of any collaboration with what it described as the religious associations and "masonic lodges." In 1898, the *Goniec* sharply criticized by name, the members of St. Hedwig's Society for breaking with the Polish custom and for participating in the general South Bend Decoration Day Parade (Swastek, 1941: 85). Participation of the Poles in any all-American associations and speaking English to their own children, met with the same criticism. Based on the available materials, I believe that the tendencies towards self-isolation and segregation, were not stimulated from the outside. The city was open for the Poles. The self-segregation within the ethnic boundaries became very difficult after World War I, and nearly impossible after World War II. Many examples were discussed here earlier.

In addition to the feasts that structured the calendar year, the South Bend Polonia also celebrated other Polish feasts that structured history in the long run. During the first decades of the functioning of this ethnic local community, there were many such feasts. They were confirming the Polishness of the group and it ties with the "old country." After World War I, the number of these celebrations began to decrease.

In 1898, the one hundredth anniversary of the birth of poet Adam Mickiewicz was celebrated. In 1910, most probably the greatest ceremony in the history of the South Bend Polonia took place. It was the 500th anniversary of the Grunwald Battle. Franciszek (Francis K. Czyzewski believes that "Nobody in South Bend has every seen such a colorful, impressive parade from different parishes to the Bendix Park, as in 1910, when the South Bend Polonia celebrated the 500th anniversary of the victory over the Germans at Grunwald" (1966). As I mentioned before, a large part of the city's Polonia came, directly or indirectly, from the German part of the partitioned Poland.

The 150th anniversary of the death of Kazimierz Pulaski took place in 1929. For the South Bend Polonia, it was something very special, particularly because their Ignatius Werwinski received from the Polish Falcons the Silver Cross of Merit, and the Polonia Restituta (Poland Reestablished), the highest Polish military award given to a civilian, from the Polish government. The Polish Consul General came especially to South Bend from Chicago (Breza and Pieszak, 1975: 20-21). Earlier in this work, I mentioned the contribution of Werwinski to the establishment of the all-American Pulaski Day.

The last great feast, celebrated by the South Bend Polonia in 1966 and coordinated by its Centrala federation, was the Millennium of the Polish State and of Christianity in Poland. I have written about it several times in this volume. A special St. Joseph County Polish Millennium Committee was appointed. It published a bilingual jubilee book (*St. Joseph County Observance*, 1966), organized many concerts and exhibitions and a grand dinner for one thousand people at Notre Dame University.

Since the early 1970s, there have been no institutions in South Bend that could serve as a basis for the everyday functioning of the Polish culture. The Polish-American culture has survived but the number of interested people is very limited now, and this culture has mostly a festive character. This is obviously not a Polish specificity, and the causes of this state of affairs lie in the processes of assimilation as well as in the rapid growth of the homogenizing mass culture, nearly totally monopolizing the cultural activities of Americans. The Polish ethnologist, Aleksander Posern-Zielinski, believes that "The expansion of the popular culture has marginalized both the so called "high" (elitist) culture and the ethnic cultures containing many folk elements" (1982: 75).

After the Millennium celebrations, there occurred several events that broke the continuity and stability of the social life of the South Bend Polonia. I will discuss them because of two, closely related reasons. The first reason is their role in the structuring of the social time, that of their role in the temporary but strong intensification of the group life, discussed on the previous pages. The second reason is the fact that, being directly linked to the normative system of the Polish-American community, rousing emotional ties with the "old country" and strongly increasing the sense of group identity, they had essentially a cultural character. The first of these events was a consequence of the situation in Poland and the second had a local character.

The social and political situation in Poland during 1980-82, i.e., the sixteen months of the so called "first Solidarity," the declaration of martial law by the Communist authorities and later, the many months of its application, all resulted in the transformation of the practical and emotional attitudes of the whole Polish emigration towards the "old country." This situation created long-lasting action for assistance for Poland, which within the host countries was simultaneously, a kind of three-year "Polish festival." The winter of 1981/82, at the beginning of martial law, was of particular significance. In the events of that time, the South Bend Polonia participated as well.

In addition to the stories told to me by the participants of the events (and their memory was sometimes treacherous), I used press clippings as a source of information. They had been collected and were later given to me by a Polonia activist. Unfortunately, they are incomplete and, therefore, difficult to identify.

In the fall of 1980, a large collection of money and gifts for example food, medicines and clothing had been conducted in South Bend. The Roman Catholic diocesan periodical published in Fort Wayne, *The Harmonizer* of 29 June 1981, and also the Polish-American, based in Chicago, Daily *Dziennik Zwiazkowy Zgoda* of 30 June of the same year, announced the activities of the local, South Bend committee, "Solidarity with Poland." This committee received great support in the form of a check for $25,000 from the ordinary bishop of the diocese of Fort Wayne - South Bend. The money had all been gathered during a special collection in all diocesan churches, held in collaboration with the above mentioned committee and the local branch of the Polish-American Congress. The *Dziennik Zwiazkowy Zgoda* of 13 July gave more information on this action. It announced that the members of the Congress had transferred help to Poland to the amount of about $30,000. The money was collected not only in churches (Polish-American and others) but also during the Ethnic Festival in the South Bend downtown on the Fourth of July, and during card parties and lotteries, specially organized. In addition to money, food and medicines were collected.

The 13 December 1981 declaration of martial law in Poland was met with a swift reaction by the Polish Americans. The *South Bend Tribune* of Saturday, 19 December 1981 published two large pictures taken at a Polish-American manifestation that had taken place one day earlier. The letterpress read: "Showing the Flags. Mrs. Sophie Romanowski...and Dr. Z.W. Sobol carry American and Polish flags at noon Friday during a rally on the downtown South Bend plaza in support of freedom and the Solidarity movement in Poland. Local government officials joined Polish-American community leaders in denouncing government suppression in Poland." And the second: "A stand for freedom. Members of South Bend's large Polish-American community display signs supporting freedom and the Solidarity movement during a noon Friday rally in downtown South Bend as they listened to government and community leaders denounce suppression by the Polish military government. More than 100 demonstrators turned out for the rally despite a snow storm."

The same demonstration was described in detail by the *Dziennik Zwiazkowy Zgoda* of 28 December. The author of the article (in Polish) entitled "A protest rally in South Bend, Indiana," was Ewa Sobocinska, an activist of the local Polonia. She believed that about 150 people gathered. The manifestation was organized by the Polish-American Congress, the Centrala and the American Relief Committee for a Free Poland. Among the participants, there were the ordinary bishop of the Roman Catholic diocese, the auxiliary bishop residing in South Bend and the city's mayor. From the article, the Polish-American community at large, learned about the activities of the South Bend Polonia.

During the winter and the following spring, the South Bend Polonia continued the collection of gifts for Poland and was preparing itself for the reception of refugees. In May 1982, the *South Bend Tribune* published a picture and a note saying that a new local committee, "Poland in Need," had joined the all-American action "Solidarity Express," collecting food to be shipped to Poland. Two refugees who had come earlier, served on the committee.

An unsigned note, difficult to identify, from the *South Bend Tribune* of spring 1982, announced that the city had expected a larger wave of refugees in the near future. I think it is worthwhile to quote a piece from this note:

"The first cases of Polish refugees, out of a projected 100 cases to be resettled in South Bend, are expected to arrive in mid-June, according to Rev. Eugene Kazmierczak, pastor of St. Adalbert Catholic Church.

Catholic Charities of the Fort Wayne-South Bend Catholic Diocese announced in late March that diocesan officials had agreed to accept up to 200 Polish refugees for resettlement in the diocese. The diocese was responding to a request from the US Catholic Conference. A case could mean a single person or a family, with up to 100 persons could be resettled in the South Bend area.

Harriet Kroll of the local Catholic Charities office and Father Kazmierczak have gathered a task force of Polish-American citizens to begin the local groundwork for the Polish refugee resettlement...the task force hopes to attract broader community support.

Task force committee members have begun recruiting volunteers to act as sponsors. In addition, the members have begun locating possible jobs and housing, fund raising and planning for transportation and English classes...."

The refugees came to South Bend and were received with honors. Within the space of one year, though, they disappeared from the city. The rumor has it that they went to big cities.

Other activities related to the situation in Poland were also undertaken. The *St. Adalbert's Parish Bulletin* of 30 May 1982 announced that the University of Notre Dame had conferred an honorary degree of doctor of laws upon Lech Walesa, chairman of the outlawed Solidarity movement. During a large "in absentia" ceremony, the first in the long history of the university, both the local Polonia and the local academic community gathered. On the first anniversary of the declaration of martial law in Poland, some members of the South Bend Polonia met downtown "to show support for Polish workers and their Solidarity movement," as the *South Bend Tribune* of the following day reported. One year later, the local TV station belonging to Notre Dame University, did broadcast a special report devoted to Poland and the Polonia for one week. A half-page advertisement published in the *South Bend Tribune* announced in advance: "Police detention, visiting with Lech Walesa, life behind the Iron Curtain, and much more will be covered in this week-long special report. Channel 16's reporter...and chief photographer...traveled with Rev. Eugene J. Kazmierczak to Poland. Their report shows how gifts of Michiana residents are used in Poland and features interviews with relatives of families from South Bend."

I have no doubt that for the South Bend Polish-American community, the historic years of 1980-82 had immense significance. They confirmed its group identity through its collective actions, through the friendly interest of the "whole world" in its "old country" and therefore in the Polish emigration at large. Clearly and positively, the Polish-American communities were distinguished from their cultural milieu. Collective actions were being organized by the stable, established ethnic associations, but also by ad hoc emerging committees. These actions were in the form of collections of money and gifts, the organization of new lives for the refugees, participation in religious services for Poland and the participation in other cultural affairs strengthening the group identity. It seems to me that in all of these activities taken together, a large part of the South

Bend Polish-American community took part. If we are to believe in the estimates of eye witnesses, no more than 1 percent of the whole South Bend Polonia participated in the rallies, however. On the pictures in periodicals and pictures shown to me by private persons, there are in total less than twenty persons.

The last event that I would like to discuss had a local character. It will be mentioned here since it broke the regular, everyday rhythm of the Polonia's social life. Because it was local, it had particular significance for the local community. It did not demand time-consuming preparations and constant effort. This event was the 75th anniversary of St. Adalbert's parish. I know the pattern of celebrations from private conversations, private photographs and from an article with pictures, published in *The Harmonizer* of 29 September 1985. In the ceremony, many local officials participated. There were among them the ordinary bishop, the auxiliary bishop, many priests, the city mayor, the US Congressman and hundreds of the faithful. The paper announced (and the pictures support this view) that in the special dinner at Notre Dame University, about six hundred people attended. *The Harmonizer* said, after the pastor, Father Kazmierczak, that 75% of his parishioners were of Polish descent.

In the next chapter, I will return to the problem of the Polish-American celebrations and to the rhythm of the social life.

3.7. The Polish-American Westside of South Bend: Summary

After having discussed the basic spheres of social life and institutions of the Polish-American community, we can look at the Westside as a whole, as a system of social interactions. Before I present this, I will return to the houses that have formed this community, houses in which the Polonia has lived.

The first Polish family that had its own home in the Western part of the South Bend's downtown of that time, most probably lived in it in 1872. During the next two decades, most of the employees of Oliver's and later of other big firms, moved into their own (or still mortgaged) one-family homes. The employers and the Polish building and loan associations helped to buy homes. Swastek believes that the first such an institution was established in 1882 and the next in 1893. Until 1900, according to this author, most of the Poles lived in their own homes. Renkiewicz thinks that the particular building booms took place in 1905-1906 and 1910-1913. He quotes data collected by the Immigration Commission in 1909. According to the statistics, two-thirds of the Poles and of Germans born abroad and one-half of the second generation of these groups lived in their own homes. In comparison, only two-fifths of the "Americans" and of the Hungarians owned their homes.

The homes of the Poles were cheap and of low quality. They provided low comfort. However, the Poles who lived in South Bend at the time, lived in much better conditions than in the same city in 1870 and than most of the Polish and other immigrants who then lived in big American cities. On the other hand, they lived in worse conditions than other ethnic groups of South Bend (see, e.g., Renkewicz, 1967: 36, 112-114; Swastek, 1941: 12-15). What was said to have distinguished their homes positively, was that they were very clean and freshly painted and the lawns around them were nicely cut.

In 1993, the Northern Indiana Historical Society started the project, "A Worker's House Museum." The focus of the house was to change every few years to reflect the many lifestyles of the groups that lived in the St. Joseph River Valley Region. The Polish house was to be the first to be opened. It was to reflect the South Bend community's Polish heritage in the 1930s. Melissa L. Olson, the Project Director, wrote in a short leaflet announcing the project: "The 1930s have been chosen because this was an active period for labor organizations, which changed the lives of many workers and their families. The interpretation of the house will address how a Polish family lived during the 1930s, including discussion of the Depression and of labor issues."

The Society appealed to all inhabitants of South Bend to lend the required objects. I will not list here everything that in the opinion of the project's authors and Committee members (Kathy Deka, the author of the often quoted paper and Professor David Stefancic who has mailed me materials concerning the House, are among them), should find itself (and actually found itself) in this Museum. I will only list the rooms of which the Worker's House consists. It is a two-story, front-gable house built around 1870. Probably it was designed and built by carpenters rather than architects. It is painted white, which was a very popular color in the 1930s. It has a living room (with the Black Madonna religious picture, the President Franklin Delano Roosevelt calendar, copies of the *Goniec Polski* and the *South Bend News Times*), dinning room (with holy pictures and framed blessings in Polish, kitchen (with a wooden ice box), a bathroom (with shower), and three bedrooms.

The Museum was dedicated on Labor Day, 5 September 1994 (see also Borlik, 1994a and Borlik, 1994b).

Around the time of the First World War, the Polish quarter of South Bend was, in its basic frameworks, shaped. The main institutions, like all of the parishes and most of the associations, already functioned. The main centers of concentration of the community, in the form of buildings of churches, schools, clubs, bars, and in the form of parks, existed too. They were continuously enlarged, improved, even moved to the better, more central sites. The Polish services like shops, banks, bars, libraries, periodicals, even the cemetery, functioned efficiently. The Polish community, concentrated in a single city quarter, speaking, reading and writing in Polish, at home but also in the streets, was a visible community, easily distinguishing itself from the social milieu. The exterior of the buildings, full of Polish language advertisements and inscriptions, contributed to the cultural separateness.

The community was constantly growing. In the period from 1868 to 1900, the growth was through a natural increase rather than by immigration (although the latter continued), but during the following years, up until World War I, the situation was the opposite. Immigration contributed to the maintenance of the ethnic identity and the separateness of the Westside. Between the two world wars, it was possible to fulfill here all of the vital needs without speaking one word of English (Breza and Pieszak, 1975: 17).

The Polish quarter, clearly distinguishing itself from its urban milieu, initially formed a small settlement, called "Bogdarka" (from "God's Gift" in Polish). Later, this name was being used solely for the original Polish social space, the territory of St. Hedwig's parish, form which the Polish quarter soon began to grow. On the eve of World War I, the Polish local community, this community of limited liability (to use terminology introduced in the first chapter of this work) was being called by inhabitants of South Bend, not only of

Polish descent, the "Polska" or "Polonia" (Poland in respectively Polish and Latin).

The "Polska" was divided into four smaller districts, as if little "villages," having the character of "defended neighborhoods," as discussed in the first chapter. Breza and Pieszak, Swastek, Stabrowski and Renkiewicz all believe that these "villages" were inhabited mostly by people coming from the same regions of Poland. This fact was reflected in the colloquial names of these "villages," being used on an everyday basis within the Westside but rather unknown outside of it.

The sequence of settlement in South Bend, originating from particular regions of Poland, coincided with the sequence of the establishment of Polish parishes. The formal parish structure of the Roman Catholic Church in the city reinforced the divisions originating from the "old country." The first Polish parish, called the "Jadwigowo." As we already know, it was also called the "Bogdarka" and the "Gniezno." Gniezno is a city in central Poland, then belonging to the German-occupied part of Poland. The first Polish settlers are said to have come from that area. The second district is the "Kazimierzowo," after St. Casimir's (St. Kazimierz in Polish) parish. Another name was the "Warszawa" (Warsaw). The parish is said to have been established by immigrants from the region occupied by the Russians, with the capital in Warsaw. The third "village" was the "Stanislawowo," after St. Stanislau's parish. It was also known as the "Poznan" (in the German-occupied Poznan Duchy) and as the "Zlote Gory" (Golden Hills). Breza and Pieszak explained the latter name in the following way: "the golden wheat on the farms nearby reminded people of the land around Poznan" (1975: 13). The last Polish district was the "Wojciechowo," after St. Adalbert's (St. Wojciech in Polish) parish, or the "Krakow" (Cracow), again after the major city in southern Poland where this wave of immigration originated from.

As far as I know, no particular name was given to the Polish-Catholic area. It was established partly in the "Krakow" and partly in the "Warszawa" districts and for half a century was kept on the martin of the social life of the South Bend Polonia.

The district names presented above are not original. For instance, the two particular neighborhoods of the Polish-American quarters in Chicago are also named after the patrons of their parishes. In South Bend, the Polish Westside neighborhoods, both being named after the parish patrons and after the cities in Poland, are still in use. Unlike in Chicago, they are used only by the old Polish Americans. These names have served an important cultural function. They have helped retain, in a symbolic way, the ties between the parishes and the districts in South Bend on the one hand, and the regions in Poland from which, according to the local myths (supported by historical investigations), their founders came, on the other hand. The old names are visible in the titles of parish periodicals and bulletins. The pictures and frescoes in churches reflect the respective regions in Poland. However, understanding of this symbolism demands a cultural competence. Now, since the Polish schools and the *Goniec Polski* have been closed, there is no institution left that could teach this competence in a systematic way.

Thanks to the churches, and particularly to their high towers, the division of the Polish quarter into four "villages" has been and continues to be visible. Because the division into four "villages" coincided with the division into four formal parish communities and four formal school districts, their social boundaries were clear and meaningful, at least for the competent observers and all of the Westside's inhabitants. The relative separation of the waves of immigration, including the differences in some immigrants' customs and the way in which they spoke Polish, was the additional factor contributing to the distinctions between the four Polish "defended neighborhoods."

The social space of the Polish quarter of South Bend was also divided in other ways. Although each of the parish communities had its own shopping center, they were not equally important. There were two big centers attended by all inhabitants of the Westside, at the Division (today Western) and Chapin streets, and two small centers, at Walnut and Washington streets. Moreover, the whole quarter has been divided into two political wards and has elected two separate councils. It is interesting that none of these divisions had contributed to any disintegration of the Westside, at least as long as it remained the Polish quarter.

In the times of its heyday, in the years of 1930-60, the Polish-American community of South Bend occupied about one-third of the city's territory and made up about one-third of its population. Therefore, it was a very important component of the city. Its significance for South Bend was visible not only in the above presented political and economic factual cases. It was also visible in more symbolic facts. In 1929, the *South Bend Tribune*, until this point actually neglecting the Poles, changed its attitude. It hired the reporter of the *Goniec*, Francis K. Czyzewski, as (among other things) its Westside correspondent. Czyzewski became an additional strong connection between the downtown and the Polonia. The improvement of the relations with the most influential institution in the city that also controlled a radio station and soon a TV station, contributed to the bringing together of the Westside and the downtown and, as a result, to the acceleration of the assimilation processes.

Close relations between the Polonia and the political center of the city and the county, including the city hall and the regional committee of the Democratic Party, had, particularly in the period of 1930-1960, a strong impact on the technical aspects of the functioning of the Westside. For the votes of the Polish Americans, the Democrats and the city hall which was controlled by them, could pay not only with the patronage of public jobs but also with the improvements of parks, streets, bridges and overpasses. These improvements were very important for the Westside Polonia.

Since the late 1950s, the Westside has undergone important transformations in its ethnic composition. In 1960, the whites constituted nearly 80% of the inhabitants of the quarter and by 1980 less than 65%. A half of the South Bend's black population lived here in 1980 (Stabrowski, 1984: 225). The Polish-Americans have not liked the lifestyles of the blacks, for example, the way in which they kept their homes and gardens. This negative attitude is still visible. It is being mentioned in each conversation with the representatives of the Polonia. It should be added that a large part of both the black and the Hispanic population were jobless and lived off unemployment benefits (off "our taxes").

Since the late 1950s, due to the immigration of blacks into the Westside, it became a site of construction of the city for the relatively high, low-income apartment houses. These houses attracted more blacks. Since then, the Polonia, which was always fighting for technical improvements in its quarter, lost this interest and became an opponent of the urban investments on the Westside. It should be added that the public houses are reasonable-looking and very well arranged from an architectural and urbanistic point of view.

Young and more prosperous whites began to move out of the Westside. The parish schools, one after another, were closed. In the 1960s and the 1970s, many old representatives of the first and the second generation of the Polonia, or immigrants and their children, died. The vast majority of the inhabitants of the Westside, even those of Polish descent, stopped speaking Polish on an everyday basis. The *Goniec Polski* was closed. Between the late 1950s and the late 1960s, the membership of the West Side Democratic and Civic Club dropped by a half. The social life of the Westside, at least that of the Polonia, moved form the political clubs to the senior citizens' clubs. They were now organized at each parish, not to mention places like the Polonaise Club at the Forever Learning Institute. Their language for conversations is English. The number of Polish-American services and stores dropped dramatically. In the early 1990s, only four relatively large firms owned by Polish Americans functioned on the Westside and were oriented towards the local patrons. They were: one bank, one insurance agency and two funeral homes. None of the owners of these firms lived on the Westside, though. I doubt if these firms have a "strictly" Polish-American character (I will return to this problem later). Based on observations like the ones above, Donald Stabrowski wrote in 1984: "The west side is no longer Polish" (1984: 289; see also 238, 257-61, 272).

It would be difficult to neglect the opinion of the above quoted scholar who was looking at the Westside with the eye of a former inhabitant and of a political scientist, knowing the previous situation very well, not only from documents but also as an eyewitness and from the stories of both the family and the neighborhood. However, I would like to stress that the vast majority of the city's inhabitants are still convinced that South Bend is a "Polish city" and its Westside is a "Polish quarter." Many of the city's citizens, active in public affairs, are able to point out which social organizations are "Polish" and which are not, even if the name in use does not suggest anything. Many Polish-American organizations keep their Polish symbolism. Many of them have the adjective "Polish" in their name and still use the symbols that refer to the Polishness. In the club bars, if looked at very carefully, one can still find posters of Polish or Polish-American entertainment groups and even copies of the picture of the Polish

Black Madonna. These symbols are here for somebody, they must refer to an existing culture, to a remaining cultural competence.

Cheap cars and cheap gas mean that people can regularly go to their parish church even though it is located very far away. The car makes it possible that the club to which one goes on a regular basis is not located so close to home. Because of the car and the telephone, one's closest friends do not have to live in the same neighborhood. This is, to a certain extent, true about the South Bend Polonia. The Westside has remained the center for the concentration of the local Polish Americans because of the existing, well developed, system of ethnic institutions. This is the new Polonia, though.

Many processes discussed in this work are contributing to the serious transformation, perhaps eventually to the complete decline of the white minorities in the modern American society, which has been proclaimed for decades. Today, however, from the point of view of the functioning of the South Bend's Westside as a center of concentration of the Polonia, this compete decline might be remote. Now, the problems depend more on the fact that the American mass culture keeps people at home watching TV and the ban on driving after drinking more than one beer or bourbon does not encourage to an everyday social life in ethnic clubs. Only when the older generation has completely disappeared, more drastic change, perhaps even the decline of the South Bend Polonia may occur.

Polish does not function in South Bend as an everyday language. As a festival language it is still partially alive, though. One does not have to know this language very well today. It is enough if one gives a public sign that he/she understands it. This sign confirms the language's significance, moreover, its usefulness in the given situation.

We can look from this perspective at two, earlier quoted jubilee books. The book published in 1980 by the West Side Democratic and Civic Club contains many greetings to the Club. Some of them are in Polish. The texts are literal translations from English and use phrases that have never existed in Polish even if they are constructed from Polish words. The texts' Polish grammar is very poor, diacritical marks are wrongly used. On the other hand, those who ordered these texts must have seen a reason to do so. They took pains to write and publish them. In the jubilee book of 1982, published by the local lodge of the Polish National Alliance, the

Polishness is a part of the name of the society. A competent reader will find Polish symbolism in the association's coat of arms. The Polish anthem can be found in the program of the ceremony. In the advertisement published here by the Sobieski Federal Savings and Loan, we can see the portrait of John III Sobieski and explanation in English that he was a Polish king. There are also some greetings here in Polish. What is interesting, is that they do not come from the Polish-American societies but were ordered by American institutions or individuals. Their Polish is quite poor and very much Americanized but they found it proper to publish these greetings in Polish and not in English. The carefulness in putting the Polish diacritical marks in the right places is visible in acknowledgment to the sponsors of the ceremonies.

At the beginning of this chapter I stressed the fact that the South Bend Polonia has undergone transformations enforced by some all-American social processes. Later, I was tying to present these processes and their impact on the local Polish-American community's life. One important all-American process was not, at least in the light of my sources, reflected in South Bend. In the 1960s and the 1970s, there was no "awakening of ethnic America " (see, e.g., Novak, 1971), no "white ethnic movement" here (see, e.g., Siemienska, 1978).

It is very difficult to point out the reasons why something has not happened. One hypothesis appears, however. "New ethnicity" of white immigrant groups could have developed in stable social milieus. The South Bend case was different. Although a strong Polish-American community had functioned there for about one century, its situation in the 1960s was not stable. In this period, the economic background of the very existence of this collectivity was in decline. It resulted in the disintegration of the whole local community. Therefore, there was no cultural space for the problematisation of its own ethnic world, there was no space for reflection upon its own ethnicity. Other problems were more important, vital for this community. These problems were not defined in ethnic terms because, on the one hand, ethnicity has already been marginalized and, on the other hand, the same problems were important for the whole local community of South Bend, whatever the ethnic origin of the particular group.

This book is evidence that Polish ethnicity in South Bend has not disappeared completely despite the lack of its "revival" movement in the 1960s and later. One mass a week, in two churches, is still read in Polish. The Christmas Eve Midnight Mass starts with Polish carols. It still is in fashion to use a Polish word during a speech at a meeting of a Polish-American organization. It still is considered appropriate to publish greetings in Polish in a jubilee book of a Polish-Association. The "Polish" breakfasts, dinners and suppers are still very popular, and it is not important that the Poles in Poland would hardly recognize them as Polish. Ethnicity continues but in a different way than it used to function. I will discuss the present times in the next chapters.

CHAPTER FOUR

THE EVERYDAY LIFE OF CONTEMPORARY POLISH-AMERICAN INSTITUTIONS

In the previous chapter, I discussed many aspects of the transformations occurring within the Polish-American community in South Bend. One of them was the institutional aspect. In the present chapter, I would like to focus only on the Polish-American institutions. I will present institutions still in operation in the years 1990 and 1991 when I had the opportunity to personally observe their activities. Among them, will be parishes, associations, and companies. They form the infrastructure of the Polish-American community in the city. My own notes based upon the observations and conversations with representatives of these institutions will constitute the basic source of information.

4. 1. Polish-American Voluntary Associations and Their Activities: Some Examples

In this section, I will discuss the activities of several associations in the second half of 1990 and the first half of 1991. Generally, I will not repeat historical and organizational information from activists, press clippings, bulletins and, when and where possible, upon participant observation. I will pay attention to the composition of these associations, particularly to such characteristics of their membership as age, place of residence in the city or its vicinity, education and occupation. This data is actually only estimated and I did not get it from registers which do not exist, but from my respondents, the activists of these organizations.

I will present here associations belonging to various categories of the Polish-American organizations. Which societies are under discussion depends mostly upon the consent of their leaders to be interviewed and to give me information on the membership. The organizations will be presented here in the same sequence in which they were discussed in the previous chapter. Two societies were not mentioned then and I will write about them at the end of this section.

The Polish-American Business and Professional Men's Association has been in operation in South Bend since the mid-1920s.

Initially, it was a society that defended the interests of businessmen of Polish descent. After the decline of the Polish-American trade and manufacturing companies in South Bend, the association had to change its constitution. It began to accept politicians and professionals. The vice-president of the society told me that the candidate had to be of Polish heritage or have a Polish wife. Polish concerns are extremely rarely discussed at the meetings but the organization occasionally gives money for Polish causes. As far as he remembered, the official language of the group has always been English. However, he believed that about 15% of the members understood Polish. These members were graduates of Polish parish schools, i.e. they were old people.

In 1991, the club had 64 members. My respondent could tell me something about 48 of them. Half of them were retired (twenty-five members were over 60 years old; only eight members were under 40). He believed that the income of the members was much higher than the city's average. Less than half of them lived on the Westside (mostly in its better, northern part). The majority lived in other quarters of the city or in the suburbs. As we can see, social relations were separated from spatial relations. Around a half of the members were actual or retired owners of various businesses, mostly small, employing less than ten persons. The remaining members were managers or office workers. Some were local politicians. What is interesting, is that four members of this club were blue-collar workers. When they were accepted though, they had their own businesses. The education of the members was on average low, but it varied from unfinished high school to completed graduate and professional school. Children of the members did not speak Polish and were not interested in Polish matters. They were better educated than their fathers. Most of them were college graduates.

The board deals with the internal matters of the association. It meets twice a month in a restaurant or at a private home. Once a month, there is a general meeting of the club. About 35 members participate regularly. The meetings are preceded by dinners. Therefore, they are organized in restaurants (the board chooses restaurants having Polish owners) or at Polish-American societies having club buildings. The best examples are the Falcons or the Polish National Alliance. During these meetings, a local politician speaks and then answers questions from the floor.

I was present at two meetings of the Businessmen's Association. The first took place in the PNA building. At the beginning, the members had small drinks, at the bar or at the tables, and talked. Later, the official part followed. The president introduced the guests. Then, dinner was served. When it was over, the city mayor, a very popular politician, gave a speech. He personally knew most of the club members. He spoke about the prospects for the city's growth in the coming few years and encouraged the audience to invest in new projects. Nobody mentioned Poland, the Westside or Polish-American matters. The second meeting in which I participated was unusual, in that I was the speaker. Poland was the topic of the presentation. There was much interest but I had not noticed more interest than at any other, all-American meeting where I had this kind of presentation.

The president of the association, a retired owner of a small firm, bought me a drink before the above mentioned meetings and later invited me to his home. He told me about the functioning of the Westside just after World War II (as an adult person, he has never returned to live there) and about the club. He thought that many members belonged to various Polish-American organizations, but also to nonethnic clubs like the Lions, Elks, Rotary. He believed that none of the Polish-American businessmen belonged to the local Chamber of Commerce: their companies were too small, rarely employing more than twenty people. The president told me about the participation of his association in the all-city project of Christmas in April.

The project depends upon aid, coordinated by the city authorities and lent by individual persons and various organizations to families in need. Some people and organizations buy old, ruined buildings and transfer them to the city, other people and/or organizations renovate them and pass them to the afore mentioned families. Every year, the Businessmen's Association takes care of one out of 30-40 houses renovated in this way. The building is usually on the Westside and will be allocated to a Polish-American family.

The Polish-American Business and Professional Men's Association continues to be an important segment of the institutional network of the Polonia. In conjunction with the decrease in the significance of the Polish-American community, the role of the association in the city has diminished too. A large part of its membership belongs, however, to the Achievement Forum, to which I will return shortly.

The second Polish-American society to be discussed here is the Chopin Fine Arts Club. The program director of the year 1990-91 told me that this was the only organization in the city that dealt primarily with Polish matters. She described it as "a club of non-working wives having cultural interests." This description did not prove to be accurate. Most of the members worked or had worked before retirement, largely in positions of responsibility. Out of the thirty-six members (on the membership list, there were sixty names, including eight men) about whom I could get information, nineteen, or a little more than half, were over 60 years of age. Only three persons were, according to my respondents, under 40. Eighteen persons, or a half of the group, had at least a two-year college education. Only two persons, advanced in years, had not finished high school. Five members were owners or co-owners of small businesses, four were nurses, five - teachers, six - office workers of various levels. It was impossible to figure out the occupation of six persons, and only the remaining ten were non-working wives. The vast majority of the members did not live on the Westside.

Since 1944, the club has continuously published a monthly, *The Keynotes*. Before each year of activity, it has also published a detailed program of events. I will present now what were the activities of the club in 1990, the year of its golden anniversary, and in the first half of 1991. The monthly meetings of the board were held almost exclusively at private homes. Meetings of the whole society were held in various educational or cultural centers in South Bend.

In March 1990, in the Logan Center, an educational center in the northern part of the city, where many club meetings were taking place, a Notre Dame University professor gave a speech on contemporary Poland. Bigos, a Polish traditional dish, was served. In April, in a recreational center outside of the city, a solemn, jubilee dinner was held. In May, in the concert hall of Indiana University at South Bend, the club presented awards in its piano competition for the youth. A piano recital followed the ceremony.

After the vacation break, in November, the Chopin Club organized a special Thanksgiving dinner in the Logan Center. In December, in a downtown cultural center, the society sponsored a concert of a Polish-American singing group from Chicago, and held a solemn Christmas Eve Supper in the Polish Heritage Center of St. Adalbert's parish. In January 1991, I was the speaker and in February, again at St. Adalbert's, a card party was organized. In April, at the same place, there was a special dinner to celebrate the 51st anniversary of the club. Besides the "Polish dishes," there was a piano recital and Polish songs were sung. The presentation of the new board of directors followed and then the awards and stipends funded by the club were presented. In May, in the city museum of neighboring Elkhart, a recital by the winners of the young pianists' competition was held.

I was invited several times to the meetings of the Chopin Club. Once, I had an official lecture, announced in *The Key Notes*. Another time, I gave a more spontaneously organized presentation. I participated with my family in the club's Thanksgiving Dinner and in its Christmas Eve Supper. This gives me the chance to describe the way in which the meetings were held.

Meetings with lectures usually begin with a blessing and a prayer by the club's chaplain or another cleric. Then, it is time for potluck dinner. This dinner lasts for about 45 minutes and has a cheery informal character. It gives an opportunity for the members to talk with each other. The official program, being a presentation with questions, answers and discussion, lasts for about 30 minutes. Later, there is a closed business meeting and still later, a raffle. In the meetings in which I participated, there were never more than twenty people and never more than three men besides myself. Once, at the Thanksgiving Dinner, a South Bend councilman at large, a person of Polish and Irish descent, came for ten minutes. He knew everybody, received a friendly welcome, drank a glass of wine and went out, most probably to another social gathering. His short presence impressed the club's members very much.

The next society is the Achievement Forum. No more than one hundred men may, in principle, belong to it simultaneously. On the membership list, made available to me and commented upon at length by one of the board members, there were 103 names, though, forty-five of them were over 60 years of age. Twenty were under 40 years. Sixty members had, according to my respondent, only high school education, twenty-one had a bachelor's degree, and the remaining ones a little lower or a little higher education than that.

Among the members under 40 years of age, the proportions were "better," but not much. A half had a high school education and another half at least two years of college.

Sixty members of the club lived on the Westside or the Northwest side and those remaining, in other parts of the city or in the suburbs. Among the persons under 40, the proportions were similar. However, among the 25 college graduates, the proportion was opposite. Ten of them lived on the Westside and fifteen somewhere else. As we can see, the Achievement Forum, and particularly its members of lower education, were in a stronger way tied with the former Polish-American quarter of South Bend, than the businessmen's club. Many members of the Businessmen's Association also belonged to the Forum. It seems to me that the Forum members who were not also the Association's members tended to live on the Westside. Most probably, they were the city or county functionaries.

There were in the Achievement Forum twenty-six office workers, eight politicians, five police officers. There were twenty-four owners (including retired) of various firms. What is interesting and similar to the situation in the Businessmen's Association, is that among the members of the Achievement Forum there were eight blue-collar workers who did not own the firms in which they worked. I did not succeed in finding a full explanation for this fact. What I learnt was that they were people of "great virtues and merits." Perhaps years ago, when they had been accepted to the club, they owned businesses or worked for the city. Acceptance by the Achievements Forum of people without college education, of owners of very small firms who worked in them as blue-collar workers, and eventually of other blue-collar workers, is a confirmation of the low educational and economic status of the whole ethnic group, and at least of the low status when the club was organized. It was impossible to choose in this group one hundred members who would have unquestionable achievements by the all-American standards, accepted by this group (see also Mucha 1984).

Once, I participated as a guest in a meeting of the Forum. It was held in a large hall of the MR Falcons in November 1990. It had an unusual character because of the issue to be discussed and because representatives of the major local Polish-American organizations were invited. There were women among them. The very nature of the meeting had a routine character, though.

The affair began at the bar. The room was overcrowded because there were more than one hundred people in it, everybody wanted to order something and to talk with others over a drink. This part lasted for about one hour. All men, regardless of their age, wore suits and ties. Some looked very well in them, but others did not feel comfortable, had loose ties, and shirt collar buttons undone. The hands of many participants clearly showed that they worked manually. I learnt later that they were construction workers, plumbers, carpenters and electricians, who worked in their own firms. The second part of the evening was the dinner. The tables were arranged so that they formed several long parallel rows. The main table stood perpendicularly to the others. The tables were covered by white, paper cloths. All plates were made of paper. Knives, forks and spoons were made of plastic. Only the coffee cups were ceramic. The "Polish dishes," i.e. sausage, chicken and sweets were served. pieces of the cake were put on the same plate, next to chicken, gravy, vegetables, etc. After everybody had finished, the young MR Falconettes, serving as waitresses, took the cups form the tables and later folded everything else into the paper cloths and put the bundles into the garbage containers (more on this kind of dinners in Mucha 1993). The second part of the evening was over.

It was the third part that was of an extraordinary character. The Achievement Forum invites local activists to its monthly club dinners. They give speeches nearly only on the local issues. This time the city mayor was also present, but the topic was not connected with the city's problems. Another guest speaker was a professor of Purdue University, the dean of the school of agriculture. He had been a member of a group of representatives of the State of Indiana (the South Bend's mayor was also there) visiting several countries of Eastern and Central Europe, including Poland. After returning home, the professor persuaded the authorities of his university to begin a collaboration with Polish farmers. This collaboration was to be quite expwnsive. He came to the conclusion that the Polonia of Northern Indiana could collect between $20,000 and $25,000 for stipends for a few young Polish farmers who would come to Purdue University for a practice. The mayor supported the initiative and announced that the city was looking for a "sister city" in Poland. After a short discussion, the first declarations appeared. The MR Falcons gave $1,000, the Businessmen's Association gave the next

$1,000. The conclusion of the meeting was that the all-city collection should start on the next day. The hosts were to coordinate the action.

Very soon, the *South Bend Tribune* published the notes and articles, warmly welcoming the Achievement Forum and its initiative. Within the Forum, the follow-up came soon, too. In March 1991, the association organized in the rooms of the Elk Club the Sixth Annual Fund Raising Dinner-Dance. Tickets cost $100. Each ticket was also eligible to participate in a drawing for the top prize of $10,000 and for five remote control, console, color TV sets as additional prizes. Those who purchased $100 tickets were entitled for a guest ticket for $40 which did not include participation in the drawing. I have never learned how many participated in the ball but I know that it was successful. The net profit was more than ten thousand dollars. The top prize was won by the Businessmen's Association, which was a collective participant of the affair. According to the *South Bend Tribune* of 17 May 1991, on the following day, the president of the Forum presented to the dean of agriculture of Purdue University a check for $17,000. The main part of this sum was the ball's profit, the rest was collected by various Polish-American organizations.

The ceremony for the presentation of the check took place during the annual Awards Night Dinner at St. Hedwig's Memorial Center. The paper wrote that about 600 people were present. The annual award went to an activist and chaplain of several Roman-Catholic Church who had three children.

The action described above was exceptional but also very successful. It showed that the Achievement Forum was a very efficient organization, having very good relations with the media and with the well-off and influential citizens of South Bend.

The Polonaise Club is a club for the older people, interested in Poland, the Polish language, trips to Polish restaurants and museums in Chicago, but also trips to Poland. In the season of 1990-91, forty-three people, including eleven men, belonged to this club. It was, therefore, an association dominated by women, similar to the earlier discussed cultural society. The vast majority of the members, according to the president of that time, did not know very much about the members, because, in her opinion, conversations about personal matters were very rare there. She did not know the occupation or the place of work of individual persons. She believed, however, that those who had a job (the vast majority, including all men) were office workers of a low level. Twenty-four people lived on the Westside, including four in its northern part. The remaining persons lived in other parts of the city or in the suburbs. The overwhelming majority were people of Polish descent. The non-Polish exceptions were people interested in Poland, who wanted to go there for vacations and the club was to help them prepare for the journey. It is difficult to say what the children of the club members were doing for a living, what were their interests. These problems were not discussed at the meetings or during the breaks. Due to the age of the members, they were more likely to discuss their grandchildren. The president believed that most of the children of the members had a college education.

The meetings of the club are held once a week, during lunch hours. The participants have coffee and cakes and talk. Later, there are lectures on Poland or Polish-American communities, language classes and discussions about the trips to be made. Everything is done in English. From time to time, some affairs are being conducted in which Polish is an equally important language. Then, Polish songs, for instance the carols, are sung. The club members are very much interested in Polish folk culture. They exchange Polish recipes, learn to paint ornamented Eastern eggs and how to make cutouts.

The last two voluntary associations I would like to discuss here, are the parish societies. They are not intentionally Polish-American societies, but are so because the parishes have been and in a sense continue to be Polish-American. The members of these associations are Polish-Americans, belonging to the parish. The first is St. Stanislau's Rosary Society. It is a female organization. At the beginning of 1991, it had 154 members, including 49 active ones, coming at least from time to time to the meetings. My information comes from a board member, formerly a president. Out of the 154 women, 105 (or two-thirds) lived within the borders of St. Stanislau's parish. The others belonged to the parish but lived in remote parts of the city. There was no one member under 40 years of age. Two women were under 50. Nineteen members were between the ages of 51 and 60, and the overwhelming majority were older than that. One hundred and eleven women were between the ages of 61 and 70, and 22 - over 70 years of age. The age structure of this association is obviously a consequence of the age structure of the whole neighborhood or even of the Westside. The Polonia of this quarter is particularly old. On the other hand, the age structure of the Rosary Society also reflects the decrease of interest of younger Polish-American women of the membership in this organization.

My informant gave me her estimates of the occupations of most of the society's members. About 40 of them had never had a job. They were housewives. Thirty women had been, before retirement, low level office workers. Three run their own businesses. Fifty women worked as manual workers, particularly in the kitchen and in the laundry of Notre Dame University. This fact illustrates two things: the occupational (and educational) structure of the Polish-American quarter of South Bend in the post World War II period and the role of Notre Dame University as the employer of the Polonia.

Among the 49 active members of the Rosary Society, the proportions regarding the age, place of residence and occupation looked similar to the whole membership. For example: one active member was under 50 years of age and thirty-eight were between the ages of 60 and 70. Forty women lived within the borders of their parish and nine outside of the Westside. The president knew that twelve women had never worked, that another twelve were office workers and fifteen were manual workers.

The Rosary Society, established relatively late at St. Stanislau's parish, in 1950, has had a religious character. It means that the meetings (attended usually by 15-25 members) were devoted mostly to prayer. The club also organized other affairs, like Christmas parties or fund-raising cake sales. The money was then used for the purchase of the chasubles for the priests and the outfits for the altar boys.

The Polishness has never been as issue, singled out in the everyday life of the society. However, a large part of the membership did understand Polish. The oldest members talked in this language. All of them were attached to the religious songs they used to sing when they were young. These hymns were sung sometimes during mass even now. Before the Christmas Eve Midnight Mass and during the Christmas parties, the women sang Polish carols. They have observed some Polish customs, like breaking the Christmas wafer or eating the Christmas Supper. My informant did not do that, though.

As I mentioned before, the St. Stanislau's Rosary Society can be described as Polish-American, due only to its ethnic composition. The neighborhood in which it functions is ethnically mixed now. This situation is not reflected in the membership of the society. Particularly interesting for me was the situation of the black Roman Catholics. Although they live in the same neighborhood, on the territory of St. Stanislau's parish, all of them go to another, "black," church. They have there their own rosary society.

The last organization to be discussed here is the Married Men's Club, at St. Casimir's parish. The club functions in its own rooms rented from the parish school. It has a bar there, a pool table and a TV set. I met its president in the club rooms and later talked there with him and other members several times. All of them stressed that the parish was Polish-American, but their society, being a parish club, was not of a Polish-American character. The Polish descent of the overwhelming majority of the membership has never been exposed and Polish matters have never been discussed.

On the membership list, there were 78 names. Only twelve of them were not Polish (in this neighborhood, there also live the Hispanic Americans, the Belgian Americans and the Hungarian Americans). The president believed that only six members (including himself) did not live on the Westside. The remaining lived on the territory of the parish. Because this was the married men's club, the members could not be very young. The president thought that only seven of them were under 30 years of age. Fourteen members were between the ages of 30 and 40 years, twenty-one between 41 and 50, thirteen between 51 and 60, and eight were over 70. Sixty-five members had only high school education, three had started college or university education. Among the sixty people whose occupation the president knew, there were nine firm owners, twenty-one office workers, one physician, two teachers, one policeman and twenty-six manual workers. Among those who were under 40 years of age, the proportions were different: two firm owners, nine office workers, one physician and four blue-collar workers.

The Married Men's Club was established in 1938. Its founders were then between the ages of 20 and 40 years. Four of them were still active at the end of 1990. Many present members were introduced to the club by their fathers. The president, who had belonged to the society for ten years, was a son and grandson of club members. As we can see, during its 42 years of activity, it was possible to have an intergenerational continuity of membership.

It is not easy to be accepted into the club. The president thought it was an exclusive club. A candidate had to be introduced to it by an actual member and be accepted by the general meeting. Initially, the candidates were recruited only from among the parish members, now this is not mandatory (even if it is true in practice). It is a parish club in the sense that it operates at the parish, the pastor is its chaplain, a part of the profits from various affairs go to the parish. As the very name suggests, bachelors are not accepted. The members are married or widowed men. Lately, a practical problem emerged, that is, what should this Roman Catholic club do with its divorced members. Tentatively, it was decided that they would not be excluded. There are two categories of membership: regular and retired. One can become a retired member when one is over 65 years of age and was a regular member for at least 15 years. It is beneficial to receive the latter status. One retains all the rights without having to do the duties.

The Married Men's Club is a recreational society. Its members go together to basketball games, organize family dance parties, card parties and raffles. There is much work to do. The bar is open one long evening a week. It is necessary to take care of the supply of the bar, of the service and of the cleaning. These are the members' duties. If one does not do his duty, he pays a fine. The retired members are free of these obligations.

Let us sum up this section. I have not dealt here with the fraternal societies that number many members in South Bend of Polish descent. Actually, their present activities were presented in the previous chapter. In this section, I have discussed small societies of a club character. All of them are Polish-American associations in the sense that they recruit their members form the Polish-American community. Only some of them are intentionally Polish-American in the sense that Polish descent, whatever its definition, is a criterion for membership. Eventually, we have to consider associations that, without stating any formal requirements for membership (Polish descent, belonging to a Polish-American parish), are of a Polish-American character in the sense that they deal with Polish matters. These various voluntary associations form an institutional network linking the ethnic community together. Because of the lasting process of declining of the old Polish-American quarter, because most of the young people move out, because of the very strong impact of the all-American mass culture, this network has become weaker and weaker.

4. 2. Today's Daily Life of the Polish-American Parishes

The second important aspects of the institutional structure of the Polish-American community are still, even if to a decreasing extent, the parishes. I mentioned them earlier in this chapter, when discussing the parish societies. Now, I will present the current method of functioning of the Polish-American churches. Their history was analyzed earlier. I will draw upon my conversations with the pastors and on the content of the parish bulletins from the years 1990 and 1991.

St. Hedwig's Church used to be addressed on the Westside by its Polish name (St. Jadwiga). Now, hardly anybody refers to it in Polish. The church building, which once found itself in the center of the Polish quarter, now stands in the Western, nearly deserted part of the downtown. Every week, the parish publishes an ample bulletin. It does not suggest in any way that we are concerned with a historic monument of the South Bend Polonia. What is visible is that the majority of parish members are people of Polish descent: every second name is Polish. The names in the bulletins are the names of the parish employees, sick and deceased parishioners, those who are going to get married the following week, those who will fulfill some parish functions in the following week, etc. We can read in the bulletins about the activities of the Polish Falcons, but to the same extent about the affairs being organized by various non-Polish societies. Some announcements advertise the firms belonging to the Polish Americans (it is necessary to have advance knowledge if one wants to recognize the "Polish-American" companies). Many more advertisements encourage us to take advantage of the services of other firms, though.

In this chapter, as in the previous one, I have already mentioned that the St. Hedwig Memorial Center has been used by some Polish-American organizations (other societies use it equally often, though). One reason can be of an ethnic sentiment, another can be that the executive director of the Center is a Polish-American activist, who was in the years 1990-91 the president of the Achievement Forum.

In the previous chapter I mentioned, that since 1964 the pastor of St. Hedwig's Church had not been a member of the Congregation of Holy Cross but a diocesan priest. Since 1975, and for ten years afterwards, the pastor was not of Polish descent. In 1990, however, the pastor was a priest coming form a Polish-American, South Bend family. His parents, according to many of my interlocutors, were born in the States but they spoke perfect Polish. The priest did not speak Polish. I ran across his name in the programs of several Polish-American religious celebrations, but he was not a Polish-American activist. He was considered a very good organizer which was confirmed by the fact that he had two full-time jobs. He was the pastor and the principal of a Roman Catholic high school in Mishawaka. In his office in this school, I had a chance to talk with him.

According to the pastor, his parish was small. It counted about 550 persons. During the last few years, the influx was bigger than the outflow, but the net increase was very small: three to four persons a year. It was a parish of old people. The average age was between 55 and 60 years. The parishioners were mostly widows and widowers, retired blue collars. They had much time for helping in the church. On the other hand, only a few of them lived in the nearest neighborhood. Most of them were going to the church from other parts of the city or even from the suburbs. Due to demographic processes, the parish school was closed in 1967. This fact accelerated the outflow of the remaining younger parishioners.

The priest was of the opinion that the vast majority of his parishioners were Polish Americans who had lived in South Bend for many generations. The whole of the parish council were people having Polish names. They were aged. Some of them still spoke some Polish. During the masses, Polish songs were still sung. Two or three times a year, the parish invited a Polish speaking priest for those who preferred Polish to English confession. More visits of the Polish speaking priests were not necessary. Polish hymns and confession were the only Polish elements in St. Hedwig's Church. Very few parishioners went to visit Poland or wrote to relatives in the old country. However, some of them assured the priest that their relatives still lived in Poland.

The parish of St. Kazimierz Krolewicz used to be the second oldest Polish-American religious institution in South Bend. It had been the living center of social life in its neighborhood. Today, it is St. Casimir's parish. Its very modest weekly bulletin reminds us about its former Polishness only by the many Polish names of its parishioners. The same is true about the names of presidents of the parish associations. In the period of 1990-91, both the pastor and the assistant were Irish-American members of the Congregation of Holy Cross. Neither of them spoke, nor understood Polish.

According to the pastor, its parish was formed by 550 households, many of which consisted of only one person. Most of the parishioners were widows and widowers. The young people did not live in that neighborhood. Some young people continued their membership in the parish but they commuted from the suburbs. New inhabitants, mostly blacks and Latin Americans were moving into the neighborhood. Blacks were rarely Roman Catholics. The Latin Americans were Catholics, but in the opinion of the pastor they "did not do anything in the way the Catholics did." They did not belong to St. Casimir's parish. They "took over" the neighboring, formerly Hungarian American parish (the Hungarian Americans were leaving the area very quickly). The pastor thought that the demographic processes would continue and in one decade, the parish would cease to exist, because there would be no parishioners. The present parishioners were nearly solely retired blue collars. He believed that there was no single person with college education in his parish, no single professional. (His opinion is not in total agreement with the information given to me by the president of the Married Men's Club about the occupational composition of his society, but the discrepancies are not significant.) It tells us a lot about the education and occupations of the post World War II Polonia in South Bend.

The pastor was totally aware of the "Polish history" of the parish. With visible pleasure, he showed me around the church and its Polish relics. He believed that no Polish traditions were continued in this church, even if some were continued in the parish societies, particularly the societies of women. However, the priest invited a Polish language confessor from the parish of the Notre Dame University once a month.

The third parish established in South Bend by the Polish immigrants was the parish of St. Stanislaw Bishop and Martyr's.

Now, it is know as St. Stanislau's (or simply St. Stan's) parish. the parish bulletin does not inform us about the Polish traditions of the institution. In 1990 and 1991, the pastor was a priest of Slovenian origin and the assistant was of Italian descent. Both were members of the Congregation of Holy Cross. None of the priests spoke Polish. The pastor, who knew the Slovenian language, understood some Polish. He told me that he did not know very much about the history of his parish, but in fact he was fully aware of the "Polish activities" of many parish societies. These activities depended mostly upon the singing of Polish hymns. The pastor paid attention to the fact that the Polish-American groups, like the Falcons or the PNA, sometimes booked special masses and sang Polish hymns during them.

St. Stanislau's is a small (about 500 households) parish of old people. Very many of them are working class women. The young people, in the opinion of the pastor, moved out either looking for jobs or because they married a non-Polish person from another area. The blacks moved in. Most of the blacks were not Catholics. The black Catholics went to another church. The pastor seemed to be sure of that, because of demographic reasons, his parish would be dissolved soon. However, because the above mentioned Polish-American societies book special masses here, and because Polish hymns are sung here, St. Stan's church is still considered by many members of the Polonia as the second most important center of the Polish religious culture in South Bend.

The fourth of the once Polish, Roman Catholic parishes of the city, is the parish of St. Wojciech's, now called by nearly everybody by its English name of St. Adalbert's. About its ample weekly bulletin, one can say exactly the same as was said about the bulletin of St. Hedwig's. There is no trace of the Polish history or the Polish-American institutional presence of the church and the parish. On the other hand, there are very many Polish names here, notes on Polish-American affairs (in addition to the notes on other affairs), advertisements of several Polish-American (and many other) businesses. Since 1972, the pastor was a diocesan priest of Polish heritage, speaking fluent Polish. Many years before he became a pastor, he was an assistant here and became well known to the Polonia. The retired resident priest was also of Polish heritage.

The pastor of St. Adalbert's (he was mentioned here several times on other occasions) was undoubtedly the most prominent leader of the Polonia in South Bend during the last few decades. His church, along with its Polish Heritage Center, was the most vivid Polish-American institution in the city. Moreover, the church itself distinguished itself from other church buildings, Polish-American or not, due to its beauty. Next to the church, there was, once a Polish, parish school. On its wall, there was a Polish language inscription inviting children. Inside the church, there were some paintings with the Polish letterpress and information on the weekdays and hours of the confession in Polish. One of the Sunday masses was read in Polish. The parish bulletin did not say anything about the Polish confession or the Polish mass.

I met the pastor (and some people who accompanied him) in the Fall of 1990 when I was invited to lunch at the rectory. The long conversation was held in Polish. Later, I spoke to the pastor often during various Polish-American affairs. In the last week of my stay in South Bend, because of poor health, the priest was moved by his authorities to a smaller parish close to South Bend. I will return to the celebrations connected with this transfer.

St. Adalbert's parish counted about one thousand families in the first half of 1991. It was the largest Polish-American parish in South Bend. Like in other parishes, its members were mostly retired. The pastor believed that their children lived in the suburbs. In his opinion, several percent of the population of the parish neighborhood were non-Catholic blacks, the rest being Roman Catholics of Polish or Mexican descent. Both of the latter groups belonged to his parish. Mexican Americans, unlike Polish Americans, were young and therefore, in about ten or twenty years, the parish would become Mexican.

St. Adalbert's Parish School, despite the language of the inscription on its wall, lost its Polish character decades ago. In 1991, it was still run by sisters of the formerly Polish Felician Order but there was no Polish program in the school. When I visited it, the second grade happened to be studying Polish culture, but the fourth grade studied Lithuanian and Latvian culture then. These topics belonged to the program of discussing world's cultures. In the school storage, there were, in the opinion of the principal, many Polish souvenirs, used from time to time by the St. Adalbert's Polish Heritage Center, located on the first floor of the school building.

Half of the students were still of Polish descent, as were a half of the school board.

The last of the Polish-American religious institutions of South Bend, being discussed in this work, is St. Mary's parish of the Polish National Catholic Church. The weekly bulletin was very modest in 1991. Most of the names to be found in it were Polish. This was the only parish bulletin in South Bend that singled out the Polishness. We could find it obviously in the name of the institution, but also in the information on the front page, saying that every week, the 10 a.m. Sunday mass was read in Polish.

Neither the first name nor the family name of the pastor suggested that he was of Polish descent. In spite of this, the priest was a Polish American, speaking fluently in Polish, without any Americanisms. He told me that he spent vacations in Poland every year. The priest used to teach Polish at the Forever Learning Institute years before. He also used to teach how to paint Easter eggs there. Nobody could question his competence in preparing traditional Polish dishes from the products available on the American grocery market. The pastor himself was an important Polish-American institution.

According to the pastor, his parish counted 480 families in 1991. (The pastor of the neighboring St. Adalbert's church, who was obviously biased in this matter but who knew the Polonia very well, believed that this number was highly overestimated.) These were the families registered and paying parish dues, but not necessarily attending mass every week. The pastor thought that only his many parishioners lived very far from their parish church and attended masses in churches of other denominations, located closer to their homes. He did not see any problem in this. In his opinion, about 75% of his parishioners were young people, mostly of Polish or Latin American descent. The turnout was smaller at the Polish language than at the English language masses.

The pastor of St. Mary's was very friendly to me. On the other hand, although I spoke with him several times, he was very reluctant to talk about his parishioners. An appointment with the chairman of the parish council proved to be impossible, in spite of my many efforts.

In the former chapter, discussing the history of the Polish religious institutions in South Bend, I presented four Roman Catholic parishes and one Polish National Catholic parish. Some people told me that there were small but organized Polish-American groups in several Protestant churches and in one Orthodox church. I have never succeeded in finding them. Therefore, in my opinion, only the five parishes presented above belong to the network of the Polish-American institutions in South Bend.

When we discussed the everyday life of the Polish-American community, it might be interesting to look at its "latent" functioning, outside of the frameworks of the Polish-American ethnic institutions. The Roman Catholic parish of Our Lady of Hungary proved to be such a place. Among the family names found in its weekly bulletin in 1991, one third were Hungarian names and another one third were Polish names. The pastor had a Polish first name and a family name (with Americanized spelling, though). Previously, he had been an assistant in one of the Polish-American parishes in South Bend. The above mentioned winner of the Achievement Forum Award for 1991, was the deacon at the Polish-Hungarian parish.

The first mission of Our Lady of Hungary was established in 1915. The parish was organized in 1916. The first church building was constructed in 1924 and the one currently in use in 1949. The parish was initially solely Hungarian. My conversation with the pastor, led partly in Polish, brought more information. The parish counted about 650 households, mostly of old, retired blue collars. There were nearly no professionals and no people with a college education. A little more than a half of the parish membership were people of Polish descent. This area was on the southern edge of the former Polish quarter of South Bend. The Polish parishioners of Our Lady of Hungary were not engaged in any ethnic activities. There were no such activities organized by the parish.

The pastor believed that the traditional inhabitants of the parish neighborhood were the Polish-Americans, the Hungarian-Americans and the Croatian-Americans who considered themselves Austrian-Americans. New inhabitants, moving in recently, were the blacks and the Mexican-Americans. In the parish school, there was not a single student of Polish or Hungarian descent. There were only black and Mexican-American kids there. The pastor thought that during the coming two decades, the parish would completely change its ethnic character.

It seems that the religious institutions formed the strongest network linking together each European ethnic group migrating to the United States. The operation of the Polish parishes in South Bend would support that opinion. The decline of traditional ethnic bond and the local ethnic communities leads to the weakening of the religious institutions of a particular group. This weakening, in turn, contributes to the further disintegration of the ethnic collectivities. In my opinion, South Bend provides a good example of this situation. It is obviously possible that the Polish-American community will continue to function there, even if there is no "iron law" saying that cultural groups must last forever. If this group continues to function, it will, most probably, be based on institutions other than the Roman Catholic parishes. They may not exist in ten or twenty years, even as the centers of ethnic concentration, to which the people would commute to a weekly mass or to participate in occasional, traditional religious ceremonies.

4. 3. Polish-American Businesses

In Chapter III, I wrote about the fast growth, glory and later decline of the Polish-American manufacturing, trade and services in South Bend. Now, I would like to present what has remained of the Polish-American business centers until today. In the Summer of 1990, the *South Bend Tribune* published, on the front page of its city section, a large article with color photographs, entitled "Looking for Polonia. On South Bend's West Side, it's tougher to find businesses that cater to Polish tastes" (Emmons 1990). The title of the article reflects the situation very well. The author paid attention to the fact that the late 1980s witnessed nearly a total decline of the many Polish-American stores. When I arrived in South Bend two weeks after the article had been published, I ran across nearly twenty big advertisements of Polish-American businesses that actually no longer existed.

In 1990 and 1991, members of the Polish-American community of South Bend owned some businesses, but nobody could have estimated how many. Most of these businesses were not concerned with Polish or Polish-American matters, they were dispersed throughout the city and even county, and their owners rarely lived on the Westside. There also existed businesses, like insurance agencies, real estate firms, or a small bank, that were located in the former Polish quarter, that worked for the population of that quarter, referred to its own Polish-American traditions, but that operated in fields and in ways which did not distinguish them from any other businesses located anywhere else in the US. I will not discuss them here. I will give only one example of this kind of business. Instead, I would like to present only those businesses that sold goods or services specific to the Polish or Polish-American population.

Two funeral homes are examples of flourishing, formerly Polish-American firms. One of them was the St. Joseph Funeral Home, established in 1901, and the second was the Kaniewski Funeral Home Inc., established in 1919. According to a letter from the manager of the second parlor (Kaniewski 1994), about 95% of deceased Polish Americans of South Bend were buried by one of these two firms. About 60% of the customers of the Kaniewski Funeral Home were Polish Americans. The Polish language was used very rarely during the ceremonies, only when the buried person belonged to the Polish Catholic parish. Its pastor celebrated everything in Polish. No other Polish symbols were used. The tombstone inscriptions were "nearly never" written in Polish, though.

The "oldest" Polish-American business, having functioned "forever," in South Bend was the Hurnon Pharmacy, located in the center of the Westside. The owner and manager was a member of several Polish-American societies. His firm first of all was selling regular American medicines, cosmetics and some basic grocery articles. Besides these, it was also possible to buy there some goods that were addressed nearly only to the needs of the Polonia and to the Poles temporarily living in the city. Good examples were the greeting cards for many occasions, printed in the US and in the American style, but in Polish. Before Christmas and Easter, the Huron Pharmacy would sell hundreds of these cards. The second kind of Polish-American items were the *Gwiazda Polarna* and the *Dziennik Zwiazkowy Zgoda*, two Polish language journals printed in America. About 10 were sold. Several years ago, the store was also selling Polish and Polish-American records. In 1990 and 1991, there was no longer demand for them.

Similar Polish-American goods had been traditionally sold by the store Gene's Dry Goods, located in the same neighborhood. It was established in 1950, by a Polish couple of Displaced Persons who came from Scotland. Since then, this had been a store with various dry goods and candies, patronized willingly by students from St. Adalbert's School "next door." Besides these goods, the store was also selling many kinds of Polish and Polish-American goods. In 1990, the store itself was sold to a non-Polish family. Respecting the tradition of the institution and paying attention to the needs of the patrons, the store continued to sell the goods representing Polishness. These goods were T-shirts with inscriptions in Polish or in English but referring to Poland and with Polish symbols, Polish flags and Polish cookbooks. The fact, that these goods were always being sold, was clearly announced on the display window. The "Polish corner" was not very large, though. It should be added that the former owners (who were very well known Polish-American activists) still ran in 1991, at their new home, a Polish trade and banking agency. People who wanted to send money or to order food parcels to Poland, could take advantage of this business.

"Regular" parcels to Poland, prepared and packed by the senders, could be shipped from South Bend by another company. Its local branch had an office and storage space in the Polish-American parish and was run by its pastor. This was a post-World War II enterprise but I did not succeed in finding out when it was established exactly.

It seems to me that these four firms were the only ones, having operated for decades, i.e. traditional, Polish-American businesses that were still linking the city to Poland and the Polishness. Only one of them had its roots in the pre-World War II period.

It was interesting for me that, despite the fast and clearly visible shrinking of the Polish-American community and the closing of many businesses, new Polish-American firms were emerging even in the late 1980s and early 1990s. In 1988, a Polish family, that had come to South Bend a few years after World War II, established a small grocery store. It was located very close to the former Polish quarter, but outside of any business center. It was not very difficult to find it, but to go there it was necessary to make a special trip. The Baker's Dozen Bake Shop had a branch, functioning on weekends on the Farmer's Market, close to the downtown. The profit was much larger here than in the main shop. In addition to the preserved food products, imported from Poland (though the wholesale companies in Chicago), the firm was selling homemade Polish-style pastry, dumplings and bread. The company was a family enterprise. The owner, a lady who had worked for many years as a cook in the Notre Dame University canteen, was the baker and pastry cook. Her husband, who had a permanent job in the technical workshops of the NDU, was responsible for the technical aspects of the operation. The daughters, when they were not in school, helped in the store. The firm advertised, manufactured and sold not only Polish but also Hungarian baking. It seems to me that on this small scale it was a very successful company. The owners were not actively engaged in any Polish-American activities, but were visible at larger meetings of the Polonia.

In the previous chapter, in the section devoted to voluntary associations, I wrote that one of them was sometimes organizing its monthly meetings in a restaurant owned by a Polish-American family. That firm did not advertise (and did not have) any ethnic character, though. It was not a "Polish" restaurant. Many Polish food places had operated in South Bend during the period of splendor of the Polish quarter. They disappeared completely, giving way to many hamburger chains and to the very popular Oriental restaurants. If these Polish places still existed in 1990 and 1991, they were very well hidden.

However, it was possible to eat out for a "Polish" breakfast or dinner in South Bend in the early 1990s. In the previous parts of this work, I mentioned that they were organized quite often by various Polish-American organizations, before their formal meetings, during some ceremonies, or as fund-raisers. They were addressed to select people and were not regular. The problem is, in my opinion, important, because "ethnic food" seems to be one of the significant and long-lasting cultural features. I will return to this issue later.

In January 1991, a modest equivalent of a "Polish restaurant" emerged. Two months earlier, on the Eastside of South Bend, at one of the main roads, a food place called The Skillet had been opened. It was run by a former bartender from the Westside, whose wife was of Polish descent. With the help of his mother-in-law, the owner began to organize once a month, on each first Saturday of the month, a "Polish buffet" (I learned about the place by accident). Despite this, according to the owner's wife, there were about 30 people each time eating "Polish food" (on Saturday afternoons, in each of the many Oriental restaurants of South Bend and Mishawaka, there were many more patrons). It was enough to make profits from this enterprise. Until the summer of 1991, the Polish buffets were organized regularly once a month. At the end of 1994 (I owe this information to David Stefancic), they were organized once a week. For $6.50 it was possible to eat soup or salad, baked sausage, baked chicken, mashed potatoes, sweet-and-sour cabbage, dumplings, beans and a roll. The owners were not engaged in any Polish-American activities, but were known to some members of the Polonia.

These six businesses formed the whole (known to me) economic infrastructure of what remained of the Polish-American community in South Bend.

4. 4. Summary

The Polish-American local community of South Bend still exists and functions in an organized way. Its institutional infrastructure is increasingly weaker, however. It is changing its character but, until now, has not died out.

The demographic changes will, most probably, result in the decay, by the end of the century, of nearly all Polish-American societies linked to the territory of the former Polish quarter. Except one, the former "Polish" parishes and parish societies will cease to exist. It seems to me that only the ethnic cultural societies and ethnic recreational societies will survive. They are on the one hand the small clubs and on the other hand the branches of big fraternal organizations.

There is no reason to believe that the Polish-American businesses, addressed to the Polish-American customers, will revive. On the other hand, several firms still in operation today will continue to have customers buying their Polish-American goods and services. In comparison to the times and places of the big immigration, and later, the big concentration of the unassimilated immigrants, who nearly totally depended on the ethnic institutions, it is now and it will be in the future a completely new situation. The Polonia differs less and less from the "native" population of the host societies and needs less and less its own institutions.

CHAPTER FIVE

FROM GENERATION TO GENERATION

5. 1. Introduction

In this chapter, I would like to present the findings of a small survey conducted in the late spring of 1991, amongst the members of the Polish-American community of South Bend. In the Introduction of this book, I discussed the financial sources of this survey, but I did not write about other technical aspects. Following Ewa Morawska (1977:4), author of a well known study of the local Polish-American community of Greater Boston, I have distributed questionnaires amongst the members of various Polish-American clubs and organizations. I also did this at a large Polish-American card party, in which not only members of the ethnic association participated. In total, I distributed about 400 questionnaires, with self-addressed and pre-paid envelopes. One hundred and fifty-fifty persons (or 40%) have returned completed questionnaires. Ewa Morawska, who collected her questionnaires through another method, received 354 of them, or twice as many (*op. cit.*:5). The small number of cases made it impossible to use advanced statistical techniques for the elaboration of the material. Even the percentages will be rounded up to five.

The above presented method of selecting respondents, seemed to be the only possible technical solution when I only wanted to reach Polish Americans and to collect empirical material in a relatively inexpensive way. This method has its significant disadvantages, though. I will not discuss here the general and particular methodological problems of the survey research, well known to sociologists for decades. I would only like to point out that the findings of my survey can be considered representative for only a part of the Polish-American community in South Bend. The questionnaire was distributed solely amongst the people who participated in the meetings of the ethnic societies (and this group is even smaller than the collectivity of the members of these associations). This means that the questionnaire was distributed only amongst the people, who were active in the organized retention of their own ethnic identity. The people who completed and returned the form were particularly active and interested. It should be added that they were relatively old.

On the other hand, as Nicos Mouzelis reminds us, not all social actors contribute to the same extent to the construction of the social realm (1993). The Polish-American local community of South Bend, like any other community of this kind, is first of all being retained and supported by social interactions of only some, particularly active people. Moreover, in this survey, I did not want to "paint a picture" of the "whole" community, but to present the way, in which some of its features last and how others transform themselves from generation to generation.

The questionnaire consisted of 35 questions, mostly with closed categories, but which gave the opportunity to provide additional information, and of six personal questions. The whole questionnaire was introduced by a preface, explaining the general idea of the survey and the suggested method of completion.

In the sample, there were 56 men and 92 women (not to count the people who did not reveal their gender). This proportion of 40% to 60% in favor of women, is also visible during Polish-American events and in the Polish-American associations in which gender is not a formal or real criterion of membership. The survey proved that gender was not an important factor, responsible for the differences in answers.

People who were below 40 years of age, formed a little more than 10% of the sample, while people between the ages of 41 and 65 years - 40%. Therefore, people over 65 years old constituted nearly a half of the sample. As I have already mentioned, the sample seems to be representative of the collectivity that has actively participated in the Polish-American public life, but in terms of age is not representative of the whole Polish ethnic community of the city. To find such a sample (in a non-expensive way) was not possible nor, in this case, necessary.

This age structure has important consequences for the possibilities of the understanding of the transmission of ethnic values from generation to generation. The parents of about a half of the sample had been born at the turn of the century. The children of most of the members of the sample are middle-aged people, or at least adults, today. Therefore, it is possible to reach quite far back into history with this survey, but it is not possible to say much about the younger generation. I will return to other features of the sample, in the third section of this chapter.

Because the scope of this survey is very limited, I will not compare my findings with other findings based on the survey research of the Polish-American local communities (see, e.g., Sanders and Morawska 1975, Morawska 1977, Sandberg 1977; in the latter case, it is not even a truly local community). They were conducted more than ten years before my survey and they refer additionally to findings obtained nearly twenty years ago. When preparing my survey and selecting (or rather limiting) the issues to be addressed, I took advantage of these important works, though. I also utilized another source, based upon the survey research conducted by Donald Pienkos in 1971 on a random sample of the Polish-Americans in Milwaukee (1977). Unfortunately, despite my many attempts, it proved to be impossible to follow the example of the Pienkos' analysis and to divide the sample into several coherent types.

5. 2. A Generation of Parents

I was interested in some of the "cultural features" of the parents of those people, who form the core of the Polish-American community of South Bend, parents, from whom those people most probably picked up their own cultural interests. Since the questionnaire had to be short, I could not ask about much.

A little more than one-third of the mothers and a little more than 40% of the fathers were born in Poland (all the rest – practically in the US). In about 45% of the respondents, at least one parent was born in Poland (similarly, in another 45% – both parents were born in the US). Among the people over 60 years old, the former percentages were much higher: nearly a half of the mothers and 55% of the fathers were born in Poland. The younger the respondents, the higher the probability, that their parents were born in America. The well known fact that the Polish-American community in South Bend has had its roots deep in the past, and that it is renewing itself to a smaller and smaller extent, is here well verified.

I asked only about the fathers' occupations, knowing from the literature and conversations that before World War II, not very many women in America had jobs outside their homes (the problem of occupations for the Polish women in South Bend was discussed earlier in this book). The fathers were nearly 60% blue collars, about 15% - the owners of small businesses, primarily the stores. Nearly 30% of the respondents mentioned (they were not asked about this) one of the well known local factories which has been presented in this book local factories: Studebaker, Singer, Oliver or Bendix, as the place where their fathers had worked. I often wrote here, that the decline of these factories brought significant consequences to all the inhabitants of the city, including the Polonia. The fathers born in Poland were more often factory workers than were the fathers born in America. What is interesting, is that the same was true about the ownership of small businesses. The fathers born in America worked in a large variety of occupations. There were more factory workers among those who spoke poor English than among those who spoke good English. Again, the same (to a smaller extent, though) was true about the fathers - businessmen. The running of a business meant, for members of the Polish-American community, isolation from the English-speaking world. In conclusion, the fathers who spoke good English and who were born in America had other jobs than factory workers and businessmen.

I will present the education of the parents now. Nearly half of the fathers and a little more than half of the mothers, had only grade-school education, and a little more than 15% of the fathers and 20% of the mothers were high-school graduates (however, every second respondent did not know anything about the education of their parents). This is an important topic, because the education of the parents seems to have influenced the education of the respondents. Nearly 60% of those whose fathers had graduated from high-school and nearly 75% of those whose mothers had graduated from the high-school, went to a college. The influence of the mothers was, therefore, much stronger.

The parents knew the Polish language very well, better than English. About 70% of both the mothers and the fathers spoke Polish fluently. Only about 5% of both the fathers and the mothers did not know the Polish language at all. In 65% of the respondents, both the father and the mother spoke Polish fluently. A little more than 50% of the fathers and (which does not correspond well with historical data presented in Chapter III) about 55% of the mothers, spoke English fluently.

The parents lived, in the vast majority of cases, on the Westside of South Bend and belonged to Polish parishes. About 70% of them belonged to one of the four Polish Roman Catholic parishes. Every second father and every second mother belonged to at least one Polish-American society. The respondents remembered primarily the membership of their parents in the all-American fraternal organizations like the Falcons or the Polish National Alliance. Some mothers belonged to the Polish-American, local parish societies, and some fathers to the local, but nonparish organizations.

A little more than 80% of the respondents remembered that their parents observed at home some Polish traditions. About 40% of the respondents stressed some particular Polish features of Christmas and Easter. Nearly 15% only listed Christmas and Easter, without giving any details. Nearly 10% listed these two occasions in addition to some other traditions. In total, about 70% of the respondents remembered mostly that the big Catholic feasts were organized in the Polish way at their family homes.

The next problems were connected with the ethnic identity of the parents. A little more than 10% of the respondents believed that their fathers considered themselves to be Poles, about 60% - to be Polish Americans and about 20% - to be Americans. As for the mothers, both the order and the frequency of categories of answers were similar. A half of the respondents had parents who, in concert, considered themselves to be Polish Americans. Among the fathers who belonged to any Polish-American organization, 70% or more than average, considered themselves to be Polish-Americans and not "simply" Americans.

5. 3. A Generation of Informants

I will return to the generation of the parents, but now I will turn to the respondents. Some initial information about them was already presented. The education of the respondents was a little better than the education of their parents. About 10% of the members of my sample said that they had not graduated from high-school. One-third of the sample were high-school graduates. The rest attained a higher level of education. Nearly 30% of the respondents began (but did not finish) college. A little more than 10% graduated from a college and another 10% finished graduate or professional school.

Nearly a half of the respondents lived on the South Bend's Westside. One-third of the sample lived in other parts of the city and the rest, i.e. about one-third of the sample, in the neighboring suburbs. As for the occupations (in a half of the cases before retirement), the most frequently occurring were: blue collars (a little more than 10%), office workers (about 10%), owners of small firms (nearly 10%), secretaries (nearly 10%), managers (nearly 10%). The rest pointed to various white collar occupations. What is visible, in the comparison with the generation of the parents, is that the percentage of blue collars decreased considerably and the percentage of owners decreased a little also. The second change is connected with the decline of the Polish-American business centers, and both of the changes are linked to the all-American transformations of the social and occupational structure. Only 5% of the sample were housewives which means, that the occupational activity of the women was very high.

If we tried to translate the declared occupation and education into class categories, valid for the analysis of the whole American society, as presented for instance in the book by Dennis Gilbert and Joseph A. Kahl (1987:326-336), the situation would look as follows. To the "upper middle class," comprising of the owners of the firms, the managers and the professionals, we could assign nearly 25% of my sample. According to the above mentioned authors, about 14% of the American households belonged to this class (*op. cit.*:332). To the "middle class," comprising of the office workers and the lower and middle level managerial positions, we could ascribe a little more than 50% of the sample, and to the "working class" - a little more than 10% (Gilbert and Kahl also assign 60% of the American households to these two classes). The remaining 10% of the sample are the "others" or people who did not answer this question (in the above quoted book, other categories are "a capitalist class," "a working-poor class" and "an underclass').

In the above presented attempt at a synthetic class ascription of the collectivity of the respondents of my survey, I did not take income into account. Gilbert and Kahl also do not treat it as a basic criterion. Besides, more than 15% of the respondents did not answer the question on family income in 1990.

The largest part, i.e. a little more than 30% of the sample, said that this income was lower than $20,000. This would mean that such a low income was attained by those who, based solely on other criteria (before retirement?) could be assigned to the "middle class." An income higher than $45,000 was given by a little more than 20% of the sample (including 15% who gave an income of more than $50,000). This would mean that to the Polish-American "upper middle class," I assigned also those whose income was lower than $45,000 (Gilbert and Kahl include here only those whose income exceeded $50,000 in 1983).

In the survey, discussed in this chapter, I was interested mostly in the ethnic tradition and its transmission. Therefore, we should return to the Polish and Polish-American considerations. More than 60% of the respondents had learned the Polish language in parish schools (as I wrote earlier, for the last several decades this has not been possible in South Bend). Nearly one-third studied this language during the whole of grade school but also later. This must mean that they attended the Polish-American high school.

Today, the level of the command of the Polish language varies. Nearly one-third of the respondents thought that they spoke Polish fluently, more than 15% believed that they understood this language but did not speak it well, nearly 20% could communicate in broken Polish, and the last 20% knew only several Polish expressions. If we consider solely the first three categories, it turns out that nearly 70% of the respondents could somehow communicate in Polish. When they were young, the whole cultural system, in which the Polish language had its "natural" place, still existed.

The above mentioned 70% proportion is more than the proportion of those who had studied Polish at school and nearly as high as the percentage of the parents who had spoken Polish fluently. The influence of the family must have been strong. I would also like to pay attention to the fact that in the generation of the parents, 70% spoke Polish fluently, and in the generation of the respondents, only about one-third spoke Polish fluently. This proportion increases to 45% among those who had studied Polish language at school (for about 40 years now) and the inadequacy of this generation of Polish-speaking parents (that will occur soon) will result in the lack of any channels for the transmission of the ethnic language.

The retention of the command of a language, learned in school or at home, is connected with the opportunities to use it regularly. As I wrote earlier, until the 1960s, there had been many chances to communicate in Polish on the South Bend's Westside. Later, these chances decreased. Despite this fact, more than 55% of the respondents (i.e. nearly all of those, who could somehow communicate in Polish), believed that they still had an opportunity to talk and read in Polish, and only 25% did not see this kind of opportunity (if we deduct the persons who did not answer this question, the percentages among the remaining people will be higher). The respondents revealed the nature of these opportunities. The most often presented instances were the conversations with close family and with friends. What was interesting for me, was that prayers and singing in church were mentioned rarely. With regards to the family, the respondents had no longer a chance to talk with their parents, who were mostly deceased. There was no chance to talk in Polish with the children (I will return to them later). The only real chance existed in the case of spouses.

A little more than 10% of the sample were people, who had never been married, but 50% of the sample were people married to Polish-Americans. Among those spouses of Polish descent, one-third did not speak Polish at all, but 40% could communicate in this language. About 20% of the spouses spoke Polish fluently.

About 45% of the respondents belonged to none of the Polish-American parishes, discussed in the previous chapters. (Seventy percent of their parents had belonged to these parishes). As I wrote earlier, about a half of the sample lived on the Westside. They were not exactly the same people. Among the inhabitants of the former Polish quarter, nearly 70% belonged to the Polish parishes. It means that close to one-third of Polish Americans from the Westside belonged to non Polish-American parishes outside of it. Nearly 75% of the Polish-American members of the Polish parishes lived on the Westside. It means that every fourth member of these parishes commuted from other areas - form the city or from the suburbs.

Those respondents, who did not belong to a Polish-American parish and who answered the next question, explained their membership, giving in one-third of the cases the argument that they had belonged there "forever," in 20% that their parents had belonged to this parish (which seems to be a variation of the former category) and in 20% that the parish was located in their closest neighborhood. Those who did not belong to any Polish-American parish and who answered the next question, explained their membership in a non-Polish parish, giving in nearly 60% of the cases the argument that they lived very far away. The remaining gave many varying reasons, like (in the order of frequency of answers): a willingness to obey the church's rules demanding membership in the parish of one's neighborhood (this means that they lived in other parts of the city; it is a variation of the above mentioned argumentation), or the habits of the spouse having belonged to another parish before the wedding.

In the questionnaire, I asked if it was still accurate to describe the Westside parishes as the Polish parishes. A little more than 55% of the respondents thought that this was still an accurate name, nearly every fourth respondent thought that it ceased to be accurate and a little more than 15% had no opinion on the matter. The explanations are interesting. Among those who answered "positively" and wanted to explain their opinion, 30% exposed the Polish tradition of the parishes, and about 20% stressed that the Polish language was somehow retained there. (As I wrote in the former chapters, this language was then used rarely in churches and mostly only in the hymns.) The remaining respondents gave many multifarious explanations of their opinions, the most frequent being the reference to the "Polish character" of the quarter in which the parishes were located, and their "Polish name." Those, who thought that the name "Polish" ceased to be adequate and who wanted to explain their opinion, in nearly 30% exposed the fact that the Polish language was no longer used in these churches, and in 25% they stressed the fact that the population of this city quarter had a new, non-Polish ethnic character. As we can see, the same arguments were being used to explain opposite opinions. Other explanations could not be categorized into any clear types.

In the questionnaire, I asked if the respondents patronized the Polish-American businesses in South Bend. Sixty percent of the sample answered that they did and 15% that they did not patronize them. The remaining persons did not know if the businesses they patronized were or were not Polish-American. Only those who were aware of the fact that they patronized Polish-American businesses, named some firms. About 55% of those who responded to this question named one or two concrete firms, and nearly 15% named three to five concrete firms. Some of these firms did not actually operate then, some kept the old name but the new management was not Polish-American. It seems to me that the respondents remembered some firms from the former times rather than referring to which really existed in 1991. The remaining people said only that they patronized the Polish-American meat markets, bakeries, etc. In the former chapters, I discussed the topic of the actually existing Polish-American business in South Bend at that time.

The respondents were asked if they belonged to any Polish-American organizations. Nearly 80% belonged to some clubs, which is not surprising since the questionnaires were distributed at the meetings of various societies. Among those who belonged to Polish-American associations and who answered the next question, the largest proportion, i.e. 40%, named only nonparish, local, nonfraternal organizations, 30% named only the local branches of the all-American fraternal organizations, and a little more than 15% named both kinds of societies. The parents of my respondents belonged to the same types of associations.

The respondents joined the Polish-American societies due to various reasons. The most frequently quoted reasons were (respectively 30% and 25%) the family tradition of the membership and the "simple fact" that they were Polish-American. Insurance was mentioned very rarely.

Membership in Polish-American organizations does not divide my sample into any interesting categories. However, these societies had particularly many (about 90%) members among those who were between the ages of 56 and 65 years. Now, I would like to present the membership of my respondents in nonethnic societies. It is a very well known fact that a large number of Americans from the social classes of the respondents, belong to various voluntary associations. The concrete class membership determines to which society one would belong (see, e.g.., Gilbert and Kahl 1987:137-139). Nearly all respondents answered the question concerning membership. About 65% of them belonged to nonethnic organizations. Class membership was not an important factor here. Those who belonged to the nonethnic associations and who answered the next question, declared mostly a membership in such formerly male (now mixed) middle-class clubs, like the Lions or the Elks (nearly one-third), to the church organizations and to the organizations somehow connected with their jobs (about 20% in each case). Social and recreational reasons were the most frequently cited motivations for membership in the nonethnic organizations. Professional reasons were mentioned by about 20% of the members. Among the other motivations, the most often declared was a willingness to help other people, to work for them. In fact, clubs like the Lions and the Elks, as well as the church societies, can be treated as charitable organizations. As I mentioned earlier, the motivation to join the Polish-American organizations was different.

A few more men (about 65%) than women (nearly 60%) belonged to the nonethnic clubs. The middle-aged people, between the ages of 31 and 50 years, belonged to them in more than 80% of the cases. Similarly, nearly 80% of the college and/or graduate and professional schools' graduates belonged to those societies. The collectivity of members of the nonethnic organizations is a little younger than the collectivity of members of the Polish-American organizations, but basically equally well educated.

Being somewhat of the periphery of ethnic matters, I will discuss the issue of local social activity. In the questionnaire, I asked about active involvement in the local problems of the city. Only about one-third of the respondents said that they were involved.

In the former chapters, I paid attention to the fact that from the late 1950s, i.e. from the times of the decline of the formerly blooming Polish quarter, the Polish Americans lost their interest in the Westside. The sample consisted mostly of old people, eyewitnesses to this decline. Amongst the younger members of the sample (those being under 50 years old, who began their adult life after the decline of the Polish quarter), the proportion of people interested in local matters was twice as high as it was in the whole sample. This proportion is slightly higher among men than among women. It also is relatively high among men than among women. It is higher among those whom we could assign the Polish-American "upper middle-class." It is 10% higher (45 to 35) among those who lived in the suburbs than among those who lived on the Westside. This fact confirms the hypothesis on the diminishing interest of the Polonia in its old quarter and even in the city as such.

The people who were interested in the local matters of South Bend, were asked to present clearly the examples of their involvement. Only a few people answered this question. The examples could be divided into two categories: political activity and charitable work.

I will now move to the issues directly linked to ethnic problems. In the questionnaire, I asked the respondents to give the ethnicity of their three closest friends. When we deduct the respondents who did not answer this question and those who said that they did not know the ethnicity of their close friends (which seems to exclude the possibility that they were of Polish descent), the situation looks as follows. The people who were named by the respondents as their friends in first place, were 70%, named in second place - 50%, and in third place - 45% of Polish descent. Using a different method of calculation, it turns out that 25% of the respondents named among their three closest friends only Polish Americans, nearly 25% - two Polish Americans, and 40% - one Polish American. Only a little more than 10% of the respondents had no single closest friend of Polish descent. It seems that the members of my sample were not completely isolated within the ethnic ghetto, but a large part of their social life was spent among friends of the same ethnicity.

Membership in the Polish-American parishes and clubs, residence on the Westside, marrying within the ethnic community, making friends mostly with other Polish Americans, could together be interpreted as a continued closing of the group. The ethnic closing, in turn, could be connected with a psychological defensive reaction, like a conviction that the Polish Americans were discriminated against. If we deduct the persons who did not answer the question, it turns out that less than 10% of the sample believed that such discrimination was a definite fact, close to 35% thought that it happened "to a certain extent." As we can see, less than a half of the respondents thought that the Polish Americans were discriminated against. Nearly the same proportion believed that no discrimination existed. The remaining 15% had no opinion. It seems to me that the latter case means that these people have never personally experienced any discrimination but were not sure if this happened to other people. The persons over 50 years of age, those who were born in Poland and those who spoke poor English believed particularly often that they were discriminated against. However, it was only a conviction that the discrimination happened "to a certain extent."

The persons who believed in discrimination were asked to give some comments. Nearly 30% of the sample gave them. I think that this is the proportion of people for whom discrimination had a real meaning. They stressed discrimination in work and in politics. No details or examples were provided (we should remember that the role of the Polish Americans in the South Bend and the St. Joseph County politics was very strong). Some respondents mentioned "Polish jokes." To conclude, we could say, that most Polish Americans did not see any real discrimination towards their own ethnic group. This could mean that the group would rather continue the assimilation processes than keep strong ethnic barriers. This majority was not vast, though. Some sense of discrimination still existed. This could mean that the ethnic boundaries and the sense of ethnic identity within the larger American context would be retained.

In the questionnaire, I asked about visits to Poland. It turned out that nearly 80% of the respondents had never been there. A little more than 10% were once in Poland, and 10% were there twice or more. Those people who visited Poland, mostly stressed their good recollections. I also asked about interests in Poland and in Polish matters. We should remember that from 1980, Poland was very often covered by the American media and that the South Bend Polonia used to organize various actions for help for Poland. It turned out that a little more than 10% of the sample were not interested in Poland at all, and nearly 15% were interested in her as much as in the situation of other European countries. One-third of the sample were interested in Poland a little more than in other European countries and nearly 40% were very much interested.

As I wrote earlier (and I will return to this in the last chapter), except for the big occasions, the Polish-American community of South Bend (and the situation in this city was not unusual) was interested in its own problems much more than in the problems of its country of origin. On the other hand, for nearly 75% of my respondents, Poland was a somehow distinguished country. Very few people (a little more than 5%) were regularly discussing what happened in Poland, and nearly two-thirds did this from time to time. The respondents were selected from among the people who were particularly active in Polish-American life. It turns out that they were also active, in the sense presented above, in Polish matters.

I will return to the Polish-American issues now. About 70% of the respondents (compared to 80% among the parents) declared that they observed Polish traditions at home. The decline was therefore very small. What was interesting for me, was that many Polish-American leaders told me earlier that, due to various reasons, Polish traditions were no longer observed at their homes. The observed traditions were similar to those of the generation of parents. If we deduct the people who did not observe any and those who did not answer the question, the situation runs as follows. Nearly 40% of the respondents stressed mostly the Polish aspects of Christmas and Easter. In total, about 70% mentioned these two occasions, sometimes describing them broadly, sometimes adding other traditions. The exposed Polish aspects were Christmas Eve supper, the breaking of the Christmas wafer, a special kind of food, the adding, at the Christmas supper, of one place setting for an unexpected visitor, the singing of Polish carols, the visiting of family and friends, the observing of the Holy Week before Easter, and the blessing of the "Easter basket."

Any different concrete Polish traditions from those mentioned above, were presented by only a little less than 10% of the respondents. They wrote about the Santa Claus gift-giving, the name day celebrations, the Polish way of organizing weddings and funerals, the celebrating of Polish patriotic occasions, like the Third May Day, listening to Polish music, the singing of Polish songs and of "One Hundred Years to You" (a Polish equivalent of "Happy Birthday to You") at birthdays.

One of the very long lasting elements of the ethnic traditions is food (see, e.g., Morawska 1977:71). Also in my survey, it turned out that 80% of the respondents liked the Polish food very much. Nearly all the rest liked it too, but not very much. Nobody disliked it. The problem to be considered, is what was Polish food for the South Bend Polonia? Nearly all of the respondents had an opinion on this matter. Only 10% did not give any examples. Nearly one-third of the sample named one to three concrete dishes, and nearly 60% - four dishes or more. I will deduct those few people who did not give any examples. Among the rest, about 20% did not use in their answers any Polish expressions, but they gave very precise descriptions in

English. As we can see, more than 80% knew the proper Polish names for the dishes. It seems that these names had a very important symbolic meaning, pointing to the membership in a cultural group (on the other hand, many people of non-Polish descent who live in South Bend, know some Polish expressions and the names of some Polish dishes also; the Polish Kiellbasa is sold in every grocery). Nearly 20% of the respondents gave one Polish expression (the correctness of the spelling was not of interest to me), one-third used tow or three Polish expressions, and 30% gave even four or more names in Polish. It means that familiarity with the Polish cuisine and the proper names was large. What was very interesting to me, was that the respondents did not name chicken as a Polish dish, even though it was very often served at the "Polish dinners" at the Polish-American clubs. On the other hand, "czernina" was named very often, but it was never served in the clubs. Grzegorz Babinski (in a private conversation on this text) suggested that there was a difference between the institutionalized and the home menu. This difference is situational, resulting from the occasions at which the particular dishes were served. unlike chicken, czernina used to be an everyday and favorite food of the relatively poor Polonia. It was never served at grand, festive occasions. Therefore, czernina is not served at the club dinners even now.

At the end of this section, I will discuss the self-identification of the respondents. Only five people did not answer this question. Among the rest, nearly 5% considered themselves to be Poles (among the parents - nearly 10%), close to 70% - to be Polish Americans (among the parents - 20%). The number of people declaring that they were Poles, decreased. The difference between the generation of the parents and the generation of the respondents has been divided between the remaining two categories that increased. Among those who considered themselves to be Polish Americans, and not "simply" Americans, there were mostly people speaking good Polish, people whose spouse was of Polish descent, people who observed the Polish traditions, who liked Polish food very much, who belonged to the Polish parishes and organizations (but also to the nonethnic associations), who were at least once in Poland, who were interested in Polish matters, who talked about Poland with their family and friends, who patronized the Polish-American business in South Bend, who had friends of Polish descent, who were over 60 years old, who had education no higher than high-school, whose family income was smaller than $30,000, and who worked as blue collars.

5. 4. A Generation of Children

As I wrote earlier, the children of the respondents were mostly middle-aged people. About 80% of the respondents had children (about 15% - one child, about 65% more than one). Later, I will not consider those who had no children and those who did not answer the next questions. In the first of them, I asked if the children spoke Polish. About 15% selected one of the five possibilities that did not exclude a positive answer: a) the child (children) was too young, b) some children speak better, some worse, c) they speak fluently, d) they understand but hardly speak, e) they can communicate in broken Polish.

One-third of the respondents said that their children knew only some Polish expressions, and a little more than half, that the children did not speak Polish at all. In comparison with their children, the respondents spoke Polish very well. As we know, nearly 70% of them could at least communicate in this language. The parents of the respondents spoke fluently in Polish in 70% of cases. Undoubtedly, even amongst the families of people actively participating in the Polish-American life in South Bend, the Polish language was dying. There was no longer a cultural system in which there would be a place for this language. One should not be surprised that there were no Polish radio programs (even if the, much numerically smaller, Hungarian-American community had its own radio show) and that no single periodical in Polish was being published.

One decade ago, Aleksander Posern-Zielinski summed up the linguistic transformations in the American Polonia in the following way: "...in the third and further generations ... the ethnic language ceases to be necessary as a means of communication within the frameworks of the ethnic community, and also within the family life. Along with the decline of the communication function, the significance of the purely symbolic functions of the ethnic language increases. These functions are expressed in the treatment of the language as an external, consciously manifested feature of ethnicity. It becomes a "sacred" language, used in the ethnic ceremonies that refer to the tradition of the group and to the culture of the country of origin" (1982:44). The observations, presented in this book several times, confirm the above quoted opinion.

More than in terms of the language, the situation amongst the children of the respondents is diversified in terms of the level of interest in Polish matters. About 30% of the respondents who had children and who answered this question, said that the children were interested in the situation in Poland as much as in the situation in any other European country. Therefore, for these children, Poland is not singled out within her European environment. A little more than 25% of the respondents said that their children were not interested in Poland at all. Nearly 20% said that their children were interested in Poland a little more than in the situation in other countries. Close to 15% said that some of their children were interested more and some less in Poland, and about 10% said that the children were too young to have this kind of interest. The latter answer means, in my opinion, that the children had not revealed any interests in Poland, but the parents believed that a chance still existed. Several times, while talking with the Polish-American leaders, I was told that they became interested in Polish matters when they were adults. The difference between the generation of these interlocutors (who belonged to the generation of the respondents) and the generation of their children depends, among other things, on the fact that the parents of the interlocutors were not Polish activists and the people who filled in the questionnaire were. If I interpret properly the latter type of answer, very few Polish-American activists hoped that their children would ever be interested in Poland.

Only four persons (among 122) answered that their children were very much interested in their country of origin. If we add to these the answers suggesting any kind of particular interest in Poland by any of the children of the respondents, it will turn out that only a little more than one-third of the respondents reported such a possibility. Thus, any kind of interest in Poland tended to take place among those respondents who considered themselves to be Polish Americans rather than "simply" Americans and who were themselves very much interested in Poland.

The respondents were asked to report the ethnic self-identification of their children. Only in one case (among 123 answers) the children were said to have been too young to have an opinion. In two cases, the children considered themselves to be Poles (among the respondents - four cases, among the parents - 19 fathers and 16 mothers), in 35% of cases - Polish Americans (among the respondents - nearly 70%, among their parents - 60%). Nearly 55% considered themselves to be Americans (among the respondents - close to 30%, among their parents - 20%). In the remaining answers, different children had different ethnic identities. Therefore, from generation to generation, the proportion of "Poles" has been declining (if we deduct the immigration - to zero) and the proportion of "Americans" has been increasing. The proportion of "Polish-Americans" was initially increasing (at the cost of the "Poles"), to decrease substantially later (in favor of "Americans," and not "Poles").

The last issue analyzed in my survey was connected with the education of the children. Actually, I asked what were the aspirations of the respondents concerning their children and to what extent these aspirations were met. Only less than 10% of the sample were of the opinion that it was enough that the children had high-school education. More than a half of the respondents wished that their children would graduate from college and nearly 30% of them wanted the children to finish a graduate or professional school. These aspirations mean that the respondents wanted their children to achieve a higher level of education than their own level, and obviously than the level of their parents.

It seems that these aspirations were fulfilled by the children. Nearly 15% of the respondents believed that the children had not yet achieved the desired level of education but it was still possible that they eventually would. More than 50% thought that their children had already achieved that level. Moreover, about 20% said that some of their children had and some had not reached the desired level. Only 10% of the respondents were disappointed with the educational achievements of their children.

5. 5. Summary

My survey had, out of necessity, a very limited character. It could not contain many questions. In practice, it reached only 155 active members of the South Bend Polonia. It was not representative for the whole Polish-American community of this city. Nevertheless,

I think that it was, to a certain extend, representative for those, who formed the core of the local Polonia, who in their everyday life and on the occasions of festivity, constructed the social world of that ethnic community. In the sample, I did not find any clear and coherent types of attitudes.

In the previous chapters, I mentioned that during the post-World War II period, the erosion of the important Polish-American institutions had taken place. Some of these eroded institutions used to be very important for the retention of the Polish identity. Parish schools, libraries, the newspaper and the radio are the best examples. A similar ethnic role was also played, "on the side," by various Polish-American businesses. Their number dropped dramatically as well. Parally, we have to consider the all-American processes of the growth of mass culture, form the movie theaters and television to the chains of cheap, nearly totally homogenized fast food restaurants. The influence of this process on the homogenization of American society is very strong. There is less and less social space for the ethnic cultures, particularly where the mass immigration had practically stopped.

The survey has shown that the Polish-American community participates in many all-American social processes. It is better and better educated and has higher and higher educational aspirations. The proportion of the blue collars within it, is continuously decreasing and the proportion of the white collars is increasing. This community has been slowly moving out of the old ethnic ghetto to the suburbs. To a decreasing degree, it belongs to the ethnic parishes, preferring now the parishes located close to the new places of residence.

The Polish-American local community, while undoubtedly retaining many aspects of ethnicity is, at the same time, losing many important "objective" ethnic features. The group traditions are increasingly rarely observed. The ethnic language (except some expressions, significant as ethnic symbols) is disappearing. The interest in the country of origin is diminishing. An increasing number of group members consider themselves to the "simply" Americans, without any ethnic adjectives.

CHAPTER SIX

THE "POLISH-AMERICAN YEAR" IN SOUTH BEND

In this last chapter of the book on the local Polish-American community in South Bend, I will discuss the questions of festivity (these problems were analyzed to some extent in the section on culture, in Chapter III). It is not easy to contrast this festivity to the everyday life. The festivity, in the form of ceremonies, rites and celebrations, is mostly predictable, prepared, routinized, conventional, formalized. On the other hand, the celebrations and other events, which gather "the whole Polonia" of South Bend, or at least its significant part, quite clearly divide the social time and give a rhythm to the collective activity.

I will first of all discuss here the "calendrical rites," but also one "rite of passage," in a broad sense of the term "rite" (see, Van Gennep 1960). These ceremonies divide not only the time but also the space, confirming the distinction between the cultural center of the group and its cultural peripheries. During the ceremonies, the social "implicit" knowledge transforms into the "explicit" knowledge, the "respected" knowledge transforms itself into the "accepted" knowledge (see, the first chapter of this book). This new type of knowledge soon becomes routinized, but the next ceremony will again make the consciousness come to the surface. The group sense of identity is strengthened.

In this chapter, I will present one concrete year, which most probably only slightly differs from other years. I mean here the period from the fall of 1990 to the summer of 1991. The fact that I begin the presentation of the year from the fall, is connected with the fact, that it is then when I began my observation of the Polonia. It has also other, much less accidental reasons. The fall is the time of the return form the summer vacations to work. It is the time when the school and academic years begin. It is the time when many associations begin a new stage of their activities. This is apparent in the club bulletins, particularly in their issues with the programs of the yearly activity. Each year, the fall is the time of the "new beginnings."

I will discuss in this chapter only some of those events which have divided the flow of the social time of the South Bend's Polonia, by giving a rhythm to its collective activity. I will ignore the closed affairs, to which only the members of the given clubs have been invited, and the affairs that are too expensive for most of the Polish Americans. I will also ignore the routine "Polish breakfasts" and "Polish dinners," which have had a slightly symbolic sheath but which belong to the everyday operations rather than to the festivity of the Polish-American associations. Instead, I will present the events, having been announced in many Polish-American bulletins, which means that "the whole Polonia" was invited to them and which were not too expensive for the average Polish Americans. Some of these events have had an entertainment character while others have been solemn patriotic celebrations. In most of them, nearly only older people have participated, but in some of them most participants have been young. My main source of information was participant observation and media coverage, and the notes in the clubs' bulletins served as an additional source.

As I wrote in the previous chapters, the efforts of Mr. Ignatius Werwinski from South Bend had led to the declaration of 11 October as the all-American Pulaski Day. In 1990, the US House of Representatives and the US Senate declared October as the Polish-American Heritage Month. The South Bend chapter of the Polish-American Congress (PAC) organized in St. Adalbert's Heritage Center, on 14 October, a special ceremony in which about 300 people participated. I will present here the course of events of the celebrations, based on participant observation and on the printed and distributed program.

The guests were welcomed by the chairwoman of the local chapter of the PAC. St. Adalbert's pastor gave the invocation. Then, the participants ate the "Polish dinner." After the dinner, one of the leaders of the Congress addressed the gathered people and suggested a collection of the change they had in their pockets. The money would be sent to Poland to help the families of the shipyard workers who had been killed by the Polish police forces in 1970. About $74 were collected. Afterwards, the celebration began.

The chairwoman of the PAC's chapter gave a short speech. She spoke about the meetings of the activists of the Congress with the Polish Ambassador and with some members of the US government. These meetings took place in Washington DC a few days earlier. The first of them was unusual in the sense that it was the first official (and, according to the speaker, warm) contact of Congress with the Polish embassy since World War II. It became possible because of the political changes occurring in Poland from 1989.

In the next part of the program, official addresses were presented. One of the two of South Bend's councilmen at large, a person of Irish and Polish descent, took the floor. On behalf of the (absent during the ceremony) city mayor, the city council and himself, he read a solemn proclamation on the occasion of the Polish Month. The next addresses were read by the (just then retiring) auxiliary bishop of Fort Wayne-South Bend Roman Catholic Diocese, and later, on behalf of the authorities of the county, by the sheriff. The sheriff was of Hungarian descent which, according to some Polish-American leaders, made him, "as a Slavic person" eligible for membership in the "Polish Falcons." The sheriff's speech stressed the Polish-Hungarian kinship and the cooperation of various ethnic communities in the city. Thus, in the formal introductory part of the ceremony, the link between South Bend's Polonia on the one hand, and the country of origin, the city, the county, the Roman Catholic church and the remaining ethnic groups of the city on the other hand, was strongly exposed.

A short break in the celebrations was filled by entertainment. A twelve-person dance group of the Sixth District of the Falcons, to which the South Bend nests belong, danced, in Polish folk (the Teshen region) outfits, the polonaise. The participants of the evening were informed that the group had been practicing for only half a year. In the six pairs, there were only four men. All the dancers were at least middle-aged.

After the entertainment break, one of the activists of the Congress, read the list of the sponsors of the ceremony (and particularly of the raffle) and of the people who helped with the organization of the affair. The next speaker was a guest, a rector of one of the seminaries in Poland. His short talk concerned the contribution of the Poles towards American achievements and contained a criticism of the consumptive civilization. It was read in Polish, but the participants received the English translation. Then, the American and the Polish anthems were sung by the participants. The Polish language appeared, thus, for the second and last time. The official part was closed with a short blessing and prayer.

At the end of the ceremony, there was a raffle and then dancing. The music was played by a local Polish-American band. There were four old musicians in it. The dancers were also quite old.

Amongst the participants of the evening, there were the representatives of all the Polish-American associations and clubs. A group of Poles, either staying in South Bend with their relatives or working at the local colleges and universities, were also present.

The next affair that exposed (this time mostly for the non-Polish public) the Polish identity of a part of the inhabitants of Michiana, was a series of exhibitions and an art fair, called collectively, Christmas Around the World. It was a traditional charitable affair, raising funds for the intensive care ward of a hospital in Mishawaka. It took place on the premises of the hospital in mid-November, i.e. just before the holiday season. In the exhibitions of the artifacts, connected, according to the organizers, with Christmas, and in the seminars and meetings that formed the whole affair, various organizations representing the local groups of Hungarian, Scandinavian, Polish, Ukrainian, Mexican, Lithuanian, Russian, Japanese, German and Scottish descent (the order of precedence is the same as in the brochure with the program) participated.

The affair had been announced in the bulletins of various Polish-American associations. The Polish aspect of the fair was organized by the Chopin Fine Arts Club. The artifacts exhibited by the Chopin Club came from the collection of one of its members. The Polish stand was very attractive, but neither the participation of the Polish-American public nor the Polish-American aspects of the accompanying affairs were significant. The brochure with the program and the posters did not reflect the demographic, cultural and political role of the Polonia in the region.

December brought the new internal, Polish-American celebrations. Many societies organized Christmas Eve Suppers almost exclusively for their members. I participated in two of them (at the Polonaise Club and at the Polish-American Congress), but will not deal with them here, because they had the above mentioned closed character. Instead, I will present a Christmas Eve Supper of the Chopin Club. It took place at St. Adalbert's Polish Heritage Center, on a Sunday afternoon, about a week before the real Christmas period. Invitations had been sent to all the Polish-American societies, but the number of seats was said to be limited. All those willing to attend, about 60, who had sent their checks of $10, were actually accepted. Most of the participants were the elderly.

The brochure with the program was printed in English but some expressions, like "Christmas Eve Supper," "the wafer," and "Merry Christmas," were in Polish. The names of dishes to be served, were also in Polish (the spelling was correct), although with English translations. These few Polish expressions and words were the important symbols of the ethnic identity and, undoubtedly, familiarity with them was a proof of the bond with the Polish cultural group. There were also two drawings (the names of the artists were not given) in the brochure. One represented Christmas Eve Supper in a Polish village cottage and the second represented a young woman in a Polish (Cracow region) folk outfit, carrying a bowl with food. Thus, the club that propagated the Polish "high culture," did not find in this culture any visual Christmas symbols, meaningful for the South Bend's Polonia and was forced to refer to folk symbolism.

The supper lasted for about two hours and consisted of three phases. The first contained a short prayer, lead by the chaplain of the club, the exchange of Christmas wishes and the breaking of the Christmas wafer. The second was the proper Christmas supper. The feast participants, who were seated at several round, large tables, came with their plates to another, long table, and took from the steel containers what they wished to eat. There was a large selection of dishes: beet root soup with dumplings, filled dumplings, fish filets, herring, potatoes, carrots with dill, sauerkraut with mushrooms, noodles with poppyseed, fruit compote, poppyseed coffee cake, and another kind of cake. Separately, wine and coffee were served. The third part of the supper consisted of the singing of Polish and American carols. Initially, only the invited pianist was singing, but soon all the participants followed suit.

Polish Christmas is not only the solemn supper (or its equivalent) but also Midnight Mass. In all the Polish-American churches on the Westside of South Bend, this mass was given. Both Polish and American carols were sung. "Everybody knew" that many particularly Polish aspects of the mass would be present at St. Adalbert's. Therefore, I participated in the mass at this church.

At this exceptionally frosty and snowy night for South Bend, about 500 people, mostly old, came to the church. From 11 pm to midnight, there was the musical part of the event. Mostly Polish, but also American carols and hymns were sung. At midnight, through the main door, the priests entered the church, led by four women and four men, all of them elderly, who wore Polish (from the Cracow region) folk outfits. When the priests took their places at the main altar, the faithful sung one carol in Polish, and the "regular," American Roman-Catholic mass began. The sermon was delivered by the pastor in English. No new Polish elements appeared until the end of the mass, although this parish is considered to be the main center of the Polish culture in the city. After the mass, in the church's lobby, the pastor was saying goodbye to the departing faithful, most of whom he knew personally. Often, he did this in Polish.

The Polish-American holiday season lasts in South Bend until mid-January. Then, a special event, called "The Oplatek" (the wafer), is usually held. The Oplatek meetings have been organized, since 1956, by the American Relief Committee for Free Poland. The profits are donated to charitable causes in Poland (see, E.E. 1986: 2). The ceremony held on a Sunday afternoon, in mid-January of 1991, was already the 35th one. It was organized in St. Adalbert's Polish Heritage Center. About 300 people participated in it. The affair consisted of the "Polish dinner" (fried chicken and fried sausage) and several speeches. The course of events was similar to the course of the Polish Heritage Day.

The meeting of 1991 had its routine elements, for example the active participation of the Roman Catholic clergy (however, no bishop was present this time; the former auxiliary bishop was already retired and the new one was not yet nominated), the prayers, or the entertainment part. There were also some new aspects. One of them was the fact that they key speaker was not an American, but a scholar from Poland. The speech, in English but later summarized in Polish, concerned anthropological and ethnographic aspects of the tradition of the breaking of the wafer in Poland.

More importantly, and to a much larger extent deviating from the routine, was the presence of the Polish Consul, who came from Chicago. This was the first case in the post-World War II history of the South Bend's Polonia, when a representative of the Polish government was invited. He was welcomed by the Polonia and by the city mayor, who gave him the symbolic keys to the city. The Consul made a short speech in Polish and in English. He promised that Polish diplomats would visit South Bend more often. His declaration was very well received. Since then, the Polish diplomats have actually come to the city several times.

The Oplatek, organized by a group of charitable and political character, fulfilled all the expectations of the participants and had various cultural meanings. It was held in connection with the Polish Christmas tradition and its religious and cultural aspects were strongly stressed. It contributed to the raising of funds for the needy people in Poland. Therefore, it expressed the link between the South Bend's Polonia and the current situation of the country of origin. It had a clear political aspect, too. While the former Oplateks had been organized in South Bend "against" the Communist authorities of Poland, the 1990 event was said not to have had any clear political sense. In 1991, the American Relief Committee for Free Poland, and with it the whole local Polonia, recognized the fact that the political liberation of the old country from the Communists had already taken place. Therefore, the Consul was invited and very warmly received. The participation of the representatives of all the Polish-American societies and of many generations (even if old people were overrepresented) stressed the unity of the ethnic community of the city.

The next important event in the "Polish-American Year" in South Bend took place in early February. It had an "ethnographic" character, connected with Easter, which was to come soon. I did not participate in it but I know of it, mostly from the TV coverage. The TV and press coverage means that the event was important for the city. Moreover, it popularized some Polish-American customs, exposing the position of the group in the city. This event was called The Paczki (doughnuts).

In Poland, about a week before Ash Wednesday, "Fat" Thursday is celebrated. According to the customs, doughnuts and other fat sweets are eaten. On the following Tuesday, it is the end of the carnival, and the "herring parties" are held. In preparation for Lent, the participants eat herrings. Both the doughnuts (in the American but also in the Polish shape) and the herrings are easily available in South Bend, but the two customs (Fat Thursday and the herring parties) merged into one tradition in this city. On the Tuesday before Ash Wednesday, the Polish Americans organize a big party called The Paczki.

In 1991, it was held in the club house of the MR Falcons. According to the local TV station, hundreds of people, mostly very young, participated in the party. What is interesting, is that The

Paczki was not announced in Polish-American bulletins other than that of the MR Falcons. However, it was an important civic affair, known to "everybody." It was known, for instance, by the city mayor, several councilmen, and at least one local TV station. One the 10 pm local news, a short live report stressed the "traditionally Polish" character of The Paczki and the contribution of the Polish Americans to the city life. The affair had, first of all, an entertainment character. However, the presence of the popular city politicians must have had another reason than their willingness to dance in the company of fellow citizens of Polish descent. The local Democratic primaries were to be held very soon, and a few months later, the local elections.

The following significant day in the "Polish-American Year" in South Bend was again indirectly connected with Easter. It was Easter Monday. In 1991, it happened to fall on the 1st of April, All Fools' Day (in Poland, this day also is "celebrated," under the Latin name of Prima Aprilis). In South Bend, Easter Monday is celebrated as Dyngus Day, a great event, once of a Polish-American, always of a political character. In 1991, because of the above mentioned local primaries, Dyngus Day was very important, even if only locally. I wrote several times about Dyngus Day in this book.

On the day before Dyngus Day, on Easter Sunday, the *South Bend Tribune* published two interesting articles. One of them, an unsigned editorial entitled "Happy Dyngus Day!", quoted a poem about the Polish sausage and recalled the Polish origins of the South Bend custom. It stressed, that nowadays Dyngus Day was celebrated in the city not only in the Polish-American clubs, but also in the Irish bars, Italian restaurants and Belgian clubs. In all of them, the kielbasa, or the Polish sausage, was offered. "Just as everybody is Irish on St. Patrick's Day, everybody is Polish and welcome on Dyngus Day," wrote the editors of the paper (p. A10).

The second article (Wensits 1991a: D1, D2) described the customs connected with Easter Monday in Poland and their transformations in America. He called the city of South Bend the American capital of Dyngus Day. The dancing of the polka (considered a Polish dance) and the eating of hard-boiled eggs and Polish sausage, were treated by the author as the most important (besides the politics) aspects of the day. He warned his readers not to drink too much alcohol. He pointed out that the Republican Party also began to celebrate the day, until now traditionally Democratic. With regret, he stressed that due to the fact, that in 1991 there would be no state or national elections, neither the Governor nor the Lieutenant Governor were expected. The paper also published, on the same pages, an article on the political affair competing with Dyngus Day, Solidarity Day, organized since 1971 by the black leaders. All the key actors of Dyngus Day were also expected in the black clubs. All participants were to eat fried chicken there, instead of sausage and hard-boiled eggs. It is interesting because for the South Bend's Polonia, chicken is a "traditional Polish dish."

According to the experts in the local tradition, Dyngus Day was to begin in the West Side Democratic and Civic Club at noon (it was a regular workday). When I arrived there punctually, I found the club overcrowded. The ticked cost $2 which covered one hotdog. Beer, fried sausage and hard-boiled eggs, were all sold in each corner of the main club hall. Moreover, beer was available in the bar on the second floor.

In the main hall on the first floor, the chairman of the county committee of the Democratic Party was loudly presenting to the audience the local politicians, both those holding offices and candidates. The crowd knew them very well. There were many known politicians in the club: the city mayor, the Democratic US Representative of the South Bend area, the city councilmen. Besides those, amongst the others, the chancellors of the local colleges and universities were present. The vast majority of the audience consisted of whites but blacks were here too. They seemed to feel very well there. In a much worse situation were some Republican politicians, regardless of color. None of them were invited to the stand and introduced. The author of the article, published the next day in the *South Bend Tribune*, also stressed this fact (Wensits 1991: b: B1, B2). On the second floor, the social atmosphere was much calmer. Most of the people here were the men, who drank beer at the bar or at the tables, and discussed things in low tones. The genetically Polish character of the affair was accentuated by the interior decoration of the club, by the Polish eagle on the tickets, and by the badges with the Polish and American flags, worn by many participants.

As I mentioned in the previous chapters, Dyngus Day begins in the West Side Democratic and Civic Club, and later moves to other clubs and bars. The politicians usually go by bus. The same things, according to the newspaper, happened in 1991. Other people were driving, even after more than one beer, from place to place. I did not go from bar to bar, but in the afternoon I went to the MR Falcons. I mentioned earlier that this nest of the Falcon society had a particularly political character. I spent more than one hour in the club. No politician came up until the moment when I left, but many were expected. The crowd did not wait inactively. The people were drinking beer and eating eggs and sausage. A band was playing and nearly twenty pairs were dancing. I did not see any Polish or Polish-American decorations or symbols. Dyngus Day was later extensively covered by the newspaper and the TV stations.

The center of the parallel black feast was the Metropolitan Civic and Democratic Club. On behalf of the black community of the city, the organizer of the event rewarded some citizens for their civic activities. One of the prizes was given to a deceased Polish-American leader and a well known local politician. On his behalf, it was presented to his daughter, also a local politician and a Polish-American leader (*op. cit.*: B2).

Dyngus Day is a very important event in the life of South Bend. It is an important affair in the life of the local Polish-American community too, not only because of the feast has a Polish origin, but also because it highlights the political significance of the group and stresses the contribution of the Polish-American culture to the culture of the whole region.

In April 1991, another Polish-American affair was held. Actually, it was a feast of only one society, the Chopin Fine Arts Club. However, it took place in St. Adalbert's Polish Heritage Center, and because of its purposes, it gathered the members of many Polish-American associations. This event was not publicized in the local media. The internal, Polish-American significance of this 51st anniversary of the club was due to the fact, that the scholarships were awarded to the competitions' winners. To win the scholarships and the prizes was difficult. It was necessary to prove familiarity with the Polish culture. The awards were given, as if, on behalf of the whole Polish-American community of the city. There were some "regular" elements of the program of the celebrations, like prayers, the "Polish dinner" and the music program. About 100 people participated in the event. It was held entirely in English.

The next interesting event of the "Polish-American Year" were the celebrations of the anniversary of the Polish Third of May Constitution of 1791. The ceremonies were organized by the local chapter of the Polish-American Congress and took place on the campus of Indiana University at South Bend. Thus, they were addressed to the academic audience as much as to the Polonia. They had two elements. First, there was a showing of documentary films about Poland. Although the show was announced in the parish bulletins, few Polish Americans were present. Secondly, in the main hall of the university library, a special exhibition, devoted to the history of Poland, was organized. The Polish-American turnout was also not great at this affair.

In June, a Polish-American ceremony of an entirely nonroutine character took place. The pastor of St. Adalbert's Church, who was mentioned in this book several times, was retiring to another parish. This "rite of passage" was a very significant event for the Polish-American group, but also for the whole city. The pastor was undoubtedly one of the most respected leaders of the local community. In connection with his retirement, a special program was broadcast by a local TV station (I did not watch it, though), and an few days before the farewell ceremony, a long article with a large picture of Father Gene Kazmierczak was published on the front page of the local newspaper (Borlik 1991).

The pastor, born in New Jersey, a graduate of the Polish-American seminary in Orchard Lake, Michigan, appeared for the first time at St. Adalbert's parish in 1951, immediately after ordination. Until 1956, he served here as the assistant. During the next years, he worked in other parishes of Indiana. In 1972, he returned to his first post, to St. Adalbert's (see, e.g., Danch 1985, Borlik 1991).

On a mid-June Sunday, 1991, Father Gene gave a mass on the occasion of the fortieth anniversary of his ordination. Many representatives of the Roman Catholic clergy assisted him. Just after the mass, in the St. Adalbert's Polish Heritage Center, there was a solemn farewell ceremony. Immediately after the celebrations, the pastor was to leave for a short vacation and rest, to become later a pastor and school teacher in a very small parish, about thirty minutes drive from South Bend.

Father Gene stood in the middle of the large hall of the Heritage Center, and hundreds of Polish Americans lined up to approach him and to personally say goodbye. The pastor talked with everybody for a short while, received gifts, shook hands, said goodbye to everybody individually and invited everybody to his new post. Thus, the line was moving very slowly. When I came to the parish, just after the end of the mass, the line was nearly twenty yards long only on the backyard, not to mention the interior of the building. New people were constantly arriving, from the church or form the parish car park. After the saying of goodbye to the pastor, most of the women sat at the tables and the men went to the Center's bar, for a beer or whisky. When all the interested people said goodbye to Father Gene, the next part of the ceremony began.

There was, first, a dinner funded by the parish, and then the collective, and not individual, farewell ceremony. The priest was in the "liminal state" of the "rite of passage." He had already ceased to be the acting and formal leader of the hundreds of representatives of the Polonia gathered there, but he did not yet take over his new post in Walkerton, Indiana. His successor was in a similar state. He did not take over St. Adalbert's parish yet, he did not yet live in the rectory, but he had already left his former post. During the ceremony under discussion, he was introducing himself to his new parishioners and to the general audience and was becoming acquainted with his new obligations.

The city mayor and the leaders of the Polonia, gave moving speeches. Then, the retiring pastor took the floor. He described his career, spoke about South Bend, the Polonia, Poland, and later he introduced his successor. He called the attention of the audience to the fact that his successor was in the eight grade of St. Adalbert's schoool in South Bend, when Father Gene appeared in the parish as assistant and teacher. As he had earlier in the interview for the *South Bend Tribune*, a dream of each pastor came true here — his student became his successor (see, Borlik 1991: A1). Moreover, the retiring pastor was a graduate of the seminary in Orchard Lake, and his successor, before coming to South Bend to take up the new position, was a professor in that seminary.

The next speech was given by the successor. He also spoke about the exchange of generations and about the return to the roots. I should add, that this priest, Rev. Leonard F. Chrobot, is an established scholar in the field of sociology of ethnicity.

The "Polish-American Year" in South Bend was to be closed with a Polish ethnic exhibition at the Ethnic Festival, organized in South Bend every year as part of the all-city, Fourth of July celebrations. Traditionally, the Centralia was in charge of the Polish-American stand. The preparations for the Festival were covered by the local TV stations, the *South Bend Tribune* and by other local papers (see, e.g., Kryder 1991). What is interesting, is that the authors of the TV programs and of the press articles did not pay much attention to the Polish-American participation in the affair.

The Festival lasted from the evening of the last Friday of June to the Sunday evening. At that time, I was no longer in the city. From the reports of my friends I know that the Polish-American stand was attractive, but it did not reflect the role of the Polonia in the cultural and social life of South Bend, at all. Actually, it was hardly visible. The press coverage of the Ethnic Festival of the next year (see, McArthur 1992) hardly even recognized the presence of the Polish-American group.

It seems to me that the Polish-American group has lost this kind of cultural distinction that could be presented in an attractive way at an ethnographically oriented festival. From this point of view, the non-European ethnic groups are much more attractive. The Polish-American group continues to exist, retains its ethnic identity, but "only" as an aspect of a relatively homogeneous cultural system.

After the Fourth of July Ethnic Festival, the vacations begin. After the summer, the next Polish-American year will start, with its everyday life and its festivity. This festivity will be mostly routinized, in the form of the foreseeable calendrical ceremonies, sometimes in the form of the rites of passage, but it will sometimes be of an unusual, unforeseeable character. Both in the Polish-American everyday life and festivity, fewer and fewer people will participate, and the above described, processes will continue to deepen.

LITERATURE AND SOURCES

Babinski, Grzegorz. 1977. *Lokalna Spolecznosc Polonijna W. Stanach Zjednoczonych Ameryki W. Procesie Przemian* (Wroclaw: Ossolineum).

_____. 1979. "Analiza przestrzenna w badaniach przemian zbiorowosci ethnicznych: teoria, metody, zastosowania," *Przeglad Polonijny*, V, 3, pp. 5-19.

_____. 1982. "Grupa mniejszosciowa a grupa ethniczna. Przeciwko ogolnej teorii grup mniejszosciowych," *Przeglad Polonijny*, VIII, 3, pp. 21-33.

_____. 1986. *Wiez ethniczna a procesy asymilacji. Przemiany organizacji ethnicznych. Zagadnienia teoretyczne I metodologiczne* (Warszawa-Krakow: PWN).

Barth, Fredrik. 1969. "Introduction," in Fredrik Barth (ed.), *Ethnic Groups and Boundaries. The Social Organization of Culture Difference.* (Boston: Little, Brown & Company), pp. 9-38.

Bell, Daniel. 1975. "Ethnicity and Social Change," in Nathan Glazer and Daniel P. Moynihan (eds.), *Ethnicity: Theory and Experience,* (Cambridge: Harvard University Press), pp. 141-174.

Bentkowski, Chester. 1990. *A Historical Story. St. Mary's Polish National Catholic Church in South Bend, Indiana, 1915-1990* (South Bend).

Berger, Peter L. and Thomas Luckmann. 1967. *The Social Construction of Reality. A Treatise in the Sociology of Knowledge* (Garden City, NY: Doubleday).

Bokszanski. Zbigniew. 1989. *Tozsamosc, Interakcja, Grupa. Tozsamosc Jednostki W Perspektywie Teorii Socjologicznej* (Lodz: Wydawnictwo Uniwersytetu Lodzkiego).

Borlik, Kathy. 1991. "Father Gene's Staying Close in New Assignment," *The South Bend Tribune*, June 19, pp. A1-A11.

Borlik, Kathy. 1994a. "Young Couple from Poland Paints House for Museum," *The South Bend Tribune,* July 21, p. C1.

_____. 1994b. "Home Museum Evokes '30s Nostalgia," *The South Bend Tribune,* August 8, p. C1.

Borowik, Irena. 1990. *Charyzma A Codziennosc. Studium Wplywu Religii Na Zycie Codzienne* (Krakow: Miniatura).

Braudel, Fernand. 1992. *Civilization and Capitalism, 15th-18th Century.* Vol. 1: *The Structure of Everyday Life* (Berkeley: University of California Press).

Breza, Kathleen and Martha Pieszak. 1975. *The Polish-American Community in South Bend* (South Bend: Indiana University of South Bend, Ethnic Heritage Studies Program).

Brown, Edythe J. 1920. *The Story of South Bend* (South Bend: South Bend Vocational School Press).

Brozek, Andrzej. 1985. *Polish Americans, 1854-1939* (Warsaw: Interpress).

Buchowski, Michal and Wojciech Burszta. 1992. *O Zalozeniach Interpretacji Antropologicznej* (Warszawa: PWN).

Buczek, Daniel S. 1980. "The Polish-American Parish as an Americanizing Factor," in Charles A. Ward, Philip Shashko and Donald E. Pienkos (eds.), *Studies in Ethnicity: The East European Experience in America* (Boulder, Colorado: East European Monographs), pp. 153-165.

Calvin, Richmond, Karen Rasmussen and Donna M. Gollnick, eds. 1975. *Ethnic Resource Guide* (South Bend: Indiana University at South Bend, Ethnic Heritage Program).

Census of Population 1980. 1983. Volume I: *Characteristics of Population.*, Chapter C: General Social and Economic Characteristics, Part 16, Indiana. (US Department of Commerce, Bureau of the Census).

Census of Population and Housing 1980. 1983. Census Tracts. South Bend, Indiana. Standard Metropolitan Statistical Area. PHC80-2-336. (US Department of Commerce, Bureau of the Census).

Chalasinski, Jozef. 1934. "Wsrod robotnikow polskich w Ameryce. Kolonia robotnicza polska w Poludniowem Chicago," *Wiedza I Zycie*, 8/9, pp. 653-68.

_____. 1935. "Parafia i szkola parafialna wsrod emigracji polskiej w Ameryce. Studium dzielnicy polskiej w Pol. Chicago," *Przeglad Socjologiczny*, III:3-4, pp. 633-711.

_____. 1936. "Zwiazek z parafia a swiadomosc narodowa emigranta," *Przeglad Socjologiczny*, IV:3-4, pp. 547-49.

_____. 1962. *Kultura Amerykanska. Formowanie Sie Kultury Narodowej W Stanach Zjednoczonych Ameryki* (Warszawa: LSW).

Cohen, Gary B. 1984. "Ethnic Persistence and Change: Concepts and Models for Historical Research," *Social Science Quarterly*, 65:4, pp. 1029-1042.

Czolem Ojczyznie, Szponem Wrogowi. Polish Falcons of America Nest No. 4. 1894-1969. Diamond Anniversary. 1969. (South Bend).

Czyzewski, Franciszek K. 1966. "Pamietny dla Narodu i Polonii w South Bend Rok Millenijny," *St. Joseph County Observance.*

Czyzewski, Marek. 1990. "Recepcja socjologii interpretatywnej w Polsce. Uwagi krytyczne," in Anna Giza-Poleszczuk and Edmund Mokrzycki (eds.), *Teoria I Praktyka Socjologii Empirycznej* (Warszawa: IFiS PAN), pp. 97-103.

Dahrendorf, Ralf. 1972. *Class and Class Conflict in Industrial Society* (London: RKP).

Danch, Elmer J. 1983. "St. Adalbert's Polish Community Celebrates 75 Years," *The Harmonizer,* September 29, p. 3.

Davies, Elmer J. 1982. *God's Playground. A History of Poland.* Volume I: *The Origins to 1795;* Volume II: *1795 to the Present* (New York: Columbia University Press).

Deka, Kathy. 1990. "Parallel Growth of St. Hedwig Church and the Polish Community in South Bend, Indiana. 1840 to 1913," *Maszynopis* (South Bend: IUSB).

Diamond Jubilee of the Polish Falcons of America. Z.B. Falcons Nest No. 80. 1972. (South Bend).

Duda-Dziewierz, Krystyna. 1938. *Wies Malopolska a Emigracja Amerykanska. Studium Wsi Babica Powiatu Rzeszowskiego* (Warszawa-Poznan: PIS).

Emmons, Becky. 1990. "Looking for Polonia: On South Bend's West Side, It's Getting Tougher To Find Businesses That Cater To Polish Tastes," *The South Bend Tribune*, 5 August, pp. G1, G7.

E. S. 1986. "'Oplatek' w South Bend, Indiana," *Dziennik Zwiazkowy Zgoda* (Chicago), 11 February, p. 2.

Fiftieth Anniversary. Saint Joseph Young Men's Society 1910-1960. 1960. (South Bend).

Fifty Years at Saint Adalbert's Parish, South Bend, Indiana 1910-1960. 1960. (South Bend).

Frysztacki, Krzysztof. 1968. *Polonia W Duzym Miescie Amerykanskim. Studium Przemian Podspolecznosci Polonijnej W Buffalo* (Wroclaw: Ossolineum).

Frysztacki, Krzysztof and Malgorzata Lesniak-Worobiak (eds.). 1990. *Szkice Bibliograficzne Z Zakresu Socjologii Miasta W Polsce 1980-1989* (Krakow: IS UJ).

Gans, Herbert J. 1979. "Symbolic Ethnicity: the Future of Ethnic Groups and Cultures in America," *Ethnic and Racial Studies,* 2:1, pp. 1-20.

Gilbert, Dennis and Joseph A. Kahl. 1987. *The American Class Structure: A New Synthesis* (Chicago: The Dorsey Press).

Giza-Poleszczuk, Anna and Edmund Mokrzycki (eds.) 1990. *Teoria I Praktyka Socjologii Empirycznej* (Warszawa: IFiS PAN).

Glazer, Nathan and Daniel P. Moynihan. 1975. "Introduction," in Nathan Glazer and Daniel P. Moynihan (eds.), *Ethnicity: Theory and Experience* (Cambridge: Harvard University Press), pp. 1-26.

Glazer, Nathan and Daniel P. Moynihan (eds.) 1975. *Ethnicity: Theory and Experience* (Cambridge: Harvard University Press).

Golden Anniversary Group 305. 1920-1970. Polish Women's Alliance of America. Zwiazek Polek W Ameryce. 1970. (South Bend).

Golden Anniversary of the Central Polish-American Organization. 1970. (South Bend).

Grathoff, Richard. 1989. "Codziennosc i swiat przezywany jako przedmiot fenomenologicznej teorii spolecznej," in Zdzislaw Krasnodebski (ed.), *Fenomenologia I Socjologia. Zbior Tekstow* (Warszawa: PWN), pp. 426-57.

Haller Post No. 125 Polish Army Veterans Association. Silver Jubilee Banquet. 1957. (South Bend).

Hillery, George A. 1955. "Definitions of Community. Areas of Agreement," *Rural Sociology* , 20:2, pp. 111-123.

Horowitz, Donald. 1975. "Ethnic Identity," in Nathan Glazer and Daniel P. Moynihan (eds.), *Ethnicity: Theory and Practice*, pp. 111-140.

Hosinski, Martha and Donald Stabrowski. 1990. *Fifty Years of Polish Culture: The History of the Chopin Fine Arts Club 1940-1990* (South Bend).

Indiana Poles in the Bicentennial Year of the United States. 1976. (Munster, Indiana: The Bicentennial Committee, Polish American Congress, Indiana Division).

Indiana. The Wander Book, 1988. 1988. (Indianapolis: Hoosier Celebration '88, Inc.).

Isajiw, Wsevolod W. 1974. "Definitions of Ethnicity," *Ethnicity*, 1:2, pp. 111-124.

Janowitz, Morris. 1961. *The Community Press in an Urban Setting: The Social Elements of Urbanism* (Chicago: University of Chicago Press).

Jubilee Book Commemorating Fiftieth Anniversary of the Dedication of the First Church 1899-1949. Saint Casimir Parish, South Bend, Indiana. 1949. (South Bend).

Kmita, Jerzy. 1982. *O Kulturzy Symbolicznej* (Warszawa: Comuk).

Kodeks Prawa Kanonicznego. Przeklad Polski Zatwierdzony Przez Konferencje Episkopatu. 1984. (Warszawa: Pallottinum).

Krasnodebski, Zdzislaw. 1989. "O zwiazkach fenomenologii i socjologii. Wprowadzenie," in Zdzislaw Krasnodebski (ed.), *Fenomenologia I Socjologia. Zbior Tekstow* (Warszawa: PWN), pp. 7-51.

Krasnodebski, Zdzislaw (ed.). 1989. *Fenomenologia I Socjologia. Zbior Tekstow* (Warszawa: PWN).

Kryder, Tom. 1991. "Ethnic Fun, Ethnic Food, Ethnic Festival," *Penny Saver* (South Bend), June 24, p.1.

Ksiega Pamiatkowa Obchodu Srebrnego Jubileuszu Towarzystkwa Gimnastycznego Sokolow Polskich Imienia Z. Balickiego No. 1 Gniazda Nr 80 ZSP 1897-1922. 1922. (South Bend).

Ksiega Pamiatkowa Obchodu Piecdziesiatej Rocznicy Gniazda Sokolow Polskich Imienia Zyg. Balickiego, Nr 1 Gniazda Nr 80, S.P.W.A 1947. (South Bend).

Kubiak, Hieronim. 1975. *Rodowod Narodu Amerykanskiego* (Krakow: Wydawnictwo Literackie).

_____. 1970. *Polski Narodowy Kosciol Katolicki W Stanach Zjednoczonych Ameryki W Latach 1897-1965. Jego Spoleczne Uwarunkowania I Spoleczne Funkcje* (Wroclaw: Ossolineum).

_____. 1980a. "Asymilacja etniczna w plaszczyznie struktury spolecznej," in Hieronim Kubiak and Andrezej K. Paluch (eds.), *Zalozenia Teorii Asymilacji* (Wroclaw: Ossolineum), pp. 53-66.

_____. 1980b. "Wspolczesne tendecje rozwojowe Polskiego Narodowego Kosciola Katolickiego w USA," *Przeglad Polonijny* VI:4, pp. 5-22.

Kwasniewski, Kryzysztof. 1986. "Tozsamosc spoleczna i kulturowa," *Studia Socjologiczne*, 3, pp. 5-15.

Les, Barbara. 1980. "Review of the Book by Stanislau A. Blejwas, *A Polish Community in Transition: The Origins and Evolution of Holy Cross Parish, New Britain, Connecticut*'," *Przeglad Polonijny,* VI:2, pp. 144-146.

Les, Barbara. 1981. *Kosciol W Procesie Asymilacji Polonii Amerykanskiej. Przemiany Funkcji Polonijnych Instytucji I Organizacji Religijnych W Srodowisku Polonii Chicagowskiej* (Wroclaw: Ossolineum).

Liberson, Stanley and Mary C. Waters. 1986. "Ethnic Groups in Flux: The Changing Ethnic Responses of American Whites." *Working Papers Series.* (Berkeley: University of California Survey Research Center).

Lipiec, Jozef. 1972. *Podstawy Ontologii Spoleczenstwa* (Warszawa: PWN).

Lecki, Kryzysztof, Kazimiera Wodz, Jacek Wodz and Piotr Wroblewski. 1992. *Swiat Spoleczny Slazakow. Rekonstrukcja Tresci Swiadomosci Potocznej* (Katowice: Wydawnictwo US1).

Map of Greater South Bend, Mishawaka and Osceola, Indiana. n.d. (Cincinnati: Spectrum Map Publishing).

McArthur, Stanley. 1992. "A Bigger Blast. This Year's Ethnic Festival Offers More Booths, A European-style Circus and Three Days of Holiday Fun," *The South Bend Tribune,* Thursday, July 2, pp. D1, D7.

McAvoy, The Reverend Thomas T., CSC. 1953. *The History of the Catholic Church in the South Bend Area* (South Bend: University of Notre Dame).

McKay James and Frank Lewins. 1978. "Ethnicity and the Ethnic Group: A Conceptual Analysis and Reformulation," *Ethnic and Racial Studies,* 1:4, pp. 412-27.

Melchior, Malgorzata. 1990. *Spoleczna Tozsamosc Jednostki (W Swietle Wywiadow Z Polakami Pochodzenia Zydowskiego Urodzonymi W Latach 1944-1955* (Warszawa: ISNS UW).

Migala, Jozef. 1984. "Historia polskich programow radiowych w Stanach Zjednoczonych," *Przeglad Polonijny*, X:1, pp. 21-37.

Mocha, Frank (ed.) 1978. *Poles in America. Bicentennial Essays* (Stevens Point, Wisconsin: Worzalla Publishing Company).

Mokrzycki, Edmund (ed.) 1984. *Kryzys I Schizma. Antyscjentystyczne Tendencje W Socjologii Wspolczesnej* (Warszawa: PIW).

Morawska, Ewa. 1977. *The Maintenance of Ethnicity: Case Study of the Polish-American Community in Greater Boston* (San Francisco: R&E Research Associates, Inc.).

_____. 1978. "Rola spolecznosci lokalnej w podtrzymywaniu etnicznych postaw i zachowan - proba interpretacji," *Prezeglad Polonijny*, IV:3, pp. 35-49.

_____. 1985. *For Bread with Butter. The Life-worlds of East-Central Europeans in Johnstown, Pennsylvania, 1890-1940* (Cambridge: Cambridge University Press).

_____. 1988. "Polonijne spolecznosci lokalne i ich przemiany. Szkic wstepny," in Hieronim Kubiak, Eugeneiusz Kusielewicz and Tadeusz Gromada (eds.), *Polonia Amerykanska. Przeszklosc I Wspolczesnosc* (Wroclaw: Ossolineum), pp. 371-398.

Mouzelis, Nicos. 1993. "The Poverty of Sociological Theory," *Sociology*, 27:4, pp. 675-695.

Mucha, Janusz. 1984. "American Indian Success in the Urban Setting," *Urban Anthropology*, 13:4, pp. 329-354.

_____. 1993. "An Outsider's View of American Culture," in Philip R. DeVita and James D. Armstrong (eds.), *Distant Mirrors. America as a Foreign Culture* (Belmont, Cal.: Wadsworth), pp. 21-28.

Novak, Michael. 1971. *The Rise of the Unmeltable Ethnics* (New York: Macmilan).

One Hundred Anniversary. 1887-1987. Polish National Alliance 83. 1987. (South Bend).

Orzechowski, Emil. 1989. *Teatr Polonijny W Stanach Zjednoczonych* (Wroclaw: Ossolineum).

Paleczny, Tadeusz. 1988. "Subiektywistyczne koncepcje ethnicznosci ich rola w socjologii," *Studia Socjologiczne,* 4 (111), pp. 177-194.

_____. 1989. *Ewolucja Ideologii I Prezemiany Tozsamosci Narodowej Polonii W Stanach Zjednoczonych W Latach 1870-1970* (Warszawa-Krakow: PWN).

Pamietnik Z Okazji Pietnasto-Letniej Rocznicy Zalozenia Placowki No. 125 Stow. Weteranow Armji Polskiej. 1947. (South Bend).

Pamietnik Srebrnego Jubileuszu Parafii Sw. Kazimierza W South Bend, Indiana. 1929. (South Bend).

Pawluczuk, Wlodzimierz. 1990. *Wiara A Zycie Codzienne* (Krakow: Miniatura).

Pienkos, Donald S. 1977. "Ethnic Orientations Among Polish Americans," *International Migration Review,* 11:3, pp. 350-362.

_____. 1984. *PNA. A Centennial History of the Polish National Alliance of the United States of North America* (Boulder: East European Monographs).

_____. 1987. *One Hundred Years Young. A History of the Polish Falcons of America, 1887-1987* (Boulder: East European Monographs).

Piotrowski, Andrzej. 1985. "Pojecie tozsamosci w tradycji inter-akcjonizmu symbolicznego," *Kultura I Spoleczenstwo,* XXIX:3, pp. 53-73.

Polish Women's Democratic Club. Golden Anniversary Banquet. 1982. (South Bend).

Posern-Zielinski, Aleksander. 1982. *Tradycja A Ethnicznosc. Przemiany Kultury Polonii Amerykanskieh* (Wroclaw: Ossolineum).

Praszalowicz. Dorota. 1986. *Amerykanska Ethniczna Szkola Para-fialna. Studium Porownawcze Trzech Wybranych Instytucji* (Wroclaw: Ossolineum).

Renkiewicz, Frank Anthony. 1967. *The Polish Settlement of St. Joseph County, Indiana 1955-1935* (Ann Arbor, Michigan: University Microfilms, Inc.).

_____. 1980. "An Economy of Self-Help. Fraternal Capitalism and the Evolution of Polish America," in Charles A. Ward, Philip Shashko and Donald E. Pienkos (eds.), *Studies in Ethnicity: The East European Experience in America,* (Boulder: East European Monographs), pp. 71-91.

Roche, Maurice. 1989. "Fenomenologiczy zwrot w socjologii" in Zdzislaw Krasnodebski (ed.), *Fenomenologia I Socjologia. Zbior Tekstow,* pp. 458-74.

Rocznica Zlotego Jubileuszu Gniazda Sokolic Im. Z. Balickiego NR. 185 Sokolstwa Polskiego W Ameryce. 1960. (South Bend).

Rokicki, Jaroslaw. 1986. "Obrzed religijny jako symbol grupy etnicznej. Konflikt o pasterke w diecezji Scranton, PA, w latach 1935-36," *Przeglad Polonijny,* XII:4, pp. 39-52.

_____. 1992. *Wiez Spoleczna A Zmiana Kultury. Studium Dynamiki Polskiej Zbiorowosci Ethnicznej W USA* (Wroclaw: Ossolineum).

Rosman, Abraham and Paula G. Rubel. 1985. *The Tapestry of Dynamiki Polskiej Zbiorowosci Ethnicznej W USA* (Wroclaw: Ossolineum).

Saint Hedwig Church, South Bend, Indiana. 100th Anniversary 1877-1977. 1977. (South Bend).

Sandberg, Neil C. 1977. *Ethnic Identity and Assimilation. The Polish-American Community. Case Study of Metropolitan Los Angeles* (New York: Praeger Publishers).

Sanders, Irvin T. and Ewa T. Morawska. 1975. *Polish-American Community Life: A Survey of Research* (Boston-New York: Boston University and Polish Institute of Arts and Sciences in America).

Sarna, Jonathan D. 1978. "From Immigrants to Ethnics: Toward a New Theory of 'Ethnicization,'" *Ethnicity,* 5:4, pp. 370-78.

Scherer, Darlene. 1975. *The Hungarian-Americans of South Bend* (South Bend: Indiana University at South Bend, Ethnic Heritage Studies Program).

Scheuer, George A. (ed.). 1982. *From Council Oak to Shopping Malls. The Ethnic Background of St. Joseph County, Indiana* (South Bend: The Forever Learning Institute).

Schwab, William A. 1982. *Urban Sociology: A Human Ecological Perspective* (Reading, Mass.: Addison-Wesley Publishing Company).

Scott, George M., Jr. 1990. "A Resynthesis Of The Primordial And Circumstantial Approaches To Ethnic Group Solidarity: Towards An Explanatory Model," *Ethnic and Racial Studies,* 13:2, pp. 147-171.

Siemienska, Renata. 1978. *Sila Tradycji I Sila Interesow. O Zrodlach Bialego Ruchu Etnicznego W Stanach Zjednoczonych* (Warszwa: PWN).

Silverman, Sydel F. 1965. "Patronage and Community-Nation Relationships in Central Italy," *Ethnology*, IV:2, pp. 172-189.

South Bend Area. n.d. R.R. Donnelly & Sons Co. Cartographic Services.

Sojka, Jacek. 1991. *Pomiedzy Filozofia A Socjologia. Spoleczna Ontologia Alfreda Schutza* (Warszawa: Fundacja Instytutu Kultury).

Spicer, Edward. 1971. "Persistent Identity Systems," *Science*, pp. 795-800.

Stabroski, Donald, J. 1984. *A Political Machine, An Ethnic Community, and South Bend's West Side 1900-1980.* Doctoral Dissertation, University of Notre Dame (Notre Dame, IN).

_____. 1991. *Holy Cross and the South Bend Polonia* (Notre Dame: Indiana Province Archives Center).

St. Adalbert Parish, South Bend, Indiana, 1910-1985. 1985. (South Bend).

St. Joseph County at a Glance. 1993. (South Bend: Institute for Applied Community Research IUSB).

St. Joseph County Observance of Poland's Millennium of Christianity. 1966. (South Bend).

Suttles, George. 1972. *The Social Construction of Communities* (Chicago: University of Chicago Press).

Swastek, Joseph V., Reverend. 1941. *The Polish Settlement in South Bend, Indiana 1868-1914.* Master of Arts Dissertation, Notre Dame University (Notre Dame, IN).

Szahaj, Andrzej. 1990. *Krytyka-Emancypacja-Dialog. Juergen Habermas W Poszukiwaniu Nowego Paradygmatu Teorii Krytycznej* (Warszawa: kolegium Otryckie).

Szawleski, Mieczyslaw. 1924. *Wychodztwo Polskie W Stanach Zjednoczonych Ameryki* (Lwow: Ossolineum).

The Golden Years of Falconry in District Six. Polish Falcons of America. Thirty-sixth Biennial Convention and Banquet. 1967. (South Bend).

Thirtieth Anniversary, Banquet and Ball. General Joseph Halle Post 125 and Auxiliary. 1962. (South Bend).

Thomas, William I. and Florian Znaniecki. 1918-1920. *The Polish Peasant in Europe and America*, 5 volumes (Boston: Richard G. Badger).

Tonnies, Ferdinand. 1963. *Community and Society* (New York: Harper and Row).

Touraine, Alain. 1977. *The Self-production of Society* (Chicago: University of Chicago Press).

_____. 1981. *The Voice and the Eye. An Analysis of Social Movements* (Cambridge: Cambridge University Press).

Turowski, Jan. 1977. "Spolecznosc lokalna," *Studia Socjologiczne,* 3 (66), pp. 105-129.

Van Gennep, Arnold. 1960. *The Rites of Passage* (Chicago: University of Chicago Press).

Walaszek, Adam. 1994. *Swiaty Imigrantow. Tworzenie Polonijnego Cleveland 1880-1930* (Krakow: NOMOS).

Wawrykiewicz, Malgorzata. 1988a. "Ethniczne organizcje ubezpieczeniowe w USA - analiza porownawcza wybranych grup," *Przeglad Polonijny,* XIV:1, pp. 49-74.

Wawrykiewicz, Malgorzata. 1988b. "Polonijne organizacje samopomocowe: organizacje etniczne czy ubezpieczeniowe?," in Grzegorz Babinski (ed.), *Studia Nad Organizacjami Polonijnym* (Wroclaw: Ossolineum), pp. 63-80.

_____. 1991. *Polonijne Organizacje Ubezpieczeniowe W Stanach Zjednoczonych* (Wroclaw: Ossolineum).

Weber, Max. 1978. *Economy and Society. An Outline of Interpretative Sociology,* Volume One (Berkeley: University of California Press).

Weingrod, A. 1968. "Patrons, Patronage And Political Parties," *Comparative Studies in Society and History*, X:4, pp. 377-400.

Wensits, James, 1991a. "Bayh Decides On Dunking Over Dyngus Day," *The South Bend Tribune,* Sunday, March 31, pp. D1, D2.

_____. 1991b. "Politics Puncuate Annual Festivities," *The South Bend Tribune,* Tuesday, April 2, pp. B1, B2.

West Side Democratic and Civic Club. 50th Anniversary Banquet. 1980. (South Bend).

Witkowski, Lech. 1988. *Tozsamosc I Zmiana. Wstep Do Epistemologicznej Analizy Kontekstow Edukacyjnych* (Torun: UMK).

Working For You. South Bend/Mishawaka. n.d. (South Bend: Area Chamber of Commerce).

Wodz, Jacek. 1986. "Spolecznosci lokalne w swietle niektorych koncepcji tak zwanej socjologii zycia codziennego," in Jacek Wodz (ed.), *Spolecznosci Lokalne. Szkice Socjologiczne* (Katowice: Wydawnictwo US1).

Wytrwal, Joseph A. 1969. *The Poles in America* (Minneapolis: Lerner Publications Company).

Wytrwal, Joseph A. 1977. *Behold: The Polish Americans* (Detroit: Endurance Press).

Zaremba, Pawel. 1992. *Historia Stanow Zjednoczonych* (Warszawa: Bellona).

Znaniecki, Florian. 1939. "Social Groups as Products of Participating Individuals," *American Journal of Sociology*, XLIV:6, pp. 799-811.

_____. 1973. *Socjologia Wychowania. T. I: Wychowujace Spoleczenstwo* (Warszawa: PWN).